Journey of the Half

A Memoir

Amy Lien Sperbeck

In memory of

ThuCuc Luong (Aunt Hai)

1937–2007

Part 1

Chapter 1
1972
Can Tho, Vietnam

This was the day I had been waiting for, the day Aunt Hai promised would happen. I didn't know how or why I had been separated from my parents, but finally we were going to meet for the first time. At that point I didn't know what my parents really looked like. Aunt Hai had some blurry black-and-white pictures of Ba taken in front of an airplane, but she had no pictures of Ma to show me.

Neighbors often asked, "Where are your parents?"

Friends would question, "Do you miss them?"

I didn't know how to answer those difficult questions. How could I miss someone I had never met? But I had created an image of my mother in my head.

"She has long black hair, delicate skin. My ma is beautiful," I told my classmate at school.

"Do you miss her?"

"Of course," I lied.

My cousins and I went to the same privileged Catholic French school where Aunt Hai used to teach before she got married. Naturally, she always made sure we worked hard at school and at home. Aunt Hai was a good parent, but she wasn't my mother. It was true Aunt Hai was really nice to me, but in my mind she saved true tenderness for her own children. I was always longing for that kind of affection and dreamt a lot about Ma.

I was told my parents lived in Saigon. It was a mystery to me why I didn't live with them. Every time I tried to ask questions about them, my aunt either changed the subject or made up some excuse.

"How far is Saigon from here?" I asked Aunt Hai. "How come my parents don't visit me? Do they miss me?"

"Of course they do. They are just very busy running their business."

"What kind of business?"

"They manage a gas station. Do you know how hard that is for your ma? Remember, your ba is handicapped, and all of your siblings are younger than you. Nannies and maids can help only so much. I'm sure when they have time, they will come to visit."

"How did Ba become handicapped?"

"He was an officer in the Air Force," Aunt Hai said. "He was injured in an off-duty accident by driving over a land mine while he was on leave. He lost his right leg but is very lucky to be alive. It was hard for him to find a job after that, so Uncle Su and I decided to set up a gas station for them. Your uncle knows how it works and helped your parents become successful business owners."

Aunt Hai's husband indeed knew how the gasoline business worked. He was the president of ESSO. He was smart—he spoke four languages—and a kind man. My grandparents loved him like he was their own son. This was another reason I envied my cousins: they had perfect parents.

Aunt Hai kissed her husband good-bye, helped my cousins get in the car, and waved as the driver took them to school. Watching her do that this morning, it made me wonder if my parents did the same for my siblings.

"Are you going to eat your breakfast, Lien?" She pointed at my now cold breakfast that the cook had prepared.

"I'm not hungry."

"Too excited to eat?"

I nodded. Yes, I was excited and nervous at the same time. What should I do when they got there? How should I act? Should I be polite but distant, or should I cry for all the years we had been apart? I had so many questions in my head, but which one should I ask first?

They arrived at the Mekong River port in the afternoon, and the driver went to pick them up. I was pacing nervously back and forth, checking myself in the mirror. I ran to the front door when I saw the car entering through the gate. Aunt Hai was by my side. There they were finally; this was the moment I had been waiting for.

The driver opened the car door and helped my ba to get out. He took tiny steps and limped slowly past me into the house. I wondered if he even saw me. A few steps behind him came a tired-looking woman. She stared at me and gave me a little sad smile, and I knew it was her. My ma looked sad; she didn't have the long black hair like I had imagined. She was not at all like I had dreamt her to be, but somehow I felt the love, and I couldn't wait to talk to her.

Everyone surrounded Ba, asking him many questions. "How was your journey? Have you gotten used to the artificial leg? How is the business?"

He said he hated traveling, business was good, and that was the reason for this visit. He just wanted to talk to Aunt Hai about renovating the gas station. He wanted to build a house in the back of it but needed Aunt Hai's signature. He said he could buy another house somewhere else, but it would be easier for him to watch over the business by living next to it. Aunt Hai gave him the approval, of course, as she always did, but Grandma didn't like the idea. She thought living next to the business was dangerous, especially a gas station. Ba said it was none of Grandma's business, and her opinion didn't matter. Grandma and Ba ended up arguing, and Aunt Hai told the maid to take me upstairs.

Ma came up about an hour later, sat down next to me, and said she was sorry Grandma and Ba didn't get along. That was why it was hard for them to visit.

"Am I going home with you?" I asked.

She looked at me with her sad eyes and said, "I think it's best for you to stay here."

"Why can't I live with you, Ma? I'm seven years old. I can take care of myself."

She said, "It's complicated. One day you'll understand."

I had so many questions to ask and things to say, but the maid came in the room and told Ma that Ba wanted her downstairs.

That night at dinner, Ba wanted a drink, but Ma had forgotten to pack his favorite liquor. He grabbed Ma's wrist and twisted it.

"I asked you to pack one thing, and you forgot. You're so useless." He was loud and angry, "Can't you do anything right?"

She was holding back tears. "I'm sorry. I was busy with the children."

"What do I pay the nannies for?" he shouted.

"There were so many things I had to do before we left. It won't happen again. Please let go of my hand. You're hurting me."

I could tell she was in pain, and I was terrified. Aunt Hai asked him to stop, handing him a bottle of brown liquid, and he let go of Ma's hand. He was still angry and started to drink heavily. He yelled at Ma some more while my aunt took me upstairs.

I was so disappointed with the way the day turned out. I was really afraid of Ba now. I didn't have a chance to talk to Ma again that night and felt so bad for her.

The next morning I got up early and went downstairs hoping to catch Ma alone before I went to school. Everyone was still asleep except for the servants, who were just getting up. I went into the kitchen and found my favorite maid, Sen, helping the cook with breakfast.

"I'm sorry about yesterday, Lien. Are you OK?" Sen asked.

I shrugged, wanting to say I was not all right. I wanted to start over; I wanted a peaceful visit from my parents, not a terrifying one.

"Do you want something to eat, child?" the cook asked.

"Can I have some coffee?" I felt grown up all of a sudden.

"You know coffee is not for children. How about some hot milk?"

"All right."

Aunt Hai entered the kitchen, and when she saw me she let out a sigh and sat down next to me.

"You're up early today." She put her arm around my shoulders. "You don't have to go to school today, Lien. Why don't you sleep some more?"

"Can I go to school? Please. I don't want to stay home."

She looked at my sad face. "All right, if that's what you want."

Later, when I came home from school, my parents had already left. Ma and I hadn't had a chance to talk, and my questions for her were left unanswered. I felt a little guilty that I hadn't stayed home to say good-bye to Ma. I just didn't like what Ba had done and felt very uncomfortable around him. When I told Aunt Hai about how afraid I was of him, she asked me to forgive him and pray for him. She told me that now that Ba was handicapped, everything was more difficult for him, and that was why he had acted that way. I thought, 'I would rather pray for Ma.'

Chapter 2
1973

It was obvious Grandma was the boss of the family. She had many rules for us to follow, and we were all intimidated by her. Her own servants were afraid of her, Aunt Hai's servants as well. We kids were instructed to fold our arms in front of our chests when we talked to her. We had to bow to her whenever she entered the house, and she would never let us walk out of the house with undone hair or wrinkled outfits.

My aunt told me stories about Grandma growing up in a privileged, noble family. Her and Grandpa's marriage had been arranged by their parents, following the old tradition of marrying within the same class. Both of their parents were land owners, and they knew each other through their famous reputations. Aunt Hai told us Grandma was old school, and we had to respect her for keeping the tradition.

My grandparents lived next door, wanting to be close to Aunt Hai and the grandchildren. They loved and respected Aunt Hai very much. It was not just because of the Vietnamese custom to love and respect the first child; Aunt Hai earned it. She always knew what to do and what to say to all of us, and we all respected her.

Honestly, I wished we lived a little farther away from Grandma. Just because she came over to our house all the time, like her own house was only for sleeping. Grandma also disciplined us often, and she was really strict. Many times she stopped me when I walked a little too fast in the house and made me walk again at a slower pace around the room as punishment. "What did I say about taking your time and walking like a lady?" She made me sit up straight every time she saw me leaning or slouching. If she thought I spoke too loudly, she would grasp my shoulder so tightly it hurt. She made me repeat what I'd said in much gentler voice—"like a lady," she would say. When I tried to speak gently to her, she couldn't hear me. "Why are you mumbling?" She turned me to face her. "A real lady would know when to speak and when to stop politely, never raising her voice. Never."

I said "yes ma'am" even though I had heard she occasionally raised her voice to everyone—except Grandpa.

Grandpa was a man of few words. Grandma said she never saw a businessman as quiet as him. Most businessmen talk till your ear falls off. Grandpa owned a lot of land, with hundreds of farmers working for him. Every morning he took a boat to the rice fields outside of Can Tho and spent his day between the fields and the factory to make sure everything ran smoothly. He came home tired most evenings and went to bed right after dinner. Whenever he took a day off, he would spend his time in the garden trimming flower bushes, even though we had a gardener. My aunts didn't understand why Grandpa liked working so much when he didn't have to.

"Why is Grandpa so quiet, and why does he always look sad?" I asked Aunt Sau.

"He wasn't always that way. He changed after his two children died. Have you heard the story about Uncle Tu and Aunt Nam?" she asked.

"I only saw pictures of them when they were children."

"Uncle Tu got a mysterious illness and died at age ten, and Aunt Nam's death was even more tragic. Your grandparents wanted the best education for us, so they sent us to the Catholic French school, even though we were Buddhist. Aunt Nam, a fourteen-year-old girl at the time, fell in love with the new religion and wanted to become a Catholic nun. Your grandparents didn't like the idea and forbade her to talk about it. They even threatened to take her out of Catholic school. Still, Aunt Nam wanted to study more about it, going to church behind our parents' backs. Grandpa decided to build a tall fence around the property with a gate, keeping it locked all the times. He hoped Aunt Nam would finally give up the idea of becoming a nun. Tragically, a few weeks after the gate was built, Aunt Nam climbed over it, trying to get to the five a.m. Mass, and fell. She hit her head on the cement driveway and passed away."

I felt goosebumps on my arms.

"Your grandparents were heartbroken," Aunt Sau continued. "I could only imagine their pain and guilt. They regretted what they had done and wanted to bury Aunt Nam with a Catholic ceremony, but the church provided the service only for Catholic families. Now my parents were willing to convert the whole family to Catholicism so their beloved daughter could receive a blessing by the church. To honor Aunt Nam, the family did become Catholic and are still really involved in the church to this day, as you know. However, there was one family member against the idea: your ba. He didn't want to convert; he didn't believe in God and didn't want to practice any religion at all."

"Did it happened here, at this gate?" I asked.

"No, it was at the old house. We moved afterward. Imagine how sad Grandpa would be if we still lived there."

Aunt Sau wiped her tears quickly, still emotional after so many years. She was only two years younger than Aunt Nam and remembered vividly what had happened. She told me the accident didn't tear the family apart but instead it made them closer. I understood now why my grandparents wanted to live close to Aunt Hai—so they could cherish all their children every single day.

Chapter 3
1974

It was just a cold, but I made a big deal out of it, pretending to have a headache and body aches. Aunt Hai allowed me to stay home, saying I had to stay in bed. Sen came upstairs to check on me periodically. After a while I got bored and wanted something to eat. I knew Sen was busy with her chores, so I decided to go to the kitchen and ask the cook myself.

Walking downstairs, I saw Grandpa was still home, which was odd. He was supposed to be at the rice fields. He had a worried look on his face and stood up abruptly when Aunt Hai walked into the dining room.

"Did you call your husband? Did you tell him it's urgent?"

"Yes, Ba, I did. He's on his way home now. What's going on?"

"What about your ma? Did you tell her?"

"I sent Sen to get her. She'll be here soon. Can you tell me what's going on?"

All of a sudden, I wasn't hungry anymore. I just wanted to know what was going on. Grandma walked into the room and I knew instantly I had to hide. I looked around and quickly hid myself behind the door.

"What is so important that you need to talk to me now? Can it wait? I was having tea with my friends, and you are interrupting us," Grandma said, sounding slightly irritated.

"Could you ask them to leave? It's very important, and I don't want anyone to know about this," Grandpa said sternly.

"Is everything OK? You aren't yourself." Grandma looked straight into his eyes with concern.

"Send your friends home. I have something very important to tell you," Grandpa repeated.

"OK! I'll ask them to leave," Grandma said.

When Grandma came back, Aunt Hai's husband had just arrived. Grandpa asked everyone to sit down. "I have something serious to tell you."

"What is it, Ba?" Aunt Hai asked.

"I just found out that the Communists from the North are coming. They're on their way. They'll be here soon, and everything will change."

"What? How do you know this? What makes you think they're on their way?" Grandma asked.

"A friend told me."

"Do you trust this friend of yours? Are you sure? If something were about to happen, don't you think our government would let us know?"

"You don't understand. This friend of mine is a Communist. We went to the same school when we were young."

Everybody was stunned.

Grandpa began to tell his amazing story, one I would never forget. "When I was young, our family lived in the countryside. At the time the French were still here. One evening when we were sleeping, a group of French soldiers banged on our door. We knew they were looking for Communists—they had been doing that all over the countryside, searching every house. We opened the door for them. My father kept telling them we were not Communists; he owned a lot of land, and he hated Communism. They didn't understand Vietnamese and kept breaking things while they were searching. My oldest brother was a teenager at the time, and he got mad when one of the French soldiers got into his room and broke some of his things. He yelled at the soldier to stop, but the soldier turned around and shot him in the chest. My brother died on the way to the hospital." Grandpa paused. "I hated the French after that."

"Ba, if you hated the French so much, then why did you send us to French school?" Aunt Hai asked.

"My brother died because he didn't speak French. That's why I wanted to make sure all of you learned the language," Grandpa said. "I can't tell you my friend's name, but we've known each other since we were in grade school. When we finished high school, he told me his secret. He had been working for the Communists. His job was to report when and where the French were. He hated the way French people were treating us, and he wanted freedom for our country. He said he would leave soon for the North, but I didn't want to join him."

Grandpa stared at his father's picture on the wall and continued. "I told him my father had already lost one son to this stupid war, and he had been sick and depressed ever since. I was all he had; he needed my help with the rice fields. I had a big responsibility taking care of the family business, besides I didn't want to be involved in politics. We said our good-byes, and went our separate ways. When my father retired, I became the new owner of his company, and business was booming. We were exporting rice outside of the country, and we were doing so well. I had forgotten about the school friend of mine, the French were gone, and my heart had healed. Recently, he came back to visit his family and wanted to see me. He told me the Communists will take over the South very soon."

"Oh my God!" Grandma said. "So this is real. They're coming, and you believe it will happen."

Grandpa nodded his head.

"What will happen when they're here, Ba?" Aunt Hai asked.

"You said everything will change. What do you mean?" Uncle Su asked. He still seemed in shock from the news.

"I don't know exactly what they'll do when they're here, but he told me you should quit your job now. If you don't, you might end up in jail because you work for the Americans."

"We're depending on that job. He can't quit. What about the American government? Aren't they supposed to help us?" Aunt Hai asked.

"You have to take this seriously because it's going to happen, and it will happen soon," Grandpa said.

"Can you transfer out of the country, honey? To America maybe?" Aunt Hai asked her husband.

"It's too late, there isn't enough time." Grandpa said. "You have to save yourself from prison. You have got to quit your job, get rid of the cars, and sell all your luxury items.

Take your money out of the bank, and buy gold. That should help you live humbly for a few years."

"What about the two of us? Will this affect us?" Grandma asked.

"I hope not. Since I didn't work for Americans, I think we're OK. But we have to keep this conversation secret. Don't tell anyone, including your siblings. No one should know but the four of us. You have to promise me you won't tell another soul about this."

All three of them promised him they would keep this secret to themselves.

All of a sudden, my legs started to shake. I was so scared they might find me listening in on their secret. I took off my shoes and carefully walked upstairs without making any noise. When I finally got into bed, I was shaking uncontrollably.

A week later my uncle quit his job, sold his cars, and let the driver go. Aunt Hai also let go all the servants including the cook, but she kept Sen. The children were still going to the same school, but we had to take the school bus now, and we had to learn how to get ready for school ourselves. There was a lot of uncertainty in our daily life, with the frustration, the worry, and the secret I'd stumbled on. I was carefully watching my aunt and her husband, but they seemed to be trying their best not to show the strain they were under.

Shortly thereafter we came home from school, and the piano was gone. My two cousins who had taken piano lessons since they were little broke down and cried. I saw my aunt's eyes were red—there was no doubt in my mind she had been crying when she'd sold that piano. Slowly the furniture kept disappearing. The grandfather clock she loved so much went too. The dining room set was also gone, replaced by a much cheaper table and chairs.

Aunt Hai and Sen did all the cooking now, and we had to help with some chores around the house. Uncle Su kept himself busy with the newspaper and radio. One day when I was helping in the kitchen, he walked in and told Aunt Hai the Americans had officially withdrawn. They both looked at each other with worry in their eyes but said nothing. Two weeks later we saw on television our president had resigned.

Chapter 4
1975

The Communist army attacked our city with force on April 30, 1975, and the South Vietnamese government ended up surrendering to avoid more bloodshed. The Northerners' tanks rolled into the city with loudspeakers blaring, telling us to take down our old yellow flags with three red stripes. They also wanted us to come outside to greet the soldiers from the North. I could see people were nervously lining up, watching the tired-looking army with cheap uniforms marching down our street. They played Communist music about Ho Chi Minh and their heroes; the sound was so strange and unpleasantly loud. Then they said all schools, banks, and businesses would be closed until further notice.

Suddenly we were no longer allowed to use our money. Thank goodness my aunts had prepared by stocking up on food and necessary items. I heard it was chaos outside. The prices of rice and produce skyrocketed. Some people traded their gold and valuable items for food.

A few days later, we got a letter saying the government would distribute food and the new Communist money for every family. But first they would apply the new law, and that was equality. Which meant they would visit every house to collect items from the rich to give to the poor. The government wanted everyone to have the same salary and the same quality lifestyle.

It didn't take long for a group of soldiers to come to Aunt Hai's house one morning and shout in their Northern accent at us. "Everybody in the living room, now!"

We all gathered in the living room, worried and scared. Some of the soldiers stayed outside by their truck, waiting. One of the soldiers, who looked like an officer in charge, walked around the house checking every single thing while another wrote down our names and dates of birth. He stopped at me and asked, "Who are your parents? Are they here?"

"She is my niece; her parents live in Saigon," Aunt Hai said.

"There is no more Saigon!" he yelled at her. "It is now Ho Chi Minh City. Do you understand?"

"Yes sir. What I'm trying to say is her father is my brother, and he is handicapped. I've been raising her since she was a baby."

He pointed at Sen. "And who is she?"

"She is a nanny to help me with the children. As you can see, I need help."

"She can't stay here anymore," he said. "She has to go home, where she belongs." He asked Aunt Hai's husband, "What is your occupation?"

Jumping in, Aunt Hai said, "He works for my father, taking care of the family business."

"I did not ask you," the soldier said, clearly irritated. "Do you have to answer for everyone?"

"I work for my father-in-law," Uncle added, "in the rice export business, I translate paperwork."

The officer came back to the living room after investigating the house and gathering all his papers. Then he looked at my aunt and uncle and said, "You have two weeks to move out. This house now belongs to the government. If you don't have a place to go, we can provide you a place in a new development in the countryside." He put his hat on and handed Aunt Hai a piece of paper. "Those are items that will stay with the house."

Aunt Hai cried, "Please, Officer, we are a big family. We need this house. It's all we have."

The officer replied flatly, "Two weeks" and left the house with the rest of the soldiers.

Uncle read the piece of paper and said, "They want the air-conditioner, television, and refrigerator to stay with the house."

***

Grandpa tried very hard to save the house for Aunt Hai, but he failed, and his friend couldn't help him. We had to move into Grandpa's house next door. Sen helped us move before she went back home for good. The night before she left, Sen and I cried on each other's shoulder like we knew we were about to lose our best friend forever. And sure enough, I never saw Sen again.

Grandma's house felt very small now that all of us lived there. There wasn't enough room for all the beds, so all the girls shared the big bedroom. Five of my cousins and I slept on thin mattresses on the floor, and it could get hectic sometimes. The most painful part was watching the soldiers move into our dear old house next door. Aunt Hai couldn't stop crying that day.

Grandpa started bringing a big bag of rice home every day and storing it in his bedroom. Grandma thought it was strange, because they never had to worry about running short of rice before—they were in the rice business. She kept asking him, "What is going on? Why do you keep storing rice in our bedroom?" Grandpa didn't answer her right away, but one night he told the family his friend couldn't save his rice fields either. All land now belonged to the government; the only thing his friend could save for him was the house we lived in. Grandpa was storing the rice before he officially lost it all. There were a lot of mouths to feed in this family, and he was worried. Grandma left abruptly to her room. I could tell that she was upset, and Grandpa started to sob right there in front of the family.

The government controlled everything from land to businesses and gave each family very little money to start. The new money had a picture of Uncle Ho (they wanted us to call Ho Chi Minh "Uncle," not President or Chairman). Every neighborhood would have a leader, and that was where we got food rations once a week. The quality of the rice we got from them was so poor and barely enough; Grandma gave ours to the neighbors. We also got seeds they wanted us to use for growing our own vegetables, which we did. It was so sad to see our street, a fine avenue of luxury homes with beautiful gardens, with misshapen vegetable plots in the front yards.

Sometime later we got another letter that said the

officers would come back to collect all books and music-related items, like albums and cassettes, to be destroyed. "What? Books?" Aunt Hai was stunned. That night she and her husband went through the bookcases to remove the gold bars they had hidden and found new hiding places for them.

The soldiers came for the books all right. They took all of ours, including children's books and cookbooks. It didn't matter. They emptied the bookcases. They were trying to control everything in our lives. I was so sad when the books were gone.

September came, and my cousins and I started in a new public school. (There were no more private schools allowed in our country.) We had to walk there; it was far, but it wasn't so bad. I actually liked to walk with my cousins. We talked and joked or teased each other. It helped us to forget the sadness surrounding us.

When we finally got our textbooks for the year, I was so disappointed. The books were so old and of poor quality, and they were all about Uncle Ho and his followers, who loved him and wanted to be like him. I really missed the good old books.

Christmas and New Year's came and went. We didn't celebrate the holidays anymore; in fact nobody did. People didn't have enough to eat. How could they afford to celebrate the holidays? Besides, the government watched everybody, and if they thought you were rich, you would be in trouble. They even came into our church to keep their eyes on the priest. We were wondering what would happen next.

Chapter 5
1976

Grandpa lost the lands that were passed down to him from his ancestors, the lands he worked so hard his whole life, planning someday to pass them down to his children. He became even more quiet, keeping to himself in his bedroom most of the time. He didn't eat with us anymore; my aunts took turns bringing food to his room, and sometimes it came back untouched. Before long Grandpa had a stroke, and after that he didn't leave his room. He refused all visitors.

Grandma became bitter about everything. She didn't want to see her friends anymore. She got upset easily, particularly when someone talked about the government. Aunt Hai's husband left for Saigon to find a job, as Aunt Hai was afraid if he stayed in Can Tho, sooner or later he would get arrested. "You can't trust friends or neighbors anymore," she said.

Aunt Sau lost her job as well. She had just graduated from law school in 1973 and worked as a lawyer for only a little over a year. The new government said they didn't need lawyers in their system. She cried sometimes and said she had turned down potential marriage proposals to focus on her career. Now she had nothing. She had no job, no husband, and no kids and still lived at home. All her friends had families of their own, which made her sad sometimes. To keep herself busy, Aunt Sau did volunteer work at the church and helped Aunt Hai around the house with cooking and taking care of the children.

Aunt Bay was an accountant and lucky enough to find a job as a tax representative. However, the tension between Aunt Bay and Aunt Sau was so high. Aunt Sau didn't like that Aunt Bay started to hang out with people from the Communist party. "Did you forget what they did to our family?" Aunt Sau asked. They argued a lot in low voices because they didn't want the soldiers next door to hear them. Finally they ended up not talking to each other for years, even though they lived in the same house.

Aunt Tam had just graduated from college with a degree in nursing in 1974, and the government sent her to Saigon to work at Cho Ray Hospital. It was the biggest hospital in the country and used to be an international hospital, with all the top medical equipment. It had now become the special hospital for government officers only. She could visit the family only a few times a year.

Grandma wished Aunt Tam would stay and work in Can Tho—Grandpa needed a nurse—but was glad that Aunt Tam got sent to the city instead of the jungle like some other nurses. The government took rich people's houses and businesses and sent the owners with their families to the jungle. They called this a new development community. There they would learn how to build houses from very little material and equipment, and they had to learn how to farm. These people were educated city people who were now punished for being successful. A lot of them got sick with malaria, and the government had to send doctors and nurses to the jungle too. Aunt Tam was relieved when she opened the letter assigning her to a hospital in Saigon.

Aunt Chin was still in college at the time, but she was struggling because she was afraid of the unknown and the uncertainty of the future.

***

The children from the public school were wild and unkind, especially the boys. They jumped up and down on the tables whenever the teachers weren't there. They wrote mean things on the blackboard all the time. They picked on me basically from the first day of school. "Where is your skirt?" They would ask and then burst out laughing. They knew we wore uniforms with skirts at French school. Sometimes they pulled my ponytail, and when I turned around they just pointed at other kids and said, "He did it. No, not him, the other guy. Oh wait, not him either." I just ignored them. Boys were stupid anyhow.

One day as I went into the classroom, everyone was

laughing. I looked around, and all eyes were on me. I didn't really know what was going on. Did I have a stain on my white shirt? I looked down and checked but found nothing. Hanh, the girl who sat next to me, said, "Read the board." I turned my eyes to the blackboard, and there it said, "Shame on you, half-American."

"I don't understand" I told her.

The principal walked in, and the classroom fell silent. He stared at the board for a bit, then looked at the children and asked, "Who did this?" No one answered him. He called on me to stand up and point out who had done this to me.

"Sir, I don't know who did it, and I don't think that message was for me."

The other children burst out laughing again, and the principal slammed his bare hand on the table. "Be quiet! I'm not tolerating a bully in this school. Shame on you. Whoever did this, consider this a warning. If I find out next time something like this happens, I will send that student home with probation."

He erased the chalkboard and told us our teacher had a personal day off. He would be our substitute teacher for that day.

At recess Hanh sat down next to me and said, "You know that message was for you, right? Who else was it for? I mean, you're the only one in the class who's, you know…half-American."

"I'm not half-American. Both of my parents are Vietnamese."

"Maybe they adopted you. Look, your hair isn't black like everyone else's, it's golden brown. Your skin is so light, and look—look at the hair on your arms."

I looked at my arms. In the sunlight the hair on them was blond. I had never noticed that before. Was it possible I was adopted? By whom? My parents? And then they sent me here to live with Aunt Hai? Why would they go through all the trouble to adopt me and then send me away? It didn't make sense.

"Do I really look half-American?" I asked Hanh.

"It's obvious," she said.

The bullying students stopped writing mean messages, but they still called me "half breed" here and there. Sometimes I wanted to ask Aunt Hai if I was actually adopted, but I was afraid to upset her. Everything changed so much, and it got worse and worse in our daily life. The adults were always worried and stressed. I wouldn't dare to put more stress on them.

***

Another summer came, with scorching heat and intense humidity. Grandma's air-conditioning had broken down the previous year, and she had decided not to fix it. She said there was no point if we could have electricity only three days a week—more work of the government mastermind. It would have been torture to have a cool house one day and hot the next. "We could save money on electric bills too," she said. Some nights it was so hot, I couldn't sleep.

The city was really dark at night; people didn't go out like they used to. There was no more strolling on the river bank, no more night market, no more food vendors. All we could do on the dark nights was surround Aunt Hai in the living room so she could tell us some fairy tales by candlelight.

Food was harder to get, even in the market; we were thankful to Grandpa for the rice he had stored. We didn't have meat for a long time, but Aunt Hai managed to get fish once a week. The rest of the time, we lived on vegetables and rice. Who knew a vegetable garden would come in so handy?

I was watering the vegetable garden one afternoon when a cyclo (a tricycle carrying passengers) dropped Aunt Tam off at the front of the house. I turned off the water and ran to her. "Aunt Tam, you're here. How long will you stay this time?"

"Just a few days, Lien," she said. "And your parents sent a letter."

"Really? To me? They never wrote before."

"No, it's for Aunt Hai," she said. "But it's about you.

Anyway, let go inside first. It's hot out here."

I helped her with her bags, and we went inside. My cousins screamed with joy. "Aunt Tam! Do you have candy for us?"

"Did I ever come home empty handed?" She took out a bag of coconut candies she had brought from Saigon for us. My cousins and I hugged her and thanked her.

Aunt Hai walked into the living room with a smile on her face. "You spoiled them again."

"I have something for you too." Aunt Tam pulled out a letter from her bag. "This one is from your husband." She handed it to Aunt Hai.

"Aunt Tam, you said my parents sent a letter too," I said nervously. "And it's about me."

"Yes, here it is." She handed Aunt Hai the letter.

"Do you know what it's about?" Aunt Hai asked.

"They want her back," Aunt Tam said, "and they asked me to accompany her on the trip to Saigon."

"No! I don't want to go," I told Aunt Tam. "I want to stay here." I tried hard not to cry, but I couldn't hold it. I wiped my tears and ran to the bedroom. I was sitting in the corner, still sobbing, when Aunt Hai came in. She handed me a handkerchief, then she gently pulled me in her arms, my head resting on her shoulder. She waited until I calmed down, then said, "Your cousins and I want you to stay here too, Lien, but your parents need you. You have to open your heart and accept them. They are your family. Besides, Uncle wants us to move to Saigon too. He's looking for a place right now, close to your parents. Soon enough we'll visit each other."

"I'm scared, Aunt Hai."

"I know. Everything will be OK. You'll see. Just open your heart and show them you love them, and you'll feel right at home in no time."

"What about school?" I asked.

"Don't worry. You'll start a new school there in September. I'll take care of the paperwork."

The next day, while I was packing, the smell of phở

surrounded me like I was in a phở restaurant. I ran downstairs to the kitchen, and everyone was excited. I saw Aunt Hai by a big pot, skimming the foam from the broth. Aunt Sau was cleaning a big piece of beef, and my cousins were busy too, picking herbs and rinsing vegetables. Everyone was in a good mood.

"Lien, go back to your room. No chores for you today," Aunt Hai said.

"How did you manage to get beef?" I asked her.

"Don't you worry, Lien. We're going to have a fine dinner tonight."

"What if the soldiers next door smell it?" Aunt Sau asked. "If it smells like phở in here, they will probably smell it over there too. Do you think they'll come over?"

Everybody looked at Aunt Hai nervously. "Yeah, what if?"

"If they come, I'll invite them to eat with us, and I will put extra hot sauce in their bowls. They won't be talking for days," Aunt Hai said.

We all laughed, and it felt good to see everyone in a good mood for a change. We had an excellent dinner that night. The phở was so good, it lifted everybody's spirits. We talked, joked, and laughed. All my cousins said they'd miss me, but we would see each other again soon.

Later that night Aunt Hai came to the bedroom with a present in her hand. I was surprised because we hadn't had any presents since we'd lost the house.

"Is it for me?" I asked.

"Yes. Open it," she said. "I hope you like it."

I opened the present. It was a beautiful leather-covered notebook with very fine, smooth paper inside. Most notebooks now were poor quality, with coarse brown paper.

"I love it. It's almost too beautiful for school," I said.

"It isn't for school. It's a journal. It's like a diary where you can write down your feelings, on a good day or a bad day. I think it'll be good for you, Lien."

"Thank you, Aunt Hai. I'm going to miss you dearly."

"Me too, sweet child." She gave me a hug, told me to go to bed early, and left the room.

The next morning Aunt Hai woke me up at five o'clock. She said Aunt Tam wanted to catch the first bus to Saigon, and she wanted me to have a good breakfast before we left. Downstairs in the kitchen, Aunt Tam fried some eggs, and we ate them with baguette while Aunt Hai brought my suitcase down. Grandma was also up; she was in the kitchen brewing coffee.

"Don't talk back to your ba. Just be careful around him," Grandma said.

"Yes, Grandma." I tried to sit up as straight as I could.

"Try your best. Be a good girl, and everything will be all right. You are the oldest sister, so you have to be a good role model for your siblings to follow."

"Ma! There is no time for this. Let her eat," Aunt Tam said. "We're going to miss the bus if you keep her from eating."

We ran out of the house because a cyclo was waiting for us in the front. We waved a brief good-bye to Aunt Hai and Grandma, and the cyclo driver started to pedal away.

***

We made it to the bus just in time. During the five-hour bus ride, Aunt Tam told me about Saigon and how it was a lot bigger and busier than Can Tho. She also told me about her job and how she had met her boyfriend at the hospital while he was a patient there, and they had been seeing each other ever since.

"Why don't you bring him home to meet the family?" I asked.

"Grandma doesn't want to meet him," she said and looked out the window.

"Do you know why she doesn't want to meet him?" I asked her.

"He's from the North, and he's a government officer."

"What are you going to do?"

"I don't know. He's a good man, and he asked me to marry him, but your grandma said she would disown me if I married him. I don't know what to do." She sounded sad.

I wanted to comfort her, but I didn't know what to say. "You know your grandma. She's so difficult sometimes. She didn't accept your ma either, when your ba wanted to marry her."

"What? She didn't accept my ma? Why?"

"Well, because she wanted your ba to marry someone else from a rich and noble family, but your ba didn't listen."

"Is Ma not from a noble family?"

"I heard she came from a very humble background," Aunt Tam said. "Her family lived near Hue; they were very poor."

"Talking about my parents, can I ask you a question?"

"Go ahead." She looked at me curiously.

"Am I adopted? A lot of kids at school made fun of me. They called me half- American, and I don't know what to make of it. I'm confused."

She let out a sigh and said, "OK, this is all I know. Eleven years ago your ba came home with a picnic basket. When I opened it, I jumped back in surprise because there was a baby inside. He told the family he had gotten married, and the baby was his stepdaughter. Your grandma was very upset. "How could you get married without your family's consent? She already has a child? Were you drunk when you got married? How could this happen so fast? Why do you never listen to me?"

Your ba shouted back, "Why should I tell you? You wouldn't accept her anyway. I'm an adult. I don't need you to tell me how to live my life."

He and Grandma argued, then he stomped out of the house and left you there. With all of that commotion, you were still lying in the basket quietly, without a fuss." Aunt Tam rubbed my head. "When Grandpa heard the story, he said, 'I know an orphanage, we can take her there.' All the women in the family said in unison, 'No! Not the orphanage.' Your Grandma stood up and said, 'She's staying with us until they sort this out.' There was no more discussion. Your parents didn't come back for you. Later Aunt Hai offered to give you a home with love and care. The rest of family agreed it was the best solution."

"So Ba isn't my father." I was still confused. "Is Ma my mother?"

"Yes, Lien, she is your mother."

"Am I half-American?" I asked and hoped she would tell me more, but she said "You have to ask your ma about that, Lien. It isn't my place to tell you about that. Just remember we love you no matter what."

I had a different feeling about Grandma now. She was strict because she meant well. She wanted me to be strong and graceful, so people outside would not look down on me. I realized what she did, she did out of love.

The bus kept on going, and I felt somewhat at peace that at least I knew this much about myself. I hoped Ma would fill in the gaps later, when I lived with her, and I couldn't wait to meet my siblings. I let myself doze off on Aunt Tam's shoulder for the rest of the bus ride.

Chapter 6
Saigon

My parents' house sat deep in the back of a big property. There was an old metal fence and weeds everywhere, suffocating a sad little vegetable garden. The property was evidently used as a gasoline station. There were two rusty old gas pumps in the front and some empty oil barrels left behind in the side yard. It looked untidy and neglected.

We let ourselves in through a half-open gate and followed the walkway to the house. Aunt Tam rang the doorbell, and Ma appeared with a baby in her arms. My siblings were surrounding Ma and stared at me like I was an alien. She opened the door wider for both of us and reached out for my suitcase.

"Hi, Lien. Let me get that for you."

"It's OK, Ma, I can handle it."

"Would you like to stay for dinner?" she asked Aunt Tam, but it sounded like she really didn't mean it.

"I would love to, but I have to go. My shift at the hospital starts in two hours," Aunt Tam replied. She turned to me and said, "Lien, from now on, this is your home. I promise I'll visit when I can. Look at the time. I have to go. Bye."

"Thank you. I really appreciate it," Ma said to Aunt Tam.

"You're welcome." And she ran to the front. I waited for Aunt Tam to get in the cyclo, then followed Ma inside. My siblings wouldn't leave me alone. Right away they started to ask questions: "What is your name?" "How old are you?" I thought they were cute.

"Lien, you have to say hi to Ba first. Come on, he's in the bedroom. Follow me," Ma said.

We entered the dark bedroom. After my eyes adjusted, I saw my stepfather lying in bed on his stomach. He didn't move. Ma elbowed me and whispered in my ear, "Say chào Ba. "

"Chào Ba," I called out, but he said nothing.

"Lien is here," Ma said. He didn't respond.

"Is he OK?" I asked.

Ma let out a sigh and pulled me out of the bedroom. "He just had a few drinks, that's all. He'll be all right. Come, meet your siblings." She called the children over and said, "Children, this is your big sister. Her name is Lien." Then she lined them up and told me their names. "This is your sister Anh, next is your brother Vu, then sisters Truc, Mai, and Lieu, and the baby's name is Trang."

"The baby's nickname is Little; we call her that at home," my sister Anh said.

"Why?" I was curious.

"Because…because she was really little when she came home from the hospital," my brother Vu said.

I laughed. They were really cute. "So Anh is the oldest next to me?" I asked Ma.

"No, Chi is the oldest after you."

"Where is she?"

"She ran away." Anh said.

"Are you serious?" I asked Anh.

"Yes, she ran away to over there." Anh pointed at the house across the street.

"How old is Chi?" I asked Ma. "Are you worried about her?"

"She's ten years old," Ma said. "Ba sent her to buy a cup of coffee for him. She accidentally tripped in a pothole and spilled half of it. Instead of telling him the truth, she filled up the coffee cup with muddy water from the pothole. Ba drank it and choked on the dirt. He yelled at her, and she ran away." She added, "Don't worry, she's safe in my friend's house across the street. Let me show you around."

She put Little down and asked Anh to watch her. I followed Ma upstairs to the bedroom I would be sharing with all of my siblings. There were two sets of bunk beds and a couple of mattresses on the floor. We went back downstairs. The kitchen had cabinets with a shiny concrete countertop, but the stove and refrigerator were missing.

"Where is the stove?" I asked Ma.

"The government took it. They took the gasoline and all

the electrical items. The fridge, electric stove, air-conditioning, rice cooker, electric kettle, everything."

"How do you cook?"

"Outside, camping style." She started to tear up but quickly recovered. "Follow me, Lien. I want to show you this." She took me to the den, where a big machine was humming. "This is the ice making machine. When the ice blocks are ready, I will teach you how to take them out and start another batch. We sell ice to coffee shops. This is our only income now."

"I thought the government took all your electrical items."

"We bought this afterward, illegally, so don't tell anyone. I sold my wedding ring for it. I brought the parts home piece by piece, and an electrician put them together for us. We had to take a risk; we really had no choice. The food rations are not enough to feed the family."

Dinner that night was boiled eggs and rice. Each one of us could have only a quarter of an egg and a small portion of the rice. My stepfather got a whole egg for himself, which he ate in silence. He sat at the table alone; he did not talk to any of us. He didn't even look at me. When he finished his dinner, he hopped back to his room. He never used his artificial leg at home, saying it was too uncomfortable. He just hopped everywhere.

Ma showed me how to do chores around the house. After washing the dishes, I did some of the laundry by hand while Ma gave baths to the children. By the time I got to bed, I was exhausted.

Ma got me up at five o'clock the next morning. She showed me how to take out the ice blocks and stack them on the back of a bicycle. We'd balance the bicycle while we were walking to the coffee shops. Ma introduced me to the coffee shop owners and said that from then on I would be the one to deliver the ice. She took the money and bought some sweet potatoes for breakfast. There were only three sweet potatoes for all of us. I wasn't full at all.

"Ma, we can plant sweet potatoes and vegetables in our yard," I told her. "That's what we did in Can Tho."

"I couldn't find the time to do it and to keep it up. Now that you're here, we can try again."

There were so many chores to do. I had to do laundry by hand and sweep and mop the house. I had to chop wood for cooking and lay it to dry in the sun. Ma wanted Anh and Vu to help me, but they were too young—Anh was nine years old, and Vu was eight. The baby and the toddlers kept Ma busy all the time. I ended up doing all the chores by myself.

Later that day Ma went to the market to get food. She came back with some tomatoes and a block of tofu. After I helped her chop the tomatoes, she realized we didn't have any cooking oil.

"Lien, can you go to Di Hue's house across the street to borrow a cup of oil? Tell her I sent you."

"OK, Ma." I crossed the street and rang the doorbell. A girl showed up at the gate, and I wondered if she was my sister Chi.

"Hi, are you Chi?" I asked her.

"Who wants to know?" She stared at me in challenge.

"My name is Lien. I'm your big sister."

"I don't have a big sister. I'm the oldest," she said forcefully.

I thought, 'She has a strong personality.' I didn't know what else to say. "Well, Ma wants to borrow some cooking oil from Di Hue." I handed her the cup; she took it and went inside without opening the gate to invite me in.

A few minutes later, a woman in her late thirties came out. She handed the cup of oil to me. "Hi, are you Lien? Nice to finally meet you. I'm Di Hue, your mom's best friend. We've talked a lot about you."

"Nice to meet you. Thank you for the oil. I better be getting back. Ma is waiting."

"OK. Tell her if she needs anything, don't hesitate to come over."

I helped Ma fry the tofu while she made tomato sauce. I set the table for my stepfather, got my siblings to sit down on the floor with me, and waited for him to come so we could eat our dinner. He hopped out from his room. As soon as he sat down, he asked Ma, "What is this?" He sounded angry.

"Fried tofu in tomato sauce," Ma said. "That's all I could find in the market today."

"Am I a freaking vegetarian to you now?" He picked up the bowl and threw it across the room. Tofu, sauce, and pieces of bowl landed all over the floor I had mopped earlier. My siblings and I were shaking with fear.

"That's all you could find to cook? Are you mocking me? You have to do better because I'm not eating this crap. Do you hear me?" he shouted.

Ma started to cry. She didn't answer him. Then he hopped toward her, grabbed her hair, and shouted in her ear, "Do you hear me?" Little was in Ma's arms, crying loudly. I went to take the baby away, and my stepfather yelled at me, "And you! Don't come near me, do you understand?"

"Yes." I grabbed Little and ran to the bedroom. I understood now why Chi had run away. My stepfather had a hot temper. I felt sorry for Ma. I wanted to go downstairs to comfort her, but I was still scared. The best I could do was comfort Little for Ma. I rocked her gently until she fell asleep. It was only my second day with my family, and I already feared for my future.

***

Our family struggled day by day. On days with no electricity, we didn't have ice to deliver, and that meant Ma couldn't go to the market to get food. We often borrowed food rations from neighbors, and basically they tried their best to avoid us. We started the vegetable garden, but it took forever to grow. Somehow my stepfather always had liquor in the house, even though we didn't have money for food. I knew Ma bought it for him. At least when he was drunk he slept, so we could breathe easier. He got up very late every day and expected coffee and lunch to be ready. He did nothing around the house.

Meanwhile Ma and I worked hard every day. The chores were endless. I hadn't gotten enough sleep since I'd gotten there. I went to bed late at night and got up early every morning. Some nights I had to get up at two o'clock in the morning to take out the ice blocks so we could have an extra batch. Extra batches of ice meant extra food.

I went to get food rations one day and saw the post office next door. I thought I should send a letter to Can Tho. I asked Ma for a stamp and started writing to the family I missed so much.

> Dear Grandma, Aunt Hai, and family,
>
> How is everybody at home? How is Grandpa? I'm still trying to adjust to my new life in Saigon. It's really hard. Ma and I work every day and still do not have enough food to eat. We have an ice making machine, but every other day the electricity gets turned off. We are struggling, and my siblings are very skinny. I will start school soon and wonder if my paperwork will be ready. When will Aunt Hai's family move here? I miss you all and hope one day I can visit.
>
> Sincerely yours,
> Lien

I mailed the letter and hoped it got to Can Tho safely.

My sister Chi finally came home. Di Hue brought her over because the school year was around the corner. Chi didn't unpack her bag; she said she wanted her belongings to stay there just in case. Happily, I got an extra pair of hands to help with the chores, but Chi was not easy to get along with. She often compared the chores and always chose an easier one. Chi told my siblings not to listen to me because I wasn't a real big sister. She gave Ma a hard time too because she thought Ma loved me more than her, which was completely untrue. I just gave in to whatever she wanted.

A week later the mailman stopped by the house to give us a letter. I thought the letter was for me from Can Tho, but it was for Ma from her parents. I didn't know a lot about her family except that they lived far away in the countryside close to Hue. She asked me to read it to her while she was feeding Little her rice soup.

"Dear daughter," I started. "Thank you so much for your help in the past. Our family could not go on without you. Your brother Thien got arrested a few months ago and was sent to a reeducation camp [he was an army officer]. We wanted to visit him but couldn't afford the bus fare. Is it possible for you to help us with bus tickets? We are forever grateful."

Ma wiped her tears and told me not to tell anybody about the letter. She said she had to find a way to help them. She would ask Di Hue to lend her some money.

The next day I heard Ma screaming and crying in her bedroom along with my stepfather yelling. There was a thumping sound between Ma's cries. My siblings and I were so scared. Chi held on to her bag, ready to flee.

I had pity for Ma when she came out of her bedroom with a bruised face. I begged her to tell me the truth. She told me she had accidentally dropped the letter in the bedroom. He had read it and beat her up for helping her family.

I hated him. He was a monster, a one-legged monster. I had no respect for him and wrote down in my diary that the monster should get arrested instead of my uncle Thien. He should be the one to get reeducated.

Two days later I heard the doorbell ring. I was really happy when I saw Grandma at the gate. She wore her fancy ao dai, even though people rarely wore them anymore. Her hair was done up neatly in a bun. My grandma still had the elegant look of a high-ranking lady.

"Grandma, I can't believe you're here." I had been expecting only a letter.

"You look skinny, Lien. Everybody misses you. Here is the paperwork for school that your Aunt Hai sent." She handed me a package.

"When will Aunt Hai's family move here, Grandma?" I asked.

"Soon, I think. I brought twenty kilos of rice for your family too. Would you help me bring the bag of rice in?"

I had never seen Grandma carry anything before. One letter from me, and there she was, carrying a big bag of rice all the way from Can Tho for us.

"Yes, Grandma, thank you. This will help us a lot," I said.

"Where is your ma? Why isn't she here to greet me?"

"I don't think she knows you're here. Let me go to get her."

"Tell her I'm waiting for her to invite me in. I don't want to intrude." Grandma was always proper.

I went inside to tell Ma that Grandma was outside waiting and that she'd brought rice. Ma looked nervous. I knew she was afraid Grandma would see her swollen and bruised face. Ma told me to hold Little and take my siblings out to greet Grandma, and she would be right out. I went outside, this time with all my siblings. Grandma asked their names and laughed too about the baby's nickname, Little. Ma came out just a bit later. I noticed she'd put on makeup, trying to cover the bruise, but Grandma was known for being a detail person. She noticed right away.

"What happened to your face?" Grandma asked.

"I tripped and fell a couple of days ago, facedown on the floor," Ma said "I'm OK."

"She's lying," Chi said. "Ba hit her."

"Chi, stop it. It isn't nice to jump into an adult conversation," Ma told her.

Ma turned to Grandma, apologized for Chi, and invited her in. She asked Grandma about the family in Can Tho and said she was sorry about Aunt Hai's house and Grandpa's land. Ma told Grandma the government had come there too and taken everything. Ma would have lost the house too, if she hadn't fought for it. Grandma wanted to know the details of how Ma had fought for the house.

"A group of soldiers came with some big trucks," Ma started. "They came inside and told us to line up against the wall. They took the TV, the refrigerator, all of the electrical items, and put everything in the trucks. Then they went into our closet and took all of our nice clothes, our suits and dresses. After they emptied the closet, they found a safe we hid in there. They yelled at my husband to open the safe. He was so nervous, he forgot the code. His hand was shaking so much, he couldn't do it quickly enough. They started to beat him, then they handcuffed him and put him in one of the trucks."

Ma continued, "The soldiers came back and dragged me to the closet. All the children started to cry. I opened the safe as quickly as possible, so I could get back to the children. The soldiers took all the gold and jewelry in the safe. The officer in charge told me to pack our belongings and get on the truck with the children. I was panicking and asked where they would be taking us. The officer said, 'We are taking you to a new development in the countryside. You will have a new life there, a new piece of land to farm on, and a new school for the children.'"

Ma stopped and asked Grandma, "Could you imagine us farming in the countryside? How would we survive? I used to live in the countryside before. I knew we wouldn't make it. We would end up dead from sickness or starvation."

"Did you tell him that?" Grandma asked.

"I told him this. 'Officer, please look at us. My husband is handicapped. He has only one leg. How can he farm? The oldest of my children is only nine years old. We can't survive in the new development because we don't know how to farm. If you have a heart, please, please let us stay here. If you don't, then go ahead and shoot us all today. I would rather die here than go there, because I know we're going to die there anyway!"

"Oh dear! I can't believe you said that," Grandma exclaimed.

"Believe it or not, they let us stay. They released my husband, emptied the house, took all the gasoline from the tank, and left."

"You are an incredible woman. I didn't know you are so strong," Grandma said.

"Who are you talking about?" My stepfather hopped out from his room finally and asked Grandma, "Who is strong?"

"Your wife. Who else?" Grandma said. "She saved the house and the children's future. You shouldn't treat her this way."

"What way?" he snapped at her.

"Look at her face. She didn't deserve that," Grandma said.

I had a feeling something bad was going to happen. I gathered all my siblings, took Little from Ma's arms, and went to our bedroom upstairs. I told the children to stay in there with me and be brave, not to cry. It didn't take long before things started to get loud. He and Grandma argued back and forth, and then the monster roared, "Get out!"

I looked outside from the upstairs window and saw Grandma wiping her eyes as she walked out of the house. I waved at her, hoping she would see me, but she didn't. We didn't have a proper good-bye. Why did he have to be like this? Why did he have to destroy every little happy moment we had? How could Ma be so strong to people outside but so weak when it came to him?

"I hate him," Chi said.

"I know," I said, still looking out the window, worried about Grandma.

"I wish she would divorce him," Chi said. "I wish we could all get together and escape in the middle of the night."

I looked at her and asked, "Did he ever hit you?"

"Yeah, he did. I try to avoid him as much as I can."

I reached out for her hand, but Chi wasn't ready to hold mine. I looked at my siblings and felt bad for all of us. I couldn't wait for school to start; school would be my escape. I hoped one day Ma would be strong and stand up for us, that she would get so sick of this and divorce him. We would be free of the monster once and for all.

Chapter 7
1977

I started the sixth grade in Saigon, and my homeroom teacher, Mrs. Hong, was kind and caring. She paid close attention to everyone, and that was trouble for me. She kept calling my name to answer questions even though I didn't raise my hand. Sometimes she yanked me out of my sleepiness. A couple of times, she was standing next to my table when I woke up due to the sudden laughing of other students. I fell asleep in class a lot. I couldn't help it due to lack of sleep at home.

I sat all the way in the back, hoping no one would look at me. I didn't want anybody staring at my hair or my face. Being half-American made me a target at that time. The other children even made a song to make fun of me. And yes, they sang it many times when the teachers weren't there.

> Blondie, Blondie
> American halfie
> Shame on your mommy
> Go home, Blondie

Sometimes I shouted back, "My hair isn't blond, it's brown." They laughed even more. I didn't know why I bothered to correct them; it didn't make any difference, really.

Another reason I didn't want anybody to look at me was my clothes. I had only two outfits for school, and they were from the previous year. They were old and too small. Luckily I was skinny, so the top sort of fit, but the pants were way too short. I felt embarrassed every time someone looked at me.

Mrs. Hong told me to stay in the classroom at recess one day, saying she wanted to talk to me.

"Oh no! Please don't change my seat," I begged her.

"Lien, you fall asleep in my class a lot. Do you find my subject boring?" She taught writing and reading.

"No, Mrs. Hong." I tried to explain. "I just don't get enough sleep at home, that's all."

"Would you care to explain why you don't get enough sleep? What would a twelve-year-old do at night except sleep?"

I told her I was the oldest in the family, and my stepfather was handicapped. We lived on ice making, and I had to get up early to deliver the ice to coffee shops. Some nights I had to get up in the middle of the night to get an extra batch of ice ready. She nodded her head like she was understanding now.

"Am I failing?" I asked her.

"If you keep sleeping in class, you will," she told me. "I need to talk to your parents about this. It sounds like child abuse to me."

"Please Mrs. Hong, give me a chance to make it up. I promise I'll do better. Please don't talk to my parents. Please don't come to my house."

"Would you like me to help you, Lien?"

"Coming to my house would not help me, Mrs. Hong. I might get punished after you leave."

She was deep in thought for a few minutes, then she said, "I like how you write, Lien. Your writing seems sad, but I like it. I think you have potential, and I want to help you. From now on I will help you with your homework here, at recess, to make up your grade. Would you like that?"

"Yes, Mrs. Hong. I like that very much. Thank you." I felt relieved.

Mrs. Hong helped me a lot with my homework—not just writing and reading but math as well. My grades went from almost failing to much improved.

***

I dragged myself out of bed at five in the morning and was on the bicycle with blocks of ice on the back, heading toward the coffee shops. It was a breezy morning; the cool air felt so good on my skin. Then, slowly, I was drifting off to sleep, not realizing I was still riding the bicycle.

Bang! The noise and the pain woke me up. There I

was, lying in the road in front of a bakery truck. My knee was bleeding, shattered blocks of ice were everywhere, and the front wheel of my bicycle was bent sideways.

The truck driver jumped down and ran to me. "What are you doing? Are you trying to get yourself killed?" He was annoyed. "I saw you aim straight at my truck and run into it. You're lucky I stopped just in time."

"I'm sorry, I didn't see you," I said to him.

"You didn't see me? It's a huge truck. It's not invisible."

"Stop yelling at her," a woman walking by said. "Can't you see she's bleeding?"

"Did you see what happened? She ran into my truck."

"There is no damage to the truck. Look at her. The poor child is shaking." Then she turned to me. "Come on, girl, let me help you up."

She helped me get to my feet, and we moved the bicycle to the side of the road. The truck driver mumbled to himself something about me ruining his morning, and he drove away.

"What is your name?" the lady asked me.

"Lien. My name is Lien. Thank you for helping me."

"It doesn't look like you broke any bones, Lien, just some scratches. Are you going to be OK by yourself? I have to get on with my day." She started to walk away and said, "You should go to the clinic and get that knee checked out." Then she was gone. I hadn't even caught her name.

I stood there for a while debating what to do. My stepfather would be furious. Should I run away? Where would I go? I didn't know anyone in Saigon and didn't have any money. I knew I would get punished when I got home. This was the only bicycle we had. I hadn't even made it to the first coffee shop, and the ice was gone.

If I ran away, he would hit Ma. So many times I had told my siblings to be brave. I had to be brave too. I walked home, enduring the pain. Dragging the bicycle by lifting the front wheel, it was hard not to hit my knee on it. Blood dripped all the way down to my foot. As I passed the school, the courtyard was empty because everybody was in class already.

I envied all the students in there; they were in a safe place.

As soon as I told Ma about the accident, she started pacing back and forth in the living room. "I have to tell him, Lien. We have no choice. He's going to find out anyway."

"Will he hit me?" I asked her.

"I don't know." Her eyes started to tear. "Let me clean up your knee, then I have to take you in to see him."

I looked out the window and regretted my decision to come home. Ma couldn't protect me even if it was an accident. After she put a bandage on my knee, she went in her bedroom to wake up the monster.

"He's waiting for you, Lien. Go on in. Explain to him what happened."

"I'm scared, Ma. Please go in there with me," I cried.

"I can't bring the baby in there, Lien."

My head told me to run, but my legs were really heavy, like they were turning to stone. My whole body started to shake when I saw him walk out with his artificial leg on. He held a big bamboo stick in his hand, and he was angry.

"You destroyed the business. You damaged this family!" He whacked me on the head with full force. "It's about time to teach you how to be useful."

"I'm sorry, Ba, it was an accident." I cried out in pain. I covered my head with both hands, and the bamboo stick kept striking me all over my body. I backed away and ended up in a corner. He continued hitting me. His eyes were like a wild animal's as it faced its prey.

"Stop it. That's enough!" Ma said.

He didn't stop. Ma jumped in and grabbed the bamboo stick. He warned Ma to let the stick go, but she didn't. He turned around and punched her in the face. Blood started to come out of her nose, but she was still holding the stick. He punched her again, and Ma fell on the floor. I ran outside.

"Help! Please, somebody help us!" I called, then used all the energy I had left to scream, "Help!"

Di Hue came running out, and I pointed to the house. "Di Hue, he's hitting Ma inside. Please help her."

She went inside and came out a few minutes later with

Ma in her arms. Neighbors stared at us from a distance, but no one came to help. Ma's face was swollen; blood was all over her top. Di Hue told us to come in her house. Then I realized Little and Lieu were still inside.

"Di Hue, the little children are still in the bedroom. What are we going to do?" I asked.

"Lien, take your ma inside. I'll go get the children."

Ma and I walked slowly to Di Hue's house. We both had been beaten up badly and felt very weak. Ma started crying again; it made me sad, and I wondered how somebody like him could be related to my sweet, loving Aunt Hai.

Di Hue came back with Lieu and Little. They cried even harder when they saw Ma's face. Lucky for us, Di Hue was a nurse at a local clinic. She put Little down on the floor and cleaned Ma's face and gave her some medicine. When Di Hue asked me to take off my top so she could treat me, she stared at my back in disbelief. I had beat marks all over my back and my arms.

"You have to report this to the police," she told Ma.

Ma shook her head no; she wouldn't do it.

"That is the only way to stop him from abusing you and the children. You have to be strong for them," Di Hue said.

"His family would blame me if he got arrested." Ma said. "They might keep him in jail for a long time if they find out he was an Air Force officer."

"Stop worrying about him. You should think about the children. I wouldn't care about his family if I were you," Di Hue said. "I'm going to boil some water for you and Lien to take warm baths. Don't wash your bloody shirt, though, keep it as evidence just in case you change your mind later."

Di Hue lived alone. She had never been married. Ma said she'd had a longtime boyfriend without knowing he was already married to somebody else. When Di Hue found out, she ended the relationship and never went out with anybody again. She was Ma's only friend.

Sometimes Di Hue gave my stepfather some pills, and Ma thought that was why he never bothered Di Hue. She gave me some of her niece's clothes to wear—she had two nieces about my age. I wished she had a long-sleeve shirt to cover my bruised arms, but they were all short sleeved.

The next day at school, everybody stared at my arms. They stopped teasing me after that. Maybe they felt sorry for me. Mrs. Hong was really upset. She wanted to talk to my parents at our house, but I told her we were temporarily living with a neighbor. Mrs. Hong gave me a new long-sleeve shirt the next day.

A few days later, Aunt Tam came to visit. I saw her from Di Hue's house and caught her before she went in. I told her the whole story, and she became really upset. How could her brother do this to his own family? She went to talk to him, and when Aunt Tam came back, she had the damaged bicycle with her. She said she would pay for the repair, and she had an idea to help us. She wanted me to meet her at the hospital so she could sneak out some food for us.

"Don't worry. I'll take the food only from patients who are not touching their meals. My coworkers do it all the time for their families."

"He wouldn't want to eat the food from hospital," Ma said.

"I'm not doing it for him. I'm risking my job for my nieces and nephew only. You don't have to tell him about it," Aunt Tam said.

I went to get food from Aunt Tam's hospital every other day. Our meeting place was under a big oak tree a block away from hospital. She came with bags of good food, like chicken, pork, and beef. The government officers were eating so well in that hospital. Aunt Tam was our angel, and I kept praying she would never get caught.

All my siblings and I were happy we had good food to eat. Ma was relieved we didn't have to bother Di Hue too much. Di Hue said to Ma that we weren't a bother to her. She even said, "Don't go home until he apologizes." Knowing him, Ma said, he would never apologize. I told Ma that Chi wished she would divorce him. After some convincing from us and Di Hue, she decided she was going to ask him for a divorce.

***

Ma went to tell him about her decision to end the marriage, but it wasn't going to be easy. The law was both husband and wife had to agree to a divorce, unless she could prove she was a victim of an abusive husband. Ma was, of course, but she didn't want to report any of it. She said she just wanted the divorce and didn't want to put him in jail.

After a few weeks of living with Di Hue, Ma decided it was time to move back home. She couldn't bother Di Hue any longer. My sister Chi and I weren't happy about Ma's decision. We liked living at Di Hue's house; we breathed a lot easier, and I slept better.

"How could you go home after that, Ma?" I asked her. "He's going to hit us again."

"We talked about it, Lien. He promised me he won't hit us anymore," Ma said. "Besides, I told him I still have the bloody shirt, and I will show it to police next time if he hits us again."

"How could you fall in love with somebody like that?" I asked.

"He wasn't like that when I met him. He changed after he lost his leg, and it was still all right when we had the gasoline business. He became angrier after we lost everything."

"I really don't want to move back with him, Ma. Can I stay here with Di Hue?"

"I need you, Lien. We sold the ice maker and bought a new business. It's a juice stand in Cho Lon. I need your help after school. You won't be around him that much, and you don't need to get up early to deliver ice anymore. Things will get better."

I didn't know what to say. I just hoped things would get better, like Ma said. I helped her pack, and we moved back home the next day.

The new juice stand we had was far from home. Every day after school, I rode the bicycle for forty-five minutes to Cho Lon to help Ma. We sold coconut, fresh orange juice, and sugarcane juice. Cho Lon was a huge wholesale market, probably the biggest market in the country. Our juice stand was very busy in the sunny seasons. There were always customers waiting in line to buy juices. It was a lot of work to run the stand. As soon as I got there, I worked nonstop until the market closed down. I had to help Ma peel coconut and sugarcane so we could be ready to serve the customers. We had to press sugarcane by hand to get the juice; it required strong muscles to do that. Despite the hard work, I was happy. I spent more time with Ma and less time at home.

Chi and Anh had to take care of the toddlers after school now. Ma cooked before work so the children could have something to eat during the day. Chi had to do some chores around the house when we weren't there. She was not happy that I went to work with Ma. She complained a lot, saying it wasn't fair for her to be home every day with him. She reported a lot to Ma about what he did during the day.

"I came home from school and saw he had tied Little's ankle to the bed and kept on sleeping," Chi said, "and he made us give him a massage."

"Well, he's in pain, Chi. Sometimes he needs a little massage to help with the pain."

"You always take his side," Chi said and walked out of the room.

Chi told Ma on another day, "He hit Vu today because Vu broke a bowl." Another day she reported, "Anh got hit today because she took too long to bring food in the bedroom for him."

"How much did he hit Anh? A lot?" Ma asked Chi.

"You can ask her yourself." She gave Ma an attitude.

Ma and I came home from work one evening, and Anh told Ma that Chi was gone.

"What do you mean gone? Anh! Tell me what happened," Ma said.

"Chi's teacher came to the house. While the teacher was talking to Ba, Chi grabbed her belongings and ran," Anh said.

It turned out Chi got into a fight at school, and the

teacher wanted to report that she got a week's probation. Ma sent Anh and me to look for her. We walked around the neighborhood in the dark calling out her name. We knocked on people's doors, but we couldn't find her. The next day I went to work and found Chi was standing in the juice stand.

"How did you get here?" I asked her in surprise.

"I walked," she said casually.

"How did you know where to go? I mean, it's really far, and you've never been here before."

"I asked people, which way is Cho Lon? They showed me. It took me more than two hours, but I got here, and I slept here last night."

"Stop talking, and start working, the two of you," Ma said.

I was happy we got extra help for the business, but Chi and I fought a lot about everything. Ma didn't tell him we found Chi at Cho Lon, and she slept at the juice stand all week. After her probation passed, Ma wanted Chi to come home for school, but Chi didn't want to. Ma tried to bribe her with new clothes; she still said no. Ma finally told him the truth about Chi staying in the juice stand and refusing to come home for school. They came up with a plan, which I didn't know about until the next day.

Chi and I were peeling sugarcane at work. All of a sudden, she dropped the peeler and ran. When I looked up, I saw my stepfather. He brought two of his friends with him, and they were chasing Chi. While I was pretending to mind my own business, I was eavesdropping on Ma when she talked to him.

"Don't hit her this time," Ma said. "I want her to stay in school."

"It depends. I can't allow her to be rude to me," he said.

His friends came back with Chi in their hands and tried to put her in one of the cyclos they brought, but Chi wasn't giving in. She kicked them, screaming that they were kidnapping her. My stepfather and Ma went to the cyclo. Ma tried to calm Chi while my stepfather told his friends to tie her up. They tied both of her hands and ankles to the cyclo.

"Chi, calm down," said Ma. "Don't worry, Ba won't hit you. He promised. We just want you to go to school."

Chi was crying and screaming about Ma not loving her at all. She just wanted to work with Ma at Cho Lon, was that too much to ask? People started forming a circle surrounding them. It was an embarrassing scene. Where were the police when you needed them? I felt bad for Chi. After his friends were done tying her up, my stepfather got into another cyclo, and they rode away together.

"He's going to hit Chi, Ma, and you won't be there to stop him," I said angrily.

"Enough, Lien! I'm doing the best I can. She needs to go to school, and I need to be here working. I don't have a choice."

I worked the rest of the day without talking to her. I just hoped he kept his promise not to hit Chi. I didn't trust him to keep promises, though, because he would still snap and slap us here and there.

We went home from work and saw my stepfather and his friends were drinking in the living room. Had they been drinking to their victory of capturing a child? How could they be in a good mood after treating Chi that way? Ma started making dinner for the captors while they were singing in their ridiculous voices. I was too upset to help Ma; I told her I didn't feel good and went to bed.

All my siblings were in the bedroom. Like me, they were avoiding him. Chi was in bed already, buried under her blanket. Anh tied Little's ankle to the bed (she learned that from him) and kept on playing with the girls. A pile of unfolded clothes was left in the middle of the room. As soon as Little saw me, she wanted to be free from the rope. She started to cry and tried to untie herself. What a mess.

Of course I couldn't go to bed like I planned to. I untied Little, had her sit next to me, and asked the girls to help me fold the clothes. Then I gave all the little ones their baths, helped Ma feed them, and washed the dishes. There was no escape, no downtime in that house. I was emotionally and physically exhausted.

The next morning Ma became sick. She looked pale and tired. I was concerned about her and asked her to see the doctor. She told me she wasn't sick—she was pregnant. What? Oh Lord, have mercy on us!

Chapter 8
1978

Aunt Hai's family finally moved to Saigon. She owned an old small house that had been abandoned when they'd moved to Can Tho. It was in a different neighborhood, so my cousins were not in school with me. I was longing for a visit with her family.

Ma and I went home from work one day, and I was so happy to see Aunt Hai and her husband in our living room. My stepfather was there too. He appeared to have an alcoholic drink right there on the dining room table while Aunt Hai and Uncle didn't have any drinks by their sides.

"Would you like some tea, Aunt Hai?" I offered, knowing Ma had just bought some. I was wondering if Ma knew about this visit.

"Yes, Lien, we would love some if you have it. You look taller. How is school?" Aunt Hai said.

"It's good." I didn't want to tell her I wasn't an honor roll student anymore. It was impossible to get on the honor roll without enough time to study.

I came back with the pot of tea for them and heard Aunt Hai talking about how small her house was. It had only two bedrooms, and the tin roof leaked every time it rained. The house was in bad shape. She felt it was not safe for her family living there.

"I was thinking since I gave you the gasoline business before when you needed help," Aunt Hai told my stepfather, "now that we need a safer place for the children to live and we don't have money anymore—"

He cut her off, saying, "You want my children to move out so your children can move in? Is that what you're trying to say? Don't forget I built this house."

"I know you built this house, but it's on my property. Why don't we work together? Try to sell this house, and divide this huge property into four lots. It would be easy to build four more houses. We can split the money—you get half, we get half. Each one of us could buy another house."

"No, I don't want to sell it. I designed this house for my needs, and if my wife hadn't saved it, the government would have taken it already."

"You're being unreasonable. We are brother and sister. We're supposed to help each other," Aunt Hai said.

"You are the one being unreasonable. You came to my house and asked me to sell it. Why don't you just build a house right next door?"

"We don't have the money to build a house. That's why we asked you to sell it. I helped you before. It's time for you to pay us back. Your house is on my property. The only way to be fair is to sell it."

"I'm not going to sell; the house is mine. All land belongs to the government now anyway. It's not your property anymore," He said stubbornly.

Aunt Hai teared up, and Uncle shook his head in disbelief. He stood up and held Aunt Hai's hand. "Come on, honey, let's go."

Ma said nothing the whole time.

"I didn't expect this from a family member, especially the one I cared for and helped in the past," Aunt Hai said. She left with her husband, without saying good-bye to any of us.

I was sad that Aunt Hai left the house before I even had a chance to catch up. All I could do was write down in my diary how much I missed her and the family. The air in this house was always heavy, hard to breathe, like it was toxic.

Another day I went home from work and saw my stepfather in the living room. He appeared to be drunk and angry. As soon as I saw my diary in his hand, I froze. He had his artificial leg on, and I knew I was in trouble. He yelled at Ma to lock the door, and she did. He threw my diary at Ma. "Read it!"

"What is it?" Ma asked him.

"Your daughter called me a monster! She called this house hell on earth, and she hates being here." He stood up abruptly, grabbed a belt from the table, and struck me. I ended up in a corner again, nowhere to run. The door was locked. I cried out at every stroke. The pain was indescribable.

Ma didn't stop him. Was it because she was pregnant or because she thought I was disrespectful to her husband? Maybe she thought I deserved the punishment. She tore up my diary into small pieces. I didn't know which one was more painful, the beating or seeing my diary torn up. The diary had been a gift from Aunt Hai, the only thing I cherished.

I went to school wearing a long-sleeve shirt, but every time someone accidentally bumped me, I would yelp out in pain. My teacher, Mrs. Hong, knew. She asked me at recess about my bruises. I cried and told her the truth about my stepfather finding my diary. He didn't like all the things I wrote about him. The result was this punishment—he had hit me with the belt. Mrs. Hong hugged me and said she was very sorry I had an abusive stepfather and she was disappointed in my ma for letting this happen.

Mrs. Hong went to the house after school that day. Ma was at work, and I should have been at Cho Lon to help her, but Mrs. Hong insisted she needed to talk to my stepfather. She said she was not afraid of him and wanted to put an end to the child abuse. Hopefully I wouldn't get hit anymore. After I pulled out a chair for Mrs. Hong, I went to his bedroom to let him know my teacher was waiting in the living room. He glared at me in anger. "How dare you?" his eyes said. He came out with his artificial leg on.

"Mr. Luong, my name is Hong, Lien's teacher," she said. "I came to talk to you about those bruises on Lien's arm. I asked her what had happened, but she didn't want to tell me. As her teacher I'm concerned about her. Do you know what happened? Did you report it to the police, or should I be the one to report it?"

"A bad child needs to be disciplined, that's all, Mrs. Hong. I have a lot of children, and I can't let them run wild," he replied.

"What did she do that you had to discipline her this way, Mr. Luong?"

"Do you have any children, Mrs. Hong?" my stepfather asked.

"Mr. Luong, I came here to find out what happened to Lien, not to answer questions."

"Well, my suggestion to you, Mrs. Hong, is that you mind your own business."

"My students are my business," Mrs. Hong said firmly.

"I have nothing else to say to you, Mrs. Hong. Lien can show you the way out."

"Mr. Luong, if I see Lien with bruises again, I will go straight to the police," Mrs. Hong said and went outside. At the gate she said, "I'll see you tomorrow, Lien." She let out a sigh. "I hope he stops hitting you." Then she left.

I went back in for the bicycle so I could go to work. My stepfather glared at me and asked, "What did you tell her?"

"Nothing," I said in fear. "I really have to go to work now. Ma is waiting." I took the bike and ran out of the house.

***

I didn't really have any friends at school or in the neighborhood. They probably didn't want to be near our strange family, and I didn't have time for friendship anyway. However, I had a friend from Cho Lon. Her name was Huong. Her family had an herbal medicine stall next to ours. We weren't friends right away because she was a few years older than I was. Slowly we became very close friends. We talked about everything when both of our businesses were slow. She even helped with my chores at work sometimes.

After Huong saw my stepfather tie Chi to the cyclo, she started to ask many questions about our family. Of course I didn't tell her anything because I didn't want to lose her as a friend. I told her everything was fine, just normal family stuff like everybody else. Chi was OK; she went to school like normal.

One day I rolled up my sleeves just a little to get ready for work. Huong grabbed my arm, pulled up my sleeve, pointed at the bruises, and demanded an answer. "What is this? You can't hide from me anymore, Lien. Friends should always tell the truth."

"Ouch!" I took my arm back. "It still hurts. Be careful."

"Are you going to tell me?"

"Look, I'll tell you later, when my ma is not here."

I told her later about my diary story that had led to the bruises. To my surprise she didn't avoid me like I thought she would. Instead she gave me some herbal medicine to put on.

"I would write the same thing and give him maybe even a worse nickname if I had a stepfather like yours. Who would read another person's diary?"

"Thank you for being my friend," I said.

"I'm going to give you my address. If you ever want to run away or something, you can stay at my house. My parents are very kind, and they like to help people."

"Running away had crossed my mind a few times, but I didn't want to leave Ma with so much to do, plus she was going to have a baby soon." I let out a sigh. "People will talk bad about me if I'm running away. Girls are not supposed to run away, right?"

"I'm just concerned about you, Lien." She wrote down her address and gave it to me. "Study it, remember it by heart, then destroy it. You can come to my house anytime, even if it's just a few days to take a break. I won't tell anybody; your ma won't find out."

I took the address, memorized it, then threw the piece of paper away. Sometimes she quizzed me just to see if I still remembered. Huong was really a good friend; she gave me her clothes and shared her food with me. Sometimes, when Ma wasn't there, I gave Huong fruit. She told me to treat her like my diary, to tell her everything without worrying someone might read it. Huong promised she would keep everything to herself, and she did.

Ma was really showing by then. Soon enough the baby would be there. She had visited the doctor only once since she became pregnant. She said it cost so much money to see the doctor, so she just left it in God's hands. Her plan was to show up at the emergency room when the baby was ready to come out. Di Hue gave her some prenatal vitamins.

Ma was still working every day, but I had to do all the heavy stuff, like pressing the sugarcane for juice, and I carried all the fruit. She took me food shopping, showing me how to get the best bargain at the end of the day, when the vendors were ready to close down. She started teaching Chi and I how to cook too.

Meanwhile my stepfather kept on drinking with his friends. He was babbling something about if Ma was having a boy this time, they would close the factory down. But if it was a girl, they would keep on trying until they had another boy. Hearing him say that, you would think he loved and spoiled my brother, Vu. He hit Vu all the time, for every little mistake Vu made. There were no mistakes allowed in that house.

We went home from work one day, and Chi reported Vu hadn't come home since my stepfather had sent him out to buy a bottle of soy sauce. Ma let out a sigh and told me to go find Vu. I walked around the neighborhood asking about him and finally found him at his friend's house. It was a shack, really, probably the poorest looking house in the neighborhood. Vu came out when I called him.

"What's happened, Vu? Why didn't you come home?" I asked him.

"I accidentally broke the soy sauce bottle. Ba is going to hit me, sister Lien. I don't want to go home. I'm scared," Vu said.

"Sooner or later you have to go home, right? Why not now, when Ma is home?"

"Ma can't stop him; he's still going to hit me. I know he will."

Vu's friend came out and stood next to him. He said, "Vu can stay here with us. My ma said it's OK."

"Can I talk to your ma?" I asked.

He took me inside their very humble home. It was one room with a cement floor, tin walls, and a thatched roof. They were probably cooking outside camping style too, because I didn't see a kitchen. The family was Chinese, and they were very friendly and kind. After a little conversation, the mother of

Vu's friend insisted he could stay there as long as he liked. Vu could go to school together with her son, and she promised he would be safe with her family.

"Do you really want to stay here, Vu?" I asked him.

"Yes! I don't want to go home. I feel safe here."

"OK. I won't tell anybody you're here. We didn't see each other tonight. Do you understand?"

"Yes, we didn't see each other," Vu said with a smile.

I said good-bye to Vu and went home, and I lied to Ma that I couldn't find him. Vu stayed there for a long time, like they were his second family.

***

The baby decided to enter the world in the middle of the night. Ma woke me up with her screaming that she needed to go to the hospital—"now!" I had to run to the neighbor who happened to drive a cyclo for a living and ask him to please take Ma to the hospital. I didn't know what to expect because our neighbors normally avoided us. I was relieved when I saw him gathering his things and pushing the cyclo to the street.

"Let's go." That was all he said. Di Hue and I helped Ma get into the cyclo; our neighbor pushed it up to speed, jumped on the seat, and started to pedal with all his strength.

Di Hue got on her bicycle and said, "I'm going to the hospital with her. You stay home to take care of your siblings. I'll let you know when I get some news."

It was still dark. I went back inside and tried to sleep, but I just couldn't. I was worried about everything. How long would Ma stay in the hospital? What was I supposed to do in the morning? Who was going to run the juice stand? Me? What about school? I was tossing and turning until the sun started to peek through the window. I got my siblings up so they could get ready for school.

Then Di Hue came to the house and told us Ma had the baby, and it was a boy. She said Ma was doing fine, but she had to stay in the hospital for two more days. I knocked on my stepfather's bedroom door. I was so scared of him, I jumped when I heard him say "yes?"

"Di Hue said Ma had the baby. It's a boy," I said through the closed door.

"You can come in," he said in a commanding voice.

I opened the door. He sat on the edge of the bed. To my surprise he was sober.

"Is Di Hue still here?" he asked.

"No, Ba, she went home. She said Ma is doing OK."

He gave me money to get coffee for him and breakfast for us.

"You and Chi are going to work at Cho Lon today. I will write a note for both of you to be excused from school for a few days," he said.

Chi and I tried our best to open the business without Ma. Some of our regular customers asked about her and said congratulations to us. The day went by fast; all of a sudden it was lunchtime. Chi wanted to order an expensive lunch for us to celebrate the baby. I refused, because first of all Ma and I would never order anything expensive and second, I was worried we would get in trouble if our parents found out.

"If you don't tell them, how would they find out?" Chi said. "I won't tell them."

"I don't know, Chi. I really don't want to get hit again."

"Come on, this is one chance we could eat something we want to eat, to celebrate the baby," Chi begged.

I gave in. We ordered grilled pork chops for lunch. We ate in silence, devouring every bite.

"I have a name for the baby," Chi said.

"Yeah? What is his name going to be?"

"Be," Chi said, nodding her head like she was satisfied with it.

"You can't call him that. It's not even a name."

"Well, I will call him Be no matter if you like it or not."

"I'm sure Ba already has a name picked out for him. We'll find out soon enough," I said. "Let's go back to work."

We went home after grocery shopping and gave him all the money we had made that day. He wasn't happy with the amount we had left, saying Ma normally made more. I was so scared and worried about our expensive lunch, but Chi told him the customers didn't want to buy juice from us. They didn't trust two little kids, and that was why we made less money. He believed her.

Chi and I cooked dinner, and we cleaned up the house. My stepfather told me to go the hospital with Di Hue. He gave me a piece of paper with the baby's name and said to give it to Ma. Di Hue and I rode bicycles to the hospital side by side. There were a lot of bicycles in the city, and Di Hue said they made the city look sad. Saigon looked very communist now without cars.

"Where are all the cars?" I asked her.

"The government took them and brought them all to the North. I miss the old Saigon. People were happier. Now everyone looks sad. Don't tell anybody I said that."

"I won't," I assured her. "Can I ask you something?"

"Go ahead, Lien. What do you want to know?"

"Does Ma ever mention who my real ba is? Do you know anything about him?"

She looked at my face, trying to read me.

"Di Hue, I know he isn't my ba. I just wonder if Ma ever talked to you about my real ba."

"No, Lien, she never did. I never asked her about it. I thought when she's ready, she will tell me. I don't want to pressure her."

I was disappointed and stayed quiet the rest of the way to the hospital. Ma looked rested. The baby was by her side. He was really cute in his sleep. Ma said he was a good baby, slept through the night and hardly cried.

Two days later Ma came home with the baby. Even though his name was Nha, Chi kept calling him Be, and it quickly became his nickname. Ma went back to work a few days later, so Be had to take bottles, and he wasn't fussy at all. Baby formula wasn't available at the market, because of government rationing so we had to feed him condensed milk mixed with a lot of water. Sometimes when we cooked white rice, we scooped out some of the hot milky liquid, waited for it to cool down, and fed him that. Despite the lack of nutrition,

Be was an easy baby, and everyone loved him.

Chapter 9
1979

Ma saved up enough money to upgrade the business. She got electricity for the juice stand, bought a machine to press the sugarcane, and a blender for fruit shakes. I was so happy, even though the electricity still turned off every other day. At least we got a break from pressing by hand.

At our house she built a small hut outside to use as a kitchen, because the camping-style cooking wasn't really working—we got rained on many times. The outdoor kitchen didn't have plumbing or a sink, so we had to use the faucet outdoors for cleaning vegetables and fish.

Ma got a few weeks of good business, so she decided to buy beef for dinner as a treat one night. I was helping her in the kitchen as usual, and she asked me to clean the beef and slice it for her. After I cleaned the beef at the outdoor faucet and realized I had forgotten the cutting board, I left the meat in the colander and went in to get the board. It was less than a minute, but when I got back I saw a big dog had taken the piece of meat and ran. I chased him to the street, but he was too fast. After a few seconds, he was gone, with our dinner in his mouth.

Why hadn't I held on to the piece of beef? My family hadn't had any meat for a long time, and I should have paid more attention. I felt so guilty I had ruined the family's dinner. I went into the hut and confessed to Ma about the dog.

Ma told me I should go in and confess to my stepfather. She grabbed my arm, pulling me toward the house. I was crying and calling Di Hue to help, but sadly for me Di Hue wasn't home. A couple of neighbors stared at us from a distance.

Ma won. She got me inside the living room, and he was there already waiting for his dinner. She told him what had happened, and he got angry instantly. He asked Ma to fetch his belt for him, but Ma said no. He struck me anyway, with an extension cord he found in the living room. I was crying, screaming, apologizing, but he didn't stop. Ma took my siblings to the other room, and the angry monster kept on hitting me.

Suddenly a miracle happened. There was something pounding the tin roof, sounding like heavy hail, and then I heard people's voices.

"Stop hitting her!" a woman's voice cried out.

"What kind of man are you?" A man's voice this time.

"You should be ashamed of yourself for hitting a defenseless child."

I realized our neighbors were outside trying to stop him from hitting me. Another wave of rocks got thrown on our roof.

Ma ran to the living room and told him to stop before the neighbors destroyed the house. She said she couldn't afford a new roof. And he stopped. He was still angry and started drinking and cursing at the neighbors. After they left he cursed at Ma, calling her names until he got too drunk and went to bed.

That night my sisters surrounded me looking concerned. They asked me if I was hurt here or there and offered me their pillows. I couldn't sleep on my back, it was so painful. There was something sharp poking me in the back, so I had to sleep on my stomach instead. Ma offered me some aspirin, but I refused. I was still mad at her.

I slowed down at work because of the pain, and honestly I didn't care anymore about working hard for the family. A few days later, I told my friend Huong what had happened, and she insisted I should run away to her house. She rubbed some herbal medicine on me and found a piece of metal stuck in my back. It turned out the extension cord's plastic cover had broken during the beating, and a piece of metal from it had lodged in my back. Huong cried when she saw it. She said it got infected and insisted I needed to go to the emergency room. Huong told Ma about it, but Ma didn't want me to go the hospital because she was afraid they might put him in jail. She asked Di Hue to treat me.

Di Hue was mad at Ma too when she saw it. They argued, and Ma left. Di Hue took me on her bicycle to the clinic where she worked. She removed the piece of metal from my back, cleaned the wound, and put on a bandage; she also gave me some antibiotics. She insisted I should stay at her house for a few days so she could keep her eye on the wound, making sure it healed properly before I went back to work. I went to school like normal, because I didn't want to be left behind.

I stayed at Di Hue's house for a week, and it felt so good to be free of my stepfather. I bumped into Chi at school, and she said she was jealous of me. She wanted to stay with Di Hue too. I asked Di Hue to let me stay with her for good, and she said she would love to have me, but she couldn't because Ma was her friend. If Ma wanted me back, then Di Hue had no choice.

When Ma came to get me, she apologized to Di Hue, and they were back to being friends again. I hated that I had to go home with Ma. I became quiet and didn't want to talk to her anymore. I also started putting my belongings in a bag like Chi, getting ready to flee. All I needed was a little money. I would have to find a way to save up.

***

As the business was getting busier, Ma had to make more trips to get fruit. Whenever I was there alone to serve the customers, I would hide a little money in a hidden pocket I sewed into my pants. Huong had been asking me about my plan, when would I be ready to flee. She told her parents about my situation, and they were eager to help. I told her I wanted to finish middle school so I could have the paperwork for high school in her area.

Vu was still staying with his friend's family. My parents knew he lived there and had been trying to take him home. Every time Ma went there, Vu ran away out the back door. Even my stepfather tried. He walked there with his friends, but they failed too. Vu was a fast runner, and his second family protected him. They told my parents to get off of their property. Vu didn't run from me; he trusted me. I went there to spend some time with Vu, then went home and lied to Ma that I couldn't catch him either.

I tried to pay more attention to my other siblings as well. I knew I would miss them when I was gone. I started to tell them fairy tales before bed and helped them with their homework when I could. My little brother, Be, had gotten bigger. He walked around so cute, and I knew I would miss him too. Still, I was prepared to leave.

One brutally hot, sticky day, the electricity was turned off. I wished we had electricity on a day like that; it was too hard to press sugarcane by hand all day. I kept the switch of the pressing machine on, as I was told to do, just so we would know when the electricity came back. It didn't come back. At the end of the day, I was exhausted and glad it was over. Like usual, Ma went to get groceries. I cleaned the juice stand and locked everything up.

The next day I was in Mrs. Hong's class. She wasn't our homeroom teacher anymore, but she still taught us reading. We were supposed to graduate middle school in two days, so she was just telling us stories about high school. Ma appeared at the classroom door. She interrupted Mrs. Hong, saying I needed to go home with her right away.

I went to the door and whispered, "Ma, I'm in class. Why do I have to go home now?"

"Lien, you burnt the juice stand. It caught on fire, and your ba wants you home now!" Ma seemed angry.

"Lien, can you tell me what's going on?" Mrs. Hong asked.

"Oh my God!" I cried. "I forgot to turn off the switch."

"You need to come home with me!" Ma said and grabbed my arm, pulling me out of the classroom.

"No! Ma, please forgive me," I cried. "You know he's going to kill me, Ma."

I grabbed a table, desperately trying to stay.

"Ma'am!" said Mrs. Hong. "I'm sorry, you can't do this in my class. You have to leave, or I will call the police."

"She is my daughter!" Ma yelled at Mrs. Hong.

"You're interrupting my class. I need you to leave."

"I'm waiting outside, Lien, at the gate," Ma said and left.

At the end of Mrs. Hong's class, I gave her a good-bye hug and fled through the school's backyard. I ran until I couldn't breathe, then I stopped, looking back to see if Ma was behind me. After I caught my breath, I walked alertly to a bus stop. I got on a bus, looking around to make sure no one there knew me. I finally calmed down after the bus drove off. It took me to the terminal, where I switched to another bus to Huong's house in district four.

I walked around asking people for directions and finally found Huong's house in the back of a long alley. I stood there not knowing what to do. Should I knock on their door now or wait for Huong to come home? I decided to wait for Huong. I wasn't good at introducing myself. I got nervous easily and probably would break down and cry.

Three hours later Huong and her mother came home. I was standing under a tree nearby when she saw me. She ran over and hugged me. "Lien, I'm glad you're here. I was worried about you."

"Did you hear what happened to the juice stand?" I asked her. "Did the whole thing burn down?"

"No, only the motor was burned. The juice stand is fine," Huong said.

I felt such relief that Ma still had her business.

"Come inside, Lien," Huong's mother told me.

I followed them inside. Their house was filled with an herbal aroma. Huong introduced me to her father and her younger brother. I felt welcome and really appreciated how they generously took me into their home. Huong showed me around and said I would be sharing a bedroom with her. That night we talked and giggled until two o'clock. It felt so good to be free from fear and worry, like a teenager should be.

***

It wasn't hard to get used to my new environment. Huong was wonderful, kind, and sweet. I felt very lucky to have a friend like her. She treated me like I was a sister she'd never had. She joked that she would rather have a sweet sister like me than her airhead brother.

Huong's mother was highly respected in their community. She was a kind person and always lent a hand when somebody was in need. A lot of ladies in the neighborhood came to get advice from her. She was really nice to me and treated me like a family member. I told her I wanted to find a job, and she went out of her way to help me.

Huong's mother got me a job in their neighborhood with her neighbor Mrs. Phu. She had a homemade candy business, and my job was to wrap the candies. During the day, while Huong and her mother went to work at Cho Lon, I would go to work at the candy place. Mrs. Phu provided lunch at work, which made things a lot easier for me. I liked to work there; my coworkers were friendly, and the owner was kind. Mrs. Phu was a single mother—she had only one child, and her daughter was half-American too. Mrs. Phu liked me instantly, often giving me an easier job and offering to let me stay with her. I preferred to stay with Huong. I offered half of my salary to Huong's mother, but she refused to take my money. She told me to save it so I could buy my own clothes.

Everyone called Huong's father a medicine man. He was always busy making medicine from herbs. He had patients come to their house for treatment and was well respected. If someone couldn't afford to pay, he treated them for free. He really listened to their problems and always tried his best to help them. He was trying to teach Huong and her brother about herbal medicine, but they weren't interested. Huong wanted to be a teacher, and her brother was interested only in girls.

Huong and I enjoyed each other's company a lot. We shared clothes, chores, and secrets. Huong was seventeen years old and very attractive, therefore many young men had been asking her out. Her father was a little over protective of her. Her mother had a soft heart, though, and often gave in when Huong asked for permission to go out. As long as she brought me along with her on a date, then the permission would be granted.

We went out on many different dates with boys Huong

chose. They didn't kiss or even hold hands; all they did was talk, but I still felt a little funny to be a third person when the other two were focused on each other. Still, I was glad to be there for Huong, and I got many free snacks and movies.

The summer was almost over. Huong would start her senior year of high school soon, and she was excited about us going to school together. I wasn't sure if I could go to high school with Huong because I didn't have any paperwork with me. I was thinking of making a trip back to the middle school to get my report card. It had been the end of the school year when I'd run away, and I'd passed all my exams, but I was still scared about going back there. It was complicated, and I certainly worried for my future.

Every day when Huong came home from work, I would ask her about Ma and the business. Who was helping my ma now? Did she say anything about my siblings? Huong said Chi had been helping Ma. Sometimes Huong asked Ma about me, pretending she knew nothing about where I was. Ma said she didn't know where I was but hoped I was OK. I couldn't help but cry; I felt so guilty and missed my siblings. I was tempted to send Ma a letter to say I was OK, but Huong said don't do it, it would hurt more than help.

Huong came home from work one day and told me Chi had run away again. While Ma had gone to get fruit, Chi had lost the tin box where we kept the money at work, and somebody stole it. She was afraid of what her father would do and ran away. Huong had no idea where Chi was. I wished I knew where she was so I could visit her. What was Ma thinking? Why didn't she stand up and protect her children? Who was going to help her now? Was she ever worried about losing her children one by one? She needed to divorce him. I wouldn't go home if she was still married to him. I hoped Chi was safe and staying with somebody nice, like Huong's family.

***

I walked all the way to Cho Lon. It was very different from how I remembered. I couldn't find anyone I knew. Where had they all gone? Where were Huong and her mother? The herbal medicine stall wasn't there either.

Then I spotted our juice stand. It was still there, covered with black smoke stains. There was a line of customers waiting to buy juice. Where was Ma? Oh! There she was, inside the juice stand, trying to press sugarcane by hand. I saw only her back; she wore a black outfit. I called out, "Ma! Ma! Do you need help?" She turned around and smiled at me. Her face was black from the smoke. Her whole body was covered in black dust. I couldn't see her clearly except for her white teeth!

I gasped, jolted out of my sleep. My heart was thumping hard, and I realized it was a dream. It was more like a nightmare, really, because I was sweating. I looked over to Huong's bed. She was sleeping peacefully. Hadn't she said the juice stand was fine? I couldn't go back to sleep and kept staring at the ceiling, worried about Ma.

The next day Huong came home from work and told me my ma hadn't come to work. The juice stand was closed, which had never happened before. What was going on? Ma never closed the business. Was she OK? The following day was the same—she didn't open up the juice stand. I was so worried about her, I told Huong's mother, "I'm going back to my neighborhood to check on her."

"Would you like Huong to go with you?" she offered.

"No, it's OK. I know you need Huong's help. Besides, I don't want my ma to find out about Huong helping me and not telling her."

"Be careful, Lien. Let me know when you get any news. I'm praying for your ma."

I took two buses back to my neighborhood and got more nervous when I walked closer to the house. I took a deep breath to calm myself, but it didn't help. I was so scared, I couldn't go any farther, so I stopped at a big tree and hid there. I wanted to go to Di Hue's house, but it was right across the street from our house; my family would see me. I would have to wait until dark. Then I could ask Di Hue what was going on.

It started to get dark. I saw Di Hue come home from work on her bicycle. As soon as she opened her gate, I ran to her, and she gasped in surprise. "Lien, where have you been?"

"Can we go inside now? I need to ask you something."

"OK, come on in." She opened the door for me.

As soon as she closed the door behind her, I breathed deeply and asked her my question. "Do you know what happened to Ma? She closed the business for two days, and I'm worried about her. You know she never closed the juice stand before. Was she sick? Did he hit her again? Is she in the hospital now?"

"Lien, she's all right. She's just sad that her husband got arrested, that's all."

"What?" I wasn't sure I had heard her right. "What did you just say?"

"He got arrested, Lien. You can come home now."

"Did he hit Ma? Did he get arrested because he was abusing Ma?"

"No, it was far more serious than that," Di Hue said. "He got arrested for political reasons. The government thinks he was a spy for the Americans. He's going to be in prison for a long time, Lien."

I could never imagine him being a spy. He was an alcoholic, and he had only one leg. I didn't believe it. Maybe someone didn't like what he did to us and framed him, but who? I had no idea. Anyway, I was glad. It sounded terrible to be happy in that situation, but I was jumping for joy.

"Yay! Free at last." I jumped into the air.

Di Hue laughed. She opened her arms, and I jumped right in. She spun me around. Then she told me not to act happy in front of Ma. She was very sad now.

"Are you ready to go home?" Di Hue reached out for my hand. "I'll walk with you."

We crossed the street to my house. As soon as the door opened, my siblings yelled out, "Sister Lien!" and ran to hug me. Ma came with Be in her arms. She didn't say much, just handed Be to me.

"I'm sorry, Ma," I said to her, but she didn't reply.

"Where are Chi, Anh?" I asked Di Hue.

"They ran away too, Lien. We have to find them and bring them home," Di Hue said. "At least we know where Vu is. We can go there tomorrow."

I was speechless. All four older children had run away. No wonder Ma couldn't work. She had to take care of the little ones. Worry no more, Ma. We would all come home for you, and everything would be all right.

***

We found Anh at her friend's house in the neighborhood. Vu knew where she was. Di Hue and I looked all over for Chi, but she was nowhere to be found. Ma wrote a letter to her family explaining the situation and asking Grandma for help. We were going to start school soon, and Ma needed someone to take care of the little ones. She went back to open the business alone because Anh and I had to babysit. We did chores like before, but we were much happier.

When Ma told me to go to Aunt Hai's house and tell them the news about my stepfather, I was surprised to find Chi was there. Chi was very happy about the news, but Aunt Hai broke down and cried. It broke my heart to see my aunt sad. She looked a lot older than I remembered. Aunt Hai had a lot of gray hair now and was very skinny. My cousins told me she was under a lot of stress. Grandpa was really sick, and Aunt Hai was worrying about him.

Chi and I walked home side by side. I told her about Huong's family helping me. She told me she hadn't wanted to stay at Cho Lon because she didn't want Ma to trick her into coming home again. She had known Aunt Hai and her ba were mad at each other, and they hadn't talked since arguing about the house. She had thought Aunt Hai's house would be a safer place for her, so she had walked the two hours it took to get there from Cho Lon.

"I want to learn karate," Chi said randomly.

"Really? Why?" I asked.

"So I can karate chop Ba if he hits me again."

I laughed. "Well, you don't have to worry anymore. We're all going to be safe from now on."

"What if the government lets him come home?"

"They won't, Chi. This is a serious charge."

"How do you know? I mean, they didn't have any proof he was a spy. Do you believe he was a spy?"

"No. Ma thinks somebody framed him."

As soon as Chi got home, she asked Ma to let her take karate classes. Ma refused, saying it cost money, and girls shouldn't learn karate because nobody wanted to marry a girl who was eager to fight. Chi would not let the idea go; she would find a way to pay for it herself, she said.

Chi started to ask around the neighborhood for odd jobs. She said she would do anything from babysitting to wood chopping, as long as she made money for karate school. Ma said she needed to help with the house chores and babysit, but Chi said no. She would do it only if Ma paid her. Chi spent all her free time peeking through a karate school's door. She threw punches at an imaginary punching bag at home or kicked the air, trying to copy what she saw in that school.

Chi saved enough money to buy a tray, an ice bucket, a few glasses, and one hundred grams of black tea. The next day she opened an iced tea stand. To everyone's surprise she actually did good business and made a profit on the first day. After a few weeks, she had enough money to go to karate school. Ma wasn't happy about it, but she was glad Chi indeed knew how to make money from nothing.

Ma seemed less sad day by day. She had all of her children back. Our life was still hectic but without fear. Di Hue came to our house often to cheer Ma up. Before school started, our grandma and Ma's youngest sister came from Hue. We were all relieved and glad we finally met Grandma. But there was one problem: Grandma and Aunt Gai spoke with a middle state accent, and we couldn't understand them. Ma had to translate back and forth. It was hilarious that we were speaking the same language but couldn't understand each other.

Grandma stayed home, taking care of Little and Be. Aunt Gai helped Ma at the juice stand. I went to high school far away, so I was allowed to use our only bicycle. I stayed home after school on weekdays to help Grandma and worked weekends at Cho Lon with Ma and Aunt Gai. Our life had moved on. I missed my friend Huong, but she was so happy for us. I saw her on the weekends when I helped Ma, until she went to college. Chi and I still had some arguments here and there, but that was normal, and I could handle that. I was secretly happy for Ma; she was finally free from her husband.

Chapter 10
1980

One night while sleeping, I was awoken by a slight knock on the downstairs window. I got up to check and see if somebody was trying to break in to our house. Ma got up as well. She was staring at the window when that knock came again.

"Who's there?" she asked.

"Open the window quick! It's me, Thien, your brother," the voice whispered.

"Oh my." Ma ran to open the window, and my uncle Thien climbed in. She closed the window and gave him a hug.

"Did they let you out?" she asked.

"No, I escaped. Don't turn on the light." He was shaking. "I need a place to stay for a few days, and I have nowhere else to go. Could you help me?"

"Of course! You can stay in the loft. We're using it only for storage, but I'll clean it up tomorrow," Ma said.

Grandma walked into the room sleepily, and then her jaw dropped. "Thien! You are here. Am I dreaming?" Then she burst out crying.

He hugged her. "Shh, Ma, it's OK. You're not dreaming. I escaped. It was bad in there. When I found my escape route, I went for it. I didn't want to go to your house because I know they will go there to look for me. I can't believe you're here too."

Ma realized I was still in the room. She told me to go to bed. I went back to bed, but I couldn't sleep. The adults downstairs were whispering all night. Uncle Thien looked exhausted. I was glad he got to our house safe and sound, but I was worried about our future. What if the government came there to look for him? Was our house still on the watch list, since they took my stepfather? We were supposed to report all visitors to a neighborhood leader. Visitors needed travel permits from where they were living before they could go anywhere. If the government was watching our house right then, Ma would be in big trouble. What was I going to do if they put Ma in jail too?

Uncle Thien had been hiding in our loft for three days, and he hadn't made a sound, even though it was really hot up there. We brought food up for him; he came down only at nighttime, while everyone was sleeping, to use the bathroom. After a few days, Uncle Thien asked Ma to find a way to let his wife know. He didn't want to send a letter because he was afraid the government would read it before it would get into his wife's hands. Ma said the best solution would be me going to deliver the letter for him. Since I was a minor, if I got caught the charge wouldn't be so serious.

"But Ma, I don't know where she lives, and I'm scared," I protested.

"Lien, he'll write down the directions on a piece of paper for you."

"I don't know. She doesn't even know me." I was still nervous about the idea.

"She does know who you are, Lien. You were there for their wedding."

"Really? I was at their wedding? How come I don't remember it?"

"You were only five or six years old at the time, that's why you don't remember. She'll remember you," Ma said.

After a day of Ma trying to convince me, I agreed to do it. The next morning I followed the directions, taking a five-hour bus ride to the coast, then a boat to the island where Uncle Thien's wife lived with their two sons. As soon as I got off the boat, I asked people to help me with the address I had in my hand. I got to the house, and my aunt recognized me right away. She cried after she read the letter and said she wanted to see him. I told her we should be careful not to get caught.

"I have a very good friend in Saigon whom I trust. She can help me," she said.

The next day my aunt took her two sons, Tuan and Tu, to her sister's house. They weren't happy about their mom going to Saigon, but after she promised that she would buy toys for them, they were OK. Tuan looked like Uncle Thien, and Tu looked just like my brother Vu. They were so cute, and I wished I had more time to spend with them. They were well fed and had nice clothes. I could tell they lived comfortably there.

We took the same way back, a boat ride then the bus to Saigon. My aunt told me about their love story. They had met on this island when Uncle Thien got an assignment there. A year after that, they got married, and he got transferred to all different places and visited his family only a few times a year. It was hard for her and the two boys as well. I felt bad for her and admired their love for each other.

We got to the house of my aunt's friend. After a quick greeting, my aunt told her friend about Uncle's situation. Her friend said she knew someone who could help him escape the country by boat. It would cost a lot of money, though. My aunt said she didn't care how much it cost. She would sell the house if she had to, in exchange for her husband's freedom. She needed to get him out of the country as soon as possible.

I went home alone with a letter for Uncle Thien. That night my uncle said good-bye to Grandma and Ma. Then he snuck out quietly through the back door and walked for hours to meet up with his wife. I felt good that I had done something to help them.

Two months later we got a letter from my aunt saying Uncle Thien had made it to Thailand. Soon he would be moving to America. The plan was as soon as Uncle Thien settled, he would sponsor his family to live with him in America. We were so happy for him that he got out safely. There were lots of stories about people trying to escape, but many didn't make it. Some got arrested; some died on the way. What a price to pay for freedom. What a price!

Chapter 11
1982

During my first year of high school, the Vietnamese government decided to make a deal with the American government to let all half-American children leave. When I found out, I told Ma about it, hoping she would let me go to America. I had always wanted to meet my real father one day. I had tried to ask Ma about him a couple of times, but she'd said she didn't want to talk about it.

After some convincing from me, saying I would be living close to Uncle Thien in New York City in the future, Ma gave in. We needed money for the application fee, translator fee, and so on. Ma said it cost a lot of money for the process, and she wasn't sure if she could trust the government on this. We decided to write to Uncle Thien for some advice.

A whole month passed by, and still no answer from my uncle. I kept begging Ma to go on with the plan before the government changed its mind. Ma wanted to see a psychic to make sure we would not waste the money. I had never been to a palm reading before and hoped maybe the fortune-teller could tell me that my future would be bright in America.

We went to one in Cho Lon. The woman asked us to sit down. While she was holding my hand, she also looked at my face, like she was reading that as well.

"What is your birthday?" the fortune-teller asked.

"I was born two days after Christmas 1966," I answered.

"Does the birthday have to be correct?" Ma suddenly looked uncomfortable.

"Yes, it has to be. Otherwise I can't read her palms."

"She wasn't born in 1966. The correct year was 1965," Ma said.

"Ma! What are you talking about?" I stared at her in surprise.

"The birth certificate said 1966, but you were born in 1965, Lien."

"OK! What's the date?" the woman asked Ma.

"I don't remember." Ma paused. "It was around December, but I don't remember the date."

I stomped out of the psychic's shop crying. Ma followed me. "Lien! Wait! I'm sorry. I should have told you before."

"How could you not remember the day your first child was born?" I was still crying. "You never tell me anything."

"It was during wartime, Lien. It wasn't easy. I had a million other things on my mind at the time, just to survive." She walked faster to keep up with me. "I couldn't get a birth certificate for you until a year later, so I forgot the date. I'm sorry!"

I kept walking faster and faster, trying to hide my tears, hoping she would leave me alone.

"Lien! Come on, talk to me." She was still chasing me.

"I'll talk to you when you're ready to tell me the truth. I've had enough secrets and lies." I stopped suddenly and faced her. "I will get a job and pay for the application fee by myself! "

I didn't talk to Ma for days, just concentrated on getting a job after school. I was eager to get out of that country in order to change my life. I wasn't happy there.

I found a waitress job at a Phở restaurant in town. After I had worked there for only a week, Ma wanted me to quit my job saying Aunt Gai was leaving for a new job that paid more.

"Wait a minute. You paid Aunt Gai all this time? I thought she was here to help you," I asked Ma in surprise.

"She is a twenty-four-year-old woman, Lien. She needed money. I had to pay her so she could stay here and help us. She found a better job now, so she is going to leave."

"I can't quit my job, Ma. I need money too."

"What are you going to need money for? You have food to eat, a roof over your head. I'm paying for your school supplies, clothes—"

"I need money for the application fees. I want to go to America. Maybe you should find somebody else to work for you," I told her straight.

"How much do they pay you? I'll pay you the same. I don't want to hire a stranger."

"I have to think about it, Ma. I really like that job."

"What if I can come up with the money right now for your application fee? Would you work for me? For your family?"

"I will quit my job if you pay for my application fee right away." I paused. "Like tomorrow."

"OK! Tomorrow it is." Ma nodded her head.

The next day we went to a government building in Saigon city center to get the paperwork done. There were so many half-American children waiting in line for the process. All the officers were cranky and mean. I told myself they were jealous of us because we would have better futures than theirs.

After hours of waiting, it was finally our turn. Ma and I got yelled at for no reason. The officer took the money and the papers we had filled out, piled them up in a box next to his table, and told us to get out.

***

I was so excited when the mailman stopped at our door, thinking finally we got a letter from Uncle Thien. Unfortunately it turned out to be a letter from my stepfather. For some reason Ma didn't want to read it privately; she told me to read it out loud for the whole family to hear.

Dear Em,

How is everybody at home? I was told you can come to visit me now. So when you come to visit, don't forget to bring these items with you.

1. 10 kilos of Jasmine rice
2. 2 kilos of beef jerky
3. 2 cartons of unfiltered cigarettes (I switched to

this kind of cigarette now,
it's not bad.)
4. 1 carton of 555 cigarettes
   (This is for the officers.)
5. A bottle of French cognac
   (This is also for the officers.
   If you can't find French
   cognac, at least try to find
   something Imported.)
6. 1 kilo of Jasmine tea
7. 2 kilos of coffee (You know
   the brand I like.)
8. 4 cans of condensed milk
9. Some nice soap (There is
   no soap in here.)
10. A few tubes of Colgate
    toothpaste (I know they're
    hard to find, but I saw a
    guy in here who has it—
    that means it's out there.)

Can you come as soon as
possible? I desperately need
those items. I will see you soon.

Your husband.

We all looked at each other like, Really? Ma said
nothing for a while, then she asked, "Who wants to visit your
ba with me?"
We all shook our heads and said, "No!"
"Come on. I need somebody to help me. I can't carry all
of that by myself." She looked at me, then Chi, Anh, and Vu.
"How can you afford to buy all of that? We don't even
eat Jasmine rice here, let alone afford French cognac and
English cigarettes," I said.
"He needs those things for the officers," Ma said.
"Why do you have to buy for the officers? We barely

make enough for a living; this is not right!"

"He wants to bribe them, so they will go easier on him. I have some money saved up for the rainy season. I can borrow money if I have to."

"But that's for the rainy season, Ma. Don't forget our business is dead during rainy season, and it's six months long. How are you going to feed us then?" I was furious.

Ma blindly went on with her plan, buying all the items on his list. I was mad at her for putting her husband before her nine children. She took a risk of starving her own children to satisfy the man who had beaten her up numerous times. Why? The letter was all about him, nothing romantic at all. Was she really that much in love with my stepfather that she went out of her way to make him happy?

Not long after, Ma went to visit him with those luxury items he wanted. We hit the rainy season, with rain almost every day. Our business was dead. There were days Ma came home with no food. Needless to say I was mad at her for spending all her savings on him. Chi and I gave Ma the silent treatment for a long time. Even Grandma was not happy with Ma. She asked Aunt Gai to send a bus ticket, and she went home to Hue.

Ma went to open the business every day anyway, even though it was slow. Chi's iced tea stand was slow too during the rainy season. Thankfully Grandma left a vegetable garden she had started in our yard. We dug some sweet potatoes to eat, then we moved on to taro, yucca, and so on. After all of that ran out, we would hold our grumbling stomachs until it passed, hoping Ma would come home with food. The government had stopped giving out food rations a long time ago. Aunt Tam got transferred to a hospital in Can Tho, so she couldn't help us anymore.

I honestly wished we had a water spinach pond like our neighbor. Her pond was thriving in the rainy season. We saw people buying water spinach every day, and the more our neighbor cut it, the more it grew back nice and thick.

"I wish we had a water spinach pond," Vu said "I would love to have some stir-fried water spinach right now."

"I know, me too," I said. "We could have enough food to eat year round. Come on, let's bring out your homework. Try not to think about food for now. Maybe Ma will bring some home today."

It was still raining when Ma came home, and she had no food with her. Vu was determined that he would sneak into the neighbor's pond and cut some water spinach. Ma didn't like the idea, of course, but everyone was hungry, so she didn't stop him when he left with a knife. We were all watching him from the window, praying he wouldn't get caught. It was rainy and dark outside. I saw Vu crawling into the pond, and he started to cut. All of a sudden, our neighbor's light came on. Vu had nowhere to hide. Our neighbor came out and caught him red handed.

"Ma! Come here. Hurry!" I shouted. "Vu got caught. Go talk to her."

Ma grabbed her raincoat, and then Chi said, "Wait! She let him go."

Vu walked in with spinach in his arms. He smiled and said, "I brought home some dinner."

"What did she say when she saw you?" I asked him. "We were so scared she might report you to the police."

"She told me if I want some spinach, all I have to do is ask."

"Really? She didn't get mad?" Chi asked.

"No, she is a cool old lady."

We laughed at his comment, but deep down we appreciated her generosity so much. We couldn't wait for the rainy season to be over.

***

Uncle Thien's letter finally arrived. Inside also was a picture of him in New York City. At first we just admired how grand the city looked, with all the Christmas decorations. Then we realized the picture was thicker than usual. I flipped it back and forth.

"Something is inside the picture," I said.

"Read the letter first, would you?" Ma said.

Dear sister,

I hope this letter gets to you safe.
Since Vietnam doesn't have a
good relationship with America,
letters take forever to get there or
sometimes go missing, I was told.

I've lived comfortably since I got
here. A friend of mine who left
before the fall of Saigon has a
couple of businesses. He helped
me to open a small restaurant in
Chinatown, New York City, so I
am doing well and willing to help
Lien when she comes. I heard
about the immigration program;
it's worth giving it a try. She needs
to learn English, and I will help her
(take a good look at my picture).

I also started paper work for my
family to come here and live with
me. I miss them and hope we will
be reunited soon.

Your brother,
Thien

"Let me see the picture again," Ma said. She bent the
corner of the picture and removed the layer of the paper.
There it was—a US one-hundred-dollar bill that Uncle Thien
had hid in there. We stared at it like a piece of art.
"It's worth nothing here, Ma," I said.
"Oh no! It's worth a lot. I'll trade it at the black market in
Cho Lon. This will help us through the rainy season for sure,"

Ma said excitedly.

"What about my English lessons?"

"You have to wait until the rainy season is over for that, Lien. Right now I need to put food on the table."

I had now learned there was a black market for everything people smuggled in from Thailand. If you could hide it, you could buy it or sell it right under the government's nose.

Despite our lack of money during the rainy season, Ma continued to visit her jailed husband once a month. She bought less stuff for him in the rainy season, but she never skipped and never went empty handed.

During that time we also went through a double tragedy. My grandpa passed away in Can Tho; he had been sick since the government took his land. Ma took Chi and Vu to the funeral, but I had to stay behind to take care of my siblings. I missed everyone in Can Tho, but deep down Chi was the real oldest girl and Vu was the oldest boy, so they had to be there.

They came back with bad news. My beloved aunt Hai was crying too much at the funeral. She ended up with a massive stroke and became paralyzed. The hospital couldn't do anything for her; they let the family bring her home, and Grandma wanted her to stay in Can Tho.

My beautiful sweet aunt. She had been my first mom, in a way. She had raised me with love, shaped me into the person I was, and I couldn't be there for her. A sadness lingered with me during that time. I felt so bad for my cousins and my uncle.

Chapter 12
1983

I started English night school as soon as the rainy season was over. It was near Cho Lon, so I went after we closed down the juice stand. I loved it right from the first night. Mr. Loi was a great teacher. He used to study abroad in America, so he told us stories about the country of my dreams, and I was just in awe.

I was biking home one day after class when a girl riding a scooter parallel to me flashed a cute smile.

"Hi. We're in the same English class." The smile was still on her face. "What is your name?"

"Lien."

"My name is Lan." She waited for me to say something. I said nothing, thinking, 'Who wants to be friends with a half-American girl like me?' She was probably just bored, and soon she would drive off on her fancy scooter. "Where do you live, Lien?"

"District 19," I answered.

"Oh, I live in District 18. We live close to each other." She sounded happy.

"Uh-huh…" I was still skeptical.

"Do you like the class?" Lan asked. "I love it. It's so interesting."

"Yes, I like it a lot." I started to warm up to her.

"My ba and my oldest brother live in California. They're sponsoring us to go to America. I thought learning English would be practical. Didn't expect that the class would be so good. What about you? Who is sponsoring you?"

"America, I guess. I'm half-American, and there is an immigration program I applied for. I'm not really sure how it'll go."

"Don't worry. I heard that's the fastest way to get out of this country right now. You'll be fine."

"Thanks."

"So I'll see you tomorrow night. Right? Nice to meet you, Lien."

"Nice to meet you too," I replied.

She sped up the scooter and was gone into the darkness of the night.

Lan and I quickly became friends. Sometimes she gave me a ride when I needed one. She stopped by the juice stand and waited for me, and we went to night school together. Lan was so much fun to be around. She made lots of jokes, and boys loved her. Of course they would love her—she was beautiful and rich. For some unknown reason, she didn't mind having a poor friend like me.

Lan invited me to her house one day, and I understood why she was so bubbly and happy all the time. Her whole family was the same. They were so much fun to talk to, like they had never been through a difficult time. How did they manage that during the Communist time? I honestly don't know. Lan had a younger sister named Diep, who became my friend too. She was funny and easygoing. Their house was filled with laughter all the time, the total opposite of my house.

I wished Lan and Diep would go to the same high school as me, but we lived in different districts. There were some girls I talked to sometimes, but I didn't really have any good friends in my high school. Since the government started allowing half-American children to emigrate, people had a different attitude toward us. All of a sudden, half- American was good. I started to get compliments about my looks. Girls wanted to hang out with me, and boys wanted to ask me out to the movies. Some girls even said they wished they were half-American too. I could only hope the Americans would accept me if I were lucky enough to get there.

Everything went well with my family and the business in the next sunny season. I started another year of high school, and all my siblings one by one started school too. I spent all my free time with Lan and Diep. Life just started to feel a little more comfortable, and then the rainy season rolled in again. Ma wanted me to stop going to English school because she couldn't afford to pay the fees. I was so sad to say good-bye to Mr. Loi.

"What do you mean by saying good-bye?" he asked.

"We can't afford the tuition in the rainy season." I told him about my big family and the juice stand.

"Lien! If you stop learning English for six months, you're going to forget everything I have taught you."

I started to tear. I loved this English class so much, but what could I do? I didn't really have a choice.

"What if I can help you?" he asked. I could tell he felt sorry for me. "I'll lend you the money for the tuition during rainy season, and you pay me back when you can."

"You would do that?" I said with surprise and wiped my tears.

"You're the best student I have in this class, Lien. I wouldn't want your talent to go to waste, would I?" Mr. Loi said. "Promise me you won't skip classes, even if it rains."

"I promise, and thank you, Mr. Loi." I couldn't believe he would help me.

I was going to write to Uncle Thien for help with the tuition, but by the time he got the letter and sent back the money, the rainy season would be over. Ma might want to use the money for food instead of paying for my English classes anyway. This was the best option to keep me in English school, and I was so grateful for Mr. Loi's kind heart.

I went to English night school even when it was stormy, just like I had promised Mr. Loi. There were a lot fewer students in the rainy season. On the stormy nights, sometimes there were only two or three students. Mr. Loi would let us listen to American music on low volume after class was over. This kind of music was prohibited in Vietnam; if he got caught he could end up in reeducation camp. I felt so nervous when I listened to American music and hoped one day I could listen to it freely anytime I wanted, without fear.

***

Word had spread around the city about the government allowing people to write love songs now. They would check, and it had to be approved, of course, before they played love songs on the radio. Slowly some young bands started to form, and music schools started opening too. Lan and Diep enrolled into a music school and learned to play guitar. They wanted me to join them, but of course I couldn't.

There was one young band that became famous and started to perform around the city. Their tickets sold out really quickly, but of course you could buy tickets on the black market for double the price. When they were scheduled to perform in my district, my sister Chi wanted to set up her iced tea stand in front of the gate of our humble district's theater. Ma thought it was a good idea to set up a small juice stand there too. She wanted me to run it right next to Chi, so we could keep an eye on each other.

I didn't like the idea because I knew Lan and Diep would be inside enjoying the concert, and I had to stay outside working. Ma said I could choose to stay home, cook dinner, feed the children, give them baths, and do laundry as well, or I could run the juice stand. In the end I chose to run the juice stand.

That night there was a big crowd of young people, including a lot of kids from my high school. Some of them had the nerve to buy juices from me. I was so embarrassed. Chi was very happy, though, because she made money for herself. Lan and Diep stopped by to say a quick hello, then they went straight inside because they wanted to sit close to the stage.

After everyone went inside and the music started, Chi and I stood there with no business. She asked me to watch her iced tea stand, and she started to wander around. Chi came back half an hour later and said she found a way to sneak inside.

"Let's close the stands and go inside to enjoy the concert," she said.

"How?" I asked her.

"There was a crack open in the backstage door. We can sneak in." Chi was really excited.

"We're going to get caught." The last thing I wanted was to get caught in front of my friends.

"Look! I'm going in first. If I get in safely, then you can

follow. If we get caught, then we're just going to say we were looking for the person who stole our fruit. We saw him go in this way."

I stared at her. Chi was brilliant sometimes. "OK! Let's do it before I change my mind."

Chi and I walked to the back of the building. It was perfectly dark; no one was around, and the music was loud. I reached to open the door, but it was locked from the inside.

"I thought you said it was half open," I said, disappointed.

"It was before. Someone just closed it, I guess." Then Chi pulled my hand. "There's another door on the other side of the building. Come on."

I followed Chi to the other side, and she was right. This door was latched at the top, but there was a crack open at the bottom. I could see the audience inside. It was an old tin door. We both got down on our knees, and in a split second Chi was inside.

"Come on, get in," she whispered.

"OK, OK!" I was so nervous.

I looked around me to make sure I was alone, then I bent the tin door back and crawled in. Everybody else was busy enjoying the concert, so no one really paid attention to us. I stood up quickly, dusted off the dirt from my clothes, and looked around. I couldn't believe I had done this.

"Did I take you to a concert or what?" Chi said.

"We'll be in trouble if Ma finds out."

"I won't tell her if you won't." She smiled a big smile.

I looked for Lan and Diep in the crowd. After a while with no luck, I was thinking of going back to find Chi in the standing-only section.

"You look lost. Are you looking for someone?" a guy sitting at the end of a row asked.

"I'm looking for my friends."

"It would be impossible to find someone in this crowd. Why don't you sit down? I have an extra seat."

I wasn't sure what to do. That seat sure looked good, but he was a stranger.

"I won't bite, I promise." He had a genuine smile. He seemed nice. He had a light Northern accent. There was something about him I felt comfortable with. I took the seat and stared straight at the stage.

"My name is Quinh," the man said.

"Lien. Nice to meet you." I kept my eyes on the stage.

"Where do you live, Lien?" He wasn't paying attention to the concert like everybody else.

I was about to ask him to leave me alone, but when I turned my head to face him, I changed my mind. He was cute, and he had given me the seat.

"I live here, in this district, and thank you for the seat." All of a sudden I was nervous.

"No problem! I was supposed to take my little sister with me, but she got grounded, so I have an extra seat. I'm glad someone could use it."

The concert was good, but I couldn't concentrate on the music. "Where are you from? You have a little accent."

"My parents are from the North, but I was born and raised here in this very same district."

"Really! I didn't see you in our high school."

"I graduated two years ago," Quinh said.

"What are you doing now, after high school?"

"I work at a motorcycle shop during the day, and I go to college at night."

"Wow! College. That sounds good." I felt silly right after I said that.

"Would you like to go for coffee tomorrow night?"

"I can't, I have English class tomorrow."

"Wow, English class. That sounds good too." He flashed a smile again.

"Are you teasing me?" I felt my cheeks burning. "If you are, then I'm not having coffee with you."

"I'm sorry, I didn't mean to. How about the day after tomorrow?"

"OK, that works. I should be free around seven thirty."

"Should I pick you up at your house?"

"No! How about the park?" I looked at him to see if he

thought that was weird.

"Perfect. I'll see you there at seven thirty p.m."

"I have to go to look for my sister. Good night, Quinh."

"Good night, Lien."

He stood up for me to get out—such a gentleman. I went back and found Chi still in the same spot.

"Let's get out of here, Chi," I said.

"Why? The concert is so good," she protested.

"I'm tired. I want to go home." I just didn't want Quinh to see me running the juice stand.

Chi and I cleaned up, quickly put everything on the bicycle, and went home. That night I kept thinking about the concert and Quinh. I couldn't wait to go out with him.

Two nights later I lied to Ma, saying I had to do group study with Lan and Diep. I walked to the park and saw Quinh was already there, standing next to a motorcycle.

"Hi there," he said.

"Hi! Nice motorcycle."

"It's not mine. I'm fixing it at the shop and just taking care of it until the owner picks it up. I hope you don't mind."

"No, not at all."

"Are you ready?" He started the engine, and I nervously climbed on the backseat. Quinh took me to a nice coffee shop in the center of Saigon. We talked for hours. He told me about his college—he was majoring in engineering. I didn't tell him a lot about myself except that I was half-American, which he probably knew anyway. I told him I took English classes because I wanted to feel closer to my American half.

When I told Lan about Quinh, she was very supportive and said I should let her dress me up before the next date. I saw Quinh every other weekend or so, and every time he had a different motorcycle. It was fun to go out with him. Sometimes I smiled to myself. I couldn't believe I had a boyfriend.

***

Ma and I came home from work one day, and there

was a woman waiting for her in the living room. As soon as she saw Ma, she started to cry, saying something really bad had happened. She told Ma that Grandma and Aunt Gai had been in a bus accident. They both got hurt really badly and were in Nha Trang hospital.

Ma dropped everything on the floor. She was so distraught, she didn't know what to do. She couldn't leave the children and go to visit Grandma and Aunt Gai.

"It's OK. You don't have to visit. Your ma and your sister will understand, but they need money for the hospital bills. That's why they sent me here, to pick up money for them," the woman explained. She said if Grandma and Aunt Gai couldn't come up with the money for the hospital, they would get kicked out.

"How much do they need?" Ma asked her.

"They need one hundred thousand đồng and I will deliver the money for you. I'm going back to Nha Trang tonight," the woman said.

Ma looked worried, and I knew why. She didn't have enough money.

"Give me a few hours to get the money." She went to Di Hue's house.

The woman didn't sit down, even though I offered her a chair. She walked around the house, which I thought was weird. I told my siblings to behave, and they all stared at her curiously. Di Hue came over with Ma.

"Hi, my name is Di Hue," she said to the woman. "What is your name?"

"Ngoc. My name is Ngoc," the woman said.

"How do you know my friend's mother and sister?"

"I work with Gai." Ngoc said. "She told me about the trip she took with her ma to visit Nha Trang. When I heard about the accident, I went to Nha Trang hospital, and sure enough they were there."

"Do you know about the trip?" Di Hue asked Ma.

"No! Maybe their letter is on the way to tell me," Ma said, sounding worried.

"Did they send a letter with you?" Di Hue asked Ngoc.

"No, they are both still unconscious."

"How did you get this address if they are both unconscious?"

"Ah, Gai was conscious for a little bit. She told me the address and asked me to come here."

"Would you excuse us?" Ma told Ngoc and grabbed Di Hue's arm, pulling her to the bedroom. They whispered for a few minutes, then they called me in.

"Lien, I want you to go with her to Nha Trang hospital," Ma said "Di Hue doesn't trust her with the money."

"I just have a weird feeling about her," Di Hue whispered.

"Would you feel better if I sent Lien with her? She could hold on to the money until it gets to my sister's hand."

"It's your call. I know you're worried about your ma and Gai, but I just don't trust this stranger."

"How far is Nha Trang from here?" I asked Ma.

"It's about an eight-hour bus ride, and if you leave tonight you'll get there in the morning."

"She can't leave tonight," Di Hue said. "She doesn't have a permit yet to travel."

"But Ngoc is leaving tonight. We can't wait till the morning." Ma turned to me. "Go get ready, Lien."

I packed my bag while Ma and Di Hue argued. In the end I left with Ngoc, holding on to the money. Ma said to guard it with my life and give it to Aunt Gai when I got there.

We got to Nha Trang in the afternoon because the bus broke down twice. During the long journey, Ngoc and I didn't talk much. She slept most of the time. I thought we should go straight to the hospital, but Ngoc wanted to check in to a motel first. I followed her around town trying to get a room, and we finally ended up in a small family run hostel.

"OK, we got a room now. Can we go to the hospital?" I was anxious to see Grandma and Aunt Gai.

"Relax. It's not visiting hours yet. I'm going to get something to eat. Why don't you take a shower or a quick nap? You look tired." And she left the room.

I was exhausted. I hadn't slept at all overnight; the bus

ride had been bumpy, and the bus had broken down twice. I took a quick shower, and Ngoc still hadn't returned. I decided to take a quick nap, assuming she would wake me up when she returned in time to go to the hospital.

I got up early the next morning, hating myself for taking a long nap. Why hadn't Ngoc gotten me up when she'd come back? I looked over to her empty bed, and it was untouched. Had she come back last night? I jumped out of bed, realizing my belongings were gone. I lifted the pillow under which I had hid the money, and it was gone too. I panicked.

"No…no, this can't happen. Ngoc is Aunt Gai's friend," I told myself.

I ran to the front to ask the owners if they knew where Ngoc was. They said she had left the previous night and hadn't come back since.

"Do you know what happened to my belongings?"

"No. She left with a pink bag, that's all I remember."

"The pink bag is mine, with all my belongings, and the money is gone too." I started to shake. "The money is for my grandma and my aunt. They're in the hospital waiting for me."

I couldn't believe what had just happened. How could she do this to poor people like us? I told the owners the whole story in tears. Mr. and Mrs. Quang listened with honest sympathy. They tried to calm me down and offered to help. Mrs. Quang took me to Nha Trang hospital to look for Grandma and Aunt Gai, but they weren't there. The receptionist said they were never registered in the hospital.

"I'm sorry, I think it is a scam. I don't think Ngoc is her real name. When she was checking in, she told me she had lost all her papers," Mrs. Quang said. "You need to report this to the police."

"I'm afraid of the police, I don't have a permit to travel. I left in a hurry because we were worried about Grandma."

"I see. What is your plan now? How are you going home to Saigon?"

"I don't know." I couldn't hold my tears.

They let me stay in the room if they didn't have a customer. I had to sleep on the wooden couch when the room was occupied. In exchange I would help them with cleaning and laundry. Mrs. Quang lent me one of her outfits. After a few days, I was brave enough to ask them to loan me money for a bus ticket. I promised I would pay them back as soon as I got home.

"I'm so sorry we can't help you more," Mrs. Quang said. "Money is really tight at the moment."

"I understand. You've both been helping me a lot already." I let out a sigh. "I'm just worried and miss my family."

"Are you willing to take a chance?" Mr. Quang said.

"What do you mean by take a chance?" Mrs. Quang asked her husband.

"If she's willing to sneak onto the train to Saigon, sometimes they don't check the tickets. I'm not saying it's a good option, but the train is a lot bigger than a bus, with more people. It's easier to sneak onto."

"What if I get caught?" I didn't like the idea.

"You can pretend you lost your ticket. They won't put you in jail for that, especially since you're a child."

"That sounds like a good idea, actually," Mrs. Quang said.

"I'm not sure. I have to think about it," I told them.

For two days I was thinking back and forth about jumping the train home. I was worried about staying there too long because I might miss the interview for America. Letters took forever to get anywhere in Vietnam. By the time Ma found out where I was, it would take months for me to get home. I had to take a chance. I couldn't afford to miss the interview.

The next night Mr. Quang took me to the train station. He waited with me until we heard the horn for departure.

"OK, Lien, this is it. Do you see that open window there?"

"The one right in front of me?" I asked him.

"Yes! I'll lift you, and you will crawl in as quickly as you can, OK? Pay attention to the uniformed people. If you see them, move to the next car."

"Thank you, Mr. Quang."

"Ready? Good luck, Lien."

He lifted me, and I crawled in as the train started to move. I walked to the end of the car, and all of a sudden the car door swung open. A conductor stepped in, and he stared at me.

"Ticket, please," he demanded.

I pretended to check my pocket with my shaking hand.

"It appears I have lost my ticket, sir," I couldn't hide my shaking voice.

"Then you have to get off the train now."

"But the train is moving." My body started to shake too.

"You have to get off the train now, before it gets to full speed."

"Please, I can't." I was crying, unable to explain. My legs were shaky and heavy, my hands covered in cold sweat. He pulled me closer to the door. I resisted, and he kicked me on my chest. People yelled at him. Everything was spinning, and I blacked out. I didn't know how long I was unconscious. When I woke up, I was in a small cabin and realized I was still on the train.

"Are you OK? I'm Doctor Linh." The nice woman seemed genuinely concerned about me. "What is your name?"

"My name is Lien."

"You're safe with me, Lien. I bought you a ticket, but I suggest you stay in here with me. You need a bed right now." She paused for a minute then asked me, "Why did your parents let you travel alone?"

I told Dr. Linh the whole story, and she insisted she would accompany me to my house. By the time we got to Saigon, I was well fed and back to normal. Thanks to Dr. Linh, I survived the panic attack. Sometimes I thought about her kindness, even though I never saw her again. Another angel had saved me. I honestly had thought I would die on that train.

Ma was glad I made it home in one piece. She wrote a letter to Aunt Gai and found out she and Grandma were both fine. They had never taken the trip to Nha Trang, an ex-coworker of Aunt Gai's had made the whole thing up to scam us. Aunt Gai reported her to the police, but she was long gone.

Chapter 13
1984

We finally got the appointment for the interview with the Vietnamese government. That was step one. If we passed that, then the next step would be the important interview with the Americans. I heard the waiting list for that interview could be two years or more. It was a long process, and I was hoping we would pass the first one with ease.

I begged Ma to tell me about my American father so we could prepare for the interview. She refused at first, saying it would upset me to find out about him. I didn't let it go and promised her that whatever happened, I wouldn't be upset about it. After all my siblings went to bed, she told me to sit down next to her.

"Lien, I'm sorry to tell you this, but I don't really know who your ba is."

"I don't understand."

"I was raped." She sighed. "By an American officer."

I was shocked, unable to say anything. For years I'd had so many questions about him. Now those went out the window. My dream to unite with him vanished. My heart sank with the news.

"I had been dating your ba—my husband now—a few months and fell in love with him. He came from a good family and was in the Air Force at the time. I was very impressed and even more so when he said I could fly for free, because he got a lot of friends to fly everywhere on a daily basis. A friend of his was flying an Air Force jet to Hue in a few days, and he offered to give me a ride. I took the opportunity to go home and visit my family. I wanted to tell my ma about my boyfriend, even though he couldn't come home with me due to his job obligations." Ma paused to wipe her tears.

"I showed up at the air base and learned his friend couldn't fly that day, but somebody else filled in for him. This new pilot said he could still fly me to Hue if I wanted to go, and

I agreed. We got to Hue at nighttime. He offered to give me a ride home, since he was heading that way. I would just have to wait a little bit while he made a stop at his boss's place to drop off paperwork. I accepted his offer again. How foolish of me. While I was waiting in the jeep, I saw an American looking at me through the window. The pilot came out and told me his boss wanted to invite me inside for a refreshment, and I thought he had a nice boss. I followed him inside to his boss's living room. He came back and handed me a drink. I drank it, then my head started spinning. I got really dizzy quickly and passed out. I woke up in the middle of the night, naked next to an American. I screamed so loudly, he jumped out of bed, grabbed his clothes, and ran out of the room. Nobody bothered to come in to see if I was OK." Ma sobbed.

"After collecting my belongings, I walked out of there in pain and took a bus to my parents' home. I didn't tell anyone about it because I was so ashamed. A month later I found out I was pregnant with you."

"I'm sorry, Ma." I didn't know what else to say.

"I had to tell my boyfriend about the rape. He felt somewhat responsible and asked me to marry him with one condition: that I put the baby up for adoption. His family was very traditional, and he couldn't accept a half-American daughter around the house. It would be too painful for him to deal with, and I accepted. After you were born, I couldn't bear to give you away and begged him to let you stay. We fought about it many times. Then, after one big argument we had, he took you to his family and let you stay there. In the end his family accepted you, and we thought that was the best option for us. At least I knew where you were. I couldn't get your birth certificate right away because we didn't know what to do at the time."

I cried, feeling sorry for Ma and myself. I was glad to know the whole story finally. At least she had fought hard to keep me. I still wanted to go to America; I wanted a better future for myself.

On the interview day, we both were very nervous. I knew it would be hard for Ma to retell the story, and it certainly wouldn't be easy for me to hear it again. When we got called to the interview room, I was glad the interviewer was a woman. But she didn't ask Ma about who my American father was at all.

"Is Lien half-American?" the interviewer asked.

"Yes ma'am," Ma answered.

"How many children do you have?"

"Nine."

"Do you all want to go to America with Lien?" She looked at Ma gently.

"Really?" Ma asked in surprise. "I thought only half-American children are allowed to go."

"The government just changed the law. You can all go together now. The only thing is you have to start again from the beginning. It'll take some time, but at least you can all go together. Is that what you want to do?"

"Yes, I think we'll do that," Ma said.

"OK. Here is Lien's file. Take it home, and add the whole family's information. Good luck."

I thought Ma was happy about the news, but she wasn't. She seemed deep in thought and was very quiet on the way home.

"What's wrong, Ma?"

"Your ba is still in reeducation camp. I don't know what to do." She seemed sad.

"Well, we don't really have a choice. He's in there for who knows how long." I waited for a bit then added, "We have to think for the whole family, not just one person."

"I have to discuss it with him, Lien. They're his children; he needs to decide about this."

"Are you saying we have to wait for him?" I got quite irritated.

"I'm going to visit him soon, and we will decide about this. I'm asking you to be patient. I can't make the decision right now."

Ma had to wait two weeks for the visiting day. She wasn't allowed to visit sooner. I was very nervous about the situation; we were back to square one now, and who knew what my stepfather would decide about it? I honestly didn't think he would let Ma go with me. She was his meal ticket. Who would bring his necessary items to the camp for him every month?

I ran to the door when I saw Ma coming home from reeducation camp. "What did he say, Ma? Did he make the decision?"

"Yes, he did," Ma answered. "He said we should all go, don't wait for him."

I was surprised by and happy with the news.

In the next few days, we went back to the government's office with the whole family's papers—all ten of us, nine children and Ma. We were very excited, even though we had to wait a long time again for the interview.

"How are you going to manage to pay for all of our English lessons, Ma?" I asked.

"Well, I'm counting on you for that, Lien. Try your best to teach your siblings what you learned from English school, because I can't afford to send them all."

"I don't know if I can handle that."

"Yes, you can. I have confidence in you."

I asked Ma for a blackboard and tried to teach English to my siblings. It wasn't easy. They were all different ages. Their levels of learning were very different too. Chi didn't want to be my student from day one. Vu didn't want to sit together with all the girls. Anh, Truc, and Mai were eager to learn, but they were impatient with Lieu when she couldn't spell the words. They yelled at her a couple of times, and she cried. I couldn't even make Little and Be sit still. I got frustrated a couple of times and almost quit, but Ma told me to be patient. Slowly we learned together to make it work. We had to prepare for America as best we could.

***

Lan lent me an outfit to go out with Quinh. It was a nice skirt and a cute top that her father had just sent her. Thank goodness we wore the same size. Lan was in fashion design school. Her father kept sending her all the latest clothes from America, and she loved to dress me up. Lucky me.

Quinh always complimented my outfits. Little did he know they weren't mine. He didn't know how poor I was either. I never did introduce Quinh to Lan because I was afraid the truth might come out. I didn't want to lose him and tried my best to keep the secret. I let Lan peek at him from her window once, and that was it. He knew nothing about my family.

"You look beautiful," he said while giving me a kiss on the cheek.

"Thank you." I smiled. I was so happy to see him.

"Lien! Is that you?" Somebody called me from the distance. They walked faster toward us in the dark, and I froze.

"Who is that? Somebody you know?" Quinh asked.

Before I could answer, Chi was right in front of me. "Hi! I recognize you," she told Quinh.

"I'm sorry, have we met?" Quinh asked her.

"At the concert. You were flirting with my sister."

Quinh raised his eyebrow in confusion.

"Chi! What are you doing here?" I growled at her.

"I was going to ask you the same question." Chi emphasized every word.

"Is everything all right?" Quinh asked me.

"I'm sorry. This is Chi, my sister."

"Oh! Hi, nice to meet you, Chi. I can't say I saw you at the concert."

"I took her to that concert, believe it or not. I saw you two from a distance. What is your name?"

"Quinh."

"Excuse us." I interrupted him and grabbed Chi's arm, pulling her a few steps away. "What on earth are you doing here?"

"Ma told me to get you. Group study, huh?"

"Listen! You can't tell Ma about this. It's going to be our secret, just like the concert."

"Yeah? I can keep the secret if you're nice to me." Chi smiled.

"Fine. Whatever you want."

"Fine. I'll let you know later." She waved at Quinh then turned to me. "I'll tell Ma you're on your way home."

"Is everything OK?" Quinh put his hands on my shoulder.

"Yes. I'm sorry, can we do this another time?"

"Of course," he said gently. "I'll walk you home."

"It's OK, you don't have to."

"I prefer to walk with you, so we can have a little more time together."

"What about your motorcycle?"

"I can handle it."

We walked side by side. He held on to the motorbike. It looked uncomfortable to walk with the heavy bike like that. He told me about his parents moving to Saigon in 1954 from the North, because they didn't want to live under the Communist government. They didn't like the idea of everyone having the same salary and everything belonging to the government. Sadly, they couldn't escape the Communists. They felt the Southerners didn't accept them, and the Northerners hated them because they had left the North. They lived quietly and focused on the family and church.

"They're really good parents, and they would love to meet you."

"Did you tell them about me?" I asked.

"Not yet." Quinh paused. "We've been together about a year now, so when you're ready, we can arrange something if you want to."

I was eighteen years old and in my last year of high school. I guessed he wanted to get even more serious. I loved Quinh for suggesting it; I just couldn't tell him the truth. I would be leaving for America when the time came. I wanted both—him and America. I was hoping somehow it would magically happen that I could have him come with me. I didn't know what to think or what to do at the moment.

We stopped at the corner near my house.

"I'm not ready to meet your parents yet. Maybe later," I said.

"I understand." He paused. "So I'll see you next week? Same time?"

"Yes, I'll see you next week. Good night, Quinh."

"Good night, love." He kissed me, then started the motorcycle's engine and disappeared into the darkness of the night.

Ma was in the living room when I walked in, mending some clothes for my siblings. Chi was there too in the corner, pouting.

"Do you want me, Ma?" I called out.

"Yes, come here." She pulled out a long piece of silk and wrapped it around my shoulder. "Do you like it?"

"It's beautiful," I said. "Who is it for?"

"For you. This fabric is going to make a beautiful ao dai."

Indeed it was pretty. I loved the design and the silk material as well, very luxurious. Ao dai was a traditional Vietnamese dress that most women would love to wear. How could she manage it? I felt a little guilty.

"It must have cost a fortune, Ma. We can't afford it."

"Every woman should own a custom-made ao dai. I got mine when I was eighteen for a special occasion. I want to give you the same experience. We will go to the tailor shop tomorrow."

"Thank you, Ma." I was so happy.

"It's not fair!" Chi yelled. "Why can she have it but I can't?"

"You have to wait for your turn. You're only sixteen. You will have one when you turn eighteen," Ma said calmly.

"I don't want to wait two years. If you buy her one, then you should buy me one too," Chi protested.

I knew Chi wouldn't give up easily, and I wasn't going anywhere fancy anyway. "I don't want it, Ma. It's OK."

"The decision is already made; you're coming with me to the tailor shop tomorrow."

Chi looked angry when she stomped out of the room. I was worried she might tell Ma about Quinh, so I went after her.

"Chi! Wait! You promised you would keep the secret, right?"

"If you want me to keep a secret for you, then you have to give me that ao dai."

"Chi! It was Ma's idea, not mine."

"Do you want me to keep the secret or not?" she said in a threatening voice.

"Fine! I'll talk to Ma." I told Ma I didn't really care about the ao dai, so Chi could have it.

"Chi is not fully developed yet, and an ao dai has to fit perfectly. Her body is still changing; she'll have to wait."

Well! What could I say? Ma had already made up her mind.

The next day we went to the tailor shop. Ma watched the seamstress measure me while joyfully sipping her complementary tea. We were told it would take a month at least to complete the ao dai. I was happy to experience it and thought Chi would understand later.

***

Ma was pacing when I came home from the English school. As soon as she saw me, she pointed at a chair.

"Sit down." She took a deep breath. "I thought the only thing on your mind was America. Why would you have a boyfriend if you know you will be leaving the country? You're too young to have a boyfriend anyway, and why on earth would you pick a Northerner?"

"He was born and raised here, in this district."

"So it is true. You have a boyfriend." Ma raised her voice.

I stayed silent, hating Chi for betraying me.

"Where does he live?"

"I don't know," I answered.

"Stop lying to me!" Ma yelled. "You said he lives in this district."

"That's all I know. I've never been to his house."

"Did you do anything foolish?" Ma continued to grill me.

"What do you mean?"

"You know what I mean. Did you go to bed with him?"

"No! He is a good man," I answered angrily.

"He's a man?" Ma was furious. "How old is he?"

I decided not to tell her any more about Quinh.

"How old is he? What is his name?"

Silence.

"You're grounded, young lady. No more friends, no more study group, and you have to stop seeing that man. Do you hear me?" She lifted my chin. "Do you hear me?"

"Yes." I turned away.

I gave Ma and Chi the silent treatment for months. I couldn't see Quinh for a long time. I knew he waited for me at the park that weekend and thought I stood him up. I was grounded, and no one could help me to send a message to him. Ma was timing me everywhere I went, and I couldn't escape. I couldn't even send him a letter because I didn't know his address.

One day, when I was studying for my exam, my sister Lieu ran inside with a letter in her hand.

"Sister Lien, there is a letter for you."

I knew it was from Quinh. I ran outside hoping he would still be there but found no one. "Who gave you this letter, Lieu?"

"It was a girl. She said to give it to you."

I opened it. Quinh wanted to see me that night. I was so happy. I had to find a way. That night I nervously asked Ma to let me study for an exam at Lan's house. Surprisingly she said yes.

I walked to our usual spot in the park. He was there already alone, without the bike.

"Hi, Quinh. How are you?"

"I don't know how I feel right now. How about you?" Quinh looked at me tenderly.

"I'm sorry for not being able to see you the last three months. Chi told Ma about us, and I got grounded."

"I know. Your ma came to my house."

"She did? How did she know where you live? What did

she say?"

"She didn't want you to go out with me anymore," Quinh said.

"I'm eighteen years old. I can go out with anybody I want."

"She told me everything, Lien."

"What did she tell you?"

"That you're going to America, and your family will come with you. Why didn't you tell me that before?"

"I'm sorry, I don't know why, but I love you, and that is true."

"I had hope before. I always thought we would grow old together, but now it's not going to work." He paused. "You have to go to America. Your family depends on you."

"Should I stay?" Tears rolled down my cheeks.

"No, you should go. My parents couldn't escape the Communists. I don't want you to stay then regret it later." He paused. "I promised your ma not to see you anymore."

"Don't give up on us. There must be something we can do," I begged him.

"I've been thinking a lot about us, Lien. No matter what we'll try, the odds are still against us. Your ma already hates me."

"She doesn't hate you. She just doesn't know you yet."

"She made it very clear that I'm not welcome. I understand. If you stayed then your whole family would be stuck here. I can't take that responsibility."

I cried. Why was my life always so complicated?

"I better go," Quinh said. "Your ma is waiting for you." He reached out for my hands, then he kissed me on my forehead. "Good-bye, Lien." He let my hands go and walked away.

It was painful watching him walk out of my life for good. I walked home with a broken heart, unable to stop the tears. There were countless nights I cried myself to sleep. My boyfriend had dumped me because he cared. Sometimes I hoped I would bump into him somewhere, but it didn't happen. I moved on slowly. Lan and Diep always tried to set me up with other guys, but I wasn't interested. My life was complicated enough. I didn't want to involve anyone else. I just wanted to leave this country in peace.

Chapter 14
1985

I graduated high school without any plans for the future. Only half of my classmates went on to college. The other half, like me, couldn't go to college due to our backgrounds. We had family members who used to work for the previous government, and the Communists were very selective about who they would give an education to. I would have loved to be a teacher, but they didn't give me that chance. I couldn't wait to leave Vietnam so I could start my education in America.

Although the government was still strict about education, books, and newspapers, they started to let the citizens open up small businesses. That was a big improvement for the country. Small business was the key to turning the country around. Saigon bounced back to being a bustling city once again. It had gone from being full of cars before the Communists to all bicycles. Now the streets started to fill with scooters and motorcycles again.

Ma wanted to change her business to something a little more stable. Something that wouldn't be affected by the rainy season. A business that could make money year round, but she didn't know yet what and how to start. She kept her eyes and ears open for an opportunity.

Di Hue quit her job as a nurse and opened a small silk store. Ma didn't think a silk store would work for her because people didn't buy silk every day. It was a luxury item. She needed something that would sell every day.

That day came when Ma heard someone wanted to sell a school-supply store, and she bought it. It was a small hut filled with school supplies. The location was perfect—it was in Cho Lon, so she could run both of her businesses.

I was delighted when Ma chose me to run the school-supply store. It was a step up from the juice stand, and I couldn't have been happier. It became my job, and I was good at it. I always organized the store and made sure we had enough supplies to sell. It was crazy busy before the school year started, then went back to normal everyday selling. Ma was happy with the new business, and so was our family. We started to eat better; each one of us got new clothes—no more patches or hand-me-downs; and we got two more bicycles for the family. Our life was improving quickly along with everyone else's in Saigon.

I was glad I could still go to English night school in the rainy season, without borrowing money for tuition from Mr. Loi. I was one of his few students still in his class. Most of them left Vietnam before they could finish the long program. I couldn't wait for my turn. Every time I got invited to going-away parties, it was bittersweet. There were countless times I went to the airport to watch my friends leave, hoping soon I would be in their shoes and leave this country for good.

***

Finally, the interview letter from the Vietnamese government arrived. We jumped and screamed with excitement. I couldn't hold back my happy tears. They wanted to see Ma and me only, not the whole family.

"I hope we get that nice lady again," Ma said.

"We're going to pass the interview, Ma, don't worry," I assured her.

There was no doubt in my mind that the government wanted to get rid of us half-American children. We would pass this interview for sure. The American interview was the one I was worried about.

I woke up early on the interview day, of course. Ma was downstairs making breakfast. She handed me a cup of coffee. We sat and looked at each other. She smiled; it was the first time I had seen her smile without a hint of sadness in it. Like me, she wanted to go to America. She hadn't wanted to before, but now she did, and I was glad to see her smile.

I rode the bicycle with Ma on the backseat to the government building. After two hours of waiting, the guy called my name. We followed him into a room.

"Have a seat," he said.

We sat down while he started to open our file. He

stared at me then asked Ma in an unfriendly voice, "Is this Lien? The half-American child?"

"Yes sir," Ma answered.

"What is her American father's first and last name?"

"I don't know his name, sir."

"You don't know his name? How could you have a child with someone without knowing his name?"

"I was raped by an American."

He put down his pen. "I need to know the whole story."

Ma started to tell him the story she had told me. I felt bad for her when she paused and wiped her tears. The officer's face was unchanged; he didn't feel bad for her. After Ma finished, he looked at her with cold eyes and asked, "How do you know for sure that your child is half-American? The Vietnamese pilot was there too, according to your story."

"I saw an American next to me when I woke up," Ma said.

"You were drugged. How do you know for sure there was just one guy who raped you?"

Ma cried. How could this man be so crude? I hated him for torturing her. I wanted to say something, but I was afraid our fate was in his hands.

"She doesn't look half-American to me." He wrote down something in our file.

"Please, officer! Look at her," Ma begged him. "She looks like me, but you can tell she is half-American."

His face was unreadable. He closed our file and put it in the "FAIL" box.

"Lien isn't half-American, so you're not going anywhere. Your interview is over. You can leave now." He walked out of the room and called the next case.

I couldn't believe what had just happened. There was a big heavy knot in my chest. I couldn't breathe. My whole life I had been teased for being half-American. Now this man said I wasn't? My dream to go to America had been crushed by this mean officer. Ma and I went home in tears. I was so angry inside for everything that had happened, I rode the bicycle into a tree. Ma and I fell down. We got a couple of cuts and bruises.

"I'm sorry, Lien," Ma said.

I said nothing. I was so angry, I couldn't speak. I was the one who should have said sorry to her. She had been through enough, and that stupid officer had rubbed more salt in her wound. Still, I was mad, confused, and disappointed at the same time. I stayed silent on the way home, no matter how many times Ma tried to talk to me.

Di Hue couldn't believe we had failed the interview either. She was upset after Ma told her all the details.

"Sounds like he wanted a bribe. He was probably jealous of you guys. Did he give you any hints?"

"Not that I noticed. Even if he did, where would I find the money?" Ma said.

"I can help you out," Di Hue offered.

"I can't keep borrowing money from you. There are ten of us in the file. If he wanted bribe money, then he would want a lot of it. I'm struggling with just the fees, let alone bribing him." Ma let out a sigh. "Maybe it's not meant to be. I just feel bad for Lien; it was her dream."

Di Hue turned to me and gave me a hug. "I'm so sorry, Lien."

I said nothing in return. Honestly I didn't even know what to say. I felt down, trapped, and I shut myself off from the world.

***

Lan took Mr. Loi to visit me at my house. I knew why: I hadn't gone to English class for three weeks. I hadn't even hung out with Lan during that time, and she was upset.

"How are you, Lien?" Mr. Loi asked after he sat down.

"I'm all right. Sorry I didn't say good-bye. But it doesn't make sense for me to continue to learn English when I failed the interview."

"You're so close to finishing the program, it doesn't make sense to stop now," he said gently.

"I just don't see how it works in the future. Why waste

money?"

"Is it the financial part you're worried about?"

"No, we're doing fine, but I'm not going to America, so..."

"I think you should finish the program, Lien. You can teach English in the future."

"The government won't let me become a teacher, Mr. Loi. I can never have a chance to teach."

"You can be a translator or a tutor. Don't give up on English, Lien. You never know what can happen in the future. Speaking two languages is always better than one."

"Getting out of the house would be good for you too, Lien," Lan jumped in. "Besides, your friends miss you. We all miss you."

Mr. Loi went to talk to Ma at the front door. Lan pulled her chair closer to me.

"It's killing me to see you like this," she said. "I know you've been through a hard time. But there are people who care about you, and you have to be strong and move on."

I took a deep breath. "You're right." We hugged. "Thank you for being here."

"Hey, that's what best friends are for." Lan smiled.

"Yeah, I think I'll go back to English class tomorrow."

"I'll pick you up. Give me a smile, pretty girl!" she demanded.

I loved her for cheering me up. Only Lan could do that. I smiled, and she lit up.

"That's what I'm talking about. See you tomorrow."

I walked Lan to the front door, where I said bye to Mr. Loi and promised him I would go back to class. After they left, I asked Ma what he had been talking to her about.

"He wanted to help us financially, to help you finish English school."

"Really? What did you say to him?"

"I said we can manage. I promised him you will finish the program, so you have to go back."

"Yeah, I'm going back tomorrow."

"Good!" She looked relieved.

I went back to night school and realized how much I loved it. It was a place for me to unwind and to connect with my friends. Mr. Loi let us listen to American music, which was still prohibited by the government. We studied and had fun at the same time. He created field trips for us—we went to beaches or the farms outside the city. We were bonding, even though everyone knew it was a temporary bond. Some of my friends were in the process of going to America, some to Australia, and others to England and Germany. Eventually everyone would be leaving except me.

I finished the program, like I had promised Mr. Loi. He recommended a tutoring job for me, which I did for a short time. I had to give it up to focus on the school-supply store. It was an important income for our family, especially now that we were staying there for good.

Chapter 15
1986

It was Lan's birthday. She was turning twenty-one. Normally she would have a big party, but not this year. She decided to celebrate with me quietly at her house. She had recently broken up with her boyfriend—not that she was upset about it. She had broken up with him before many times and then gotten back together again and again. Still, I thought that was the reason she didn't want a party.

Lan specifically requested a sleepover, and Ma was OK about it. She liked Lan's family. I bought her a wallet and put a picture of us in there. We had dinner with her family; they usually laughed and teased each other, but they were quiet that night. After we were alone in her bedroom, I gave her the gift. She teared up as soon as she opened it.

"Hey! It's just a silly picture of us. It's supposed to make you laugh," I said.

"I know." She wiped her tears. "I'm going to miss you, Lien."

"You're going to miss me? Is there something you want to tell me? Did you get an interview?"

"No, but I'm leaving in a few days by boat," Lan said.

"You're planning to escape? Why? Your ba is sponsoring you. Why escape when you can leave legally?"

"Waiting for paperwork is taking too long. We've been waiting for seven years. My ba is longing for us. He sent money for two of us to escape, so my brother Tien and I will leave by boat in a few days."

"Why didn't you tell me this before?" I was upset about the news.

"I'm not supposed to tell anyone. Even my boyfriend doesn't know." She couldn't hold her tears.

I understood now why she had broken up with him. It was difficult to say good-bye without telling him the truth. Lan's boyfriend, Nho, was a police officer, but he wasn't Communist. He had gone in to avoid the draft for the army after he'd finished high school. Nho was the only son, and his family had to bribe his way in, so he could stay local. Lan kept the secret from him to protect him as well. If Nho knew about Lan's escape plan but did not report it, he could go to jail himself.

Escaping Vietnam was expensive and very dangerous. I had heard that if people got caught, they would be put in jail for a very long time. Also there were a lot of pirates on the open sea. They raped and kidnapped people for ransom. I was worried for Lan.

"I don't know what to say. Everyone wants to go to America, but escaping is so dangerous." I sat down next to her. "Are you sure you want to do this?"

"I'm not sure if it's the right decision, but I want to do it. I miss my ba and my oldest brother. I don't want to wait anymore."

I envied her. I wished somebody would send money for me to escape too. I would do it. I would take a chance to escape like Lan, even though it was dangerous. I might get lucky, and the plan would go smoothly, and I would live happily in America with my best friend.

I cried because in reality my best friend was leaving me for good, and I may never have seen her again. If her plan went well, then Lan wouldn't have a chance to come back to Vietnam. Lan promised she would write to me. We stayed up till three o'clock in the morning that night talking, promising.

I visited Lan daily until one day she wasn't there. Her family told me she and Tien had gone to visit her grandma, and I knew Lan was on her way to escape the country. She had left me a box. Inside were the outfits she had dressed me in and a couple of pictures of us. I missed Lan already and hoped she made it to America safely.

I visited Diep at least once a week to see if there was any news about Lan. After a few times, Diep finally told me Lan had escaped.

"I know, Lan told me," I whispered. "Any news? Did she get out?"

"No news yet. We're very worried." Diep paused. " I will let you know as soon as we have news."

Three months later Diep came to my house. She

looked distressed, and I knew the news was not good.

"We just got a letter from Lan. They didn't get out. They were arrested. Lien, they have been in jail for three months now." Diep cried. "Who knows what will happen to them?"

"Oh no! I'm so sorry." I hugged her. "When can you visit her?"

"In two weeks. I'll go with my ma."

"Can I visit her too?"

"I'm sorry, Lien, they said family only."

"Can you hand Lan a letter for me?"

"Yes, of course. She would like that."

"They're going to be OK, Diep! Your siblings have an incredible family to lean on. They'll be all right."

Lan and her brother stayed in jail for six months. During that time her mother tried everything in her power to get them out. She bribed many politicians, police, and prison officials. It was an ordeal, but in the end Lan and Tien were released and came back home to their family. I was so happy to see Lan home safe and sound.

Lan and Nho got back together again. He loved her, wanted to marry her, but Lan had to stay single in order to go to America. The immigration rule was if the daughter or son married, then she or he had to stay behind. Lan wanted to leave; Nho knew that, but he didn't give up. He was always there when she needed him. They were dating on and off for ten years. Lan broke his heart then put it back and broke it again and again.

I envied Lan. She had everything. She was rich and had a wonderful family. She was always happy, and her boyfriend loved her to death. Quinh had broken up with me as soon as he'd heard I was going to America. Deep down I wished Lan would marry Nho so she could stay in Vietnam. I never told her that; I knew it was selfish of me to wish it, but it would be nice if she stayed in Vietnam too. She was my best friend, and she made me laugh. Who was going to make me laugh when she was gone?

Chapter 16
1987

I was working at the school-supply store when my sister Anh showed up unexpectedly. She looked pale and nervous.

"Anh! What's wrong?"

"Ba is home. I came home from school, and there he was. They let him come home, sister Lien. He told me to get Ma."

"Oh my God! Go get Ma. She's at the juice stand."

It was bad news indeed. We were doing great without him, and now he came home to tear us apart. My chest felt heavy all of a sudden. I was worried for our future.

Ma closed the juice stand early and went home with Anh. I told her I had to wait for a client to pick up an order. I lied. As soon as they left, I closed the store and biked to Lan's house. I collapsed in her chair, mentally exhausted with fear.

"Hey! What's going on?" Lan asked. "You don't look yourself."

"I'm in deep trouble."

"You're pregnant?" She laughed.

"Stop! It's not funny. I'm not in the mood for joking."

"I'm sorry, what is it?"

"My stepfather came home. They released him."

"When, today?" Her face tensed up immediately.

"Yes! I haven't been home yet. I don't want to see him. Remember those terrible stories I told you? It may happen again, and I'm afraid of him."

"I'm so sorry. What are you going to do?"

"I don't know. Really, I would like to run away, but I'm too old for that."

"You're welcome here anytime. If he hits you again, you can come here to live with us."

"Lan, he is very controlling. He might not let me hang out with you. I don't know when I will see you next, and don't stop by my house, because I don't know what he will do. I'll visit you when I can."

"I'm not afraid of him, Lien! If I don't see you for a while,

I'm going to stop by just to make sure you're OK. I'll bring Nho with me. He's a police officer. I'll make sure he wears his uniform when I visit."

"Lan! I'm serious, you can't do that. You don't know what happens after you leave. He'll torture me. Do you understand?"

"I'm sorry, I'm just trying to help." She paused. "You need to get out of there. It sounds like hell to me."

"Trust me. I don't want to live there, not with him in that house. I just don't know how to get out."

We hugged. It was time for me to go home. I biked home in a nervous state, scared and worried. What would happen to us and Ma? Would he hit us again? Would he still hit me even though I was now twenty-one years old?

I walked in the living room and saw him at the table eating his dinner. Ma sat next to him. She seemed happy and kept on putting more food in his bowl like he couldn't help himself. He looked a lot skinnier, a lot older too, but he was still scary looking to me.

"Chào Ba, Ma." I had to say hello even though I wanted to keep my distance from him.

"Come, sit down and eat," Ma said.

"I want to finish the sales totals for today first. I'll eat later."

My four youngest siblings, Mai, Lieu, Little, and Be, were there eating with them. I went to the bedroom, which I still shared with all the girls. Chi, Anh, and Truc were there too, hiding from him again, like the old times.

"Where is Vu?" I asked them.

"He's not coming home." Truc told me quietly. "He moved back to his friend's house."

"At least he had a place to move to. We're stuck," Chi said.

There! We had lost one already.

***

Even though my stepfather had stopped drinking, he

120

still yelled at Ma and us a lot. Either the coffee was too cold or dinner was too late. I got in trouble a couple of times for not remembering to buy him a newspaper. He stayed in his bedroom most of the time. When he came out, he seemed to suck all the oxygen out of the house. The air was suddenly stiff, heavy, and hard to breathe. We didn't smile or laugh anymore since he came home. I felt like we were fish out of water.

Ma, Chi, and I went to work each day, and he wanted a report on the businesses every day, just like before.

"How much did you make today? Why was it so little profit? Did you try to grab more customers today?"

Like we didn't know how to run the businesses. We did fine when he wasn't there. What did he know about running businesses in Cho Lon anyway? He was never there. I wished he would leave us alone, let us breathe a little. I felt bad for Anh; she had to stay home after school to take care of the house chores. Staying around him wasn't easy, I knew that. She seemed sad every day, and I wouldn't dare to ask her what was wrong. I knew what was wrong.

We came home from work one day, and Anh was gone. She hadn't come home from school. We went to look for her, but she wasn't in the neighborhood. Ma and I were concerned about her last year of high school. If she ran away, then she couldn't graduate. The next morning I went to the high school early to talk to her friends, hoping they knew where she was. Her best friend, Thanh, told me Anh had gotten married the previous day at city hall.

"She what?" I was shocked. I didn't even know she had a boyfriend.

"She married her high school sweetheart. His name is Nghia."

"How long have they been dating?" I asked Thanh.

"Five, six months, I think."

"Do you know where Nghia lives?"

"Yes, but I promised Anh not to tell anyone."

"Please, Thanh, I need to see my sister. I just want to know if she is OK."

Thanh hesitated, but in the end she gave me the address. I couldn't believe it. Anh was so quiet. Nobody knew she had a boyfriend, and boom! She got married. She had just turned eighteen. She got herself a ticket to get out of the house legally—the marriage certificate. I wasn't sure if it was good or bad. Should I be happy for her or worried?

I gave Ma Anh's new address. I didn't tell her Anh had gotten married at city hall. Anh probably wanted to tell Ma herself, so I pretended I knew nothing about it.

Ma went to see Anh with Chi. When they came back, Ma was upset, and Chi had cuts and bruises on her.

"What's happened to you?" I asked Chi.

"We got into a fight."

"With who?"

"Anh's sisters-in-law. Can you believe it? She got married to a dumb family."

"Ma! What's happened?" I turned to her.

"We just want Anh to come home, but they were a very aggressive family. They're claiming Anh belongs to them now. They said mean things to me, and Chi lost her patience."

"What a mess! What are you going to do?" I asked Ma.

"She's too young to be married. I don't like her mother-in-law; she seemed to have a hot temper like her daughters. What was Anh thinking?"

"Did you talk to Anh?"

"They didn't let her come out to talk to us. I don't know what to do." She sighed.

Ma had to tell him about Anh. He prohibited us from seeing or contacting her in any way. He said Anh dishonored the family by getting married in secret, and she wasn't allowed to come home to visit us either. Ma said nothing. I wished she would stand up and say, "No! You can't stop me from seeing my daughter." But she just sat there, head down, and accepted his decision.

We didn't see Anh for a long time. Eventually we got a note from her saying she'd just had a baby boy, and she wanted us to visit. Ma and I visited them in secret. Anh looked happy. I couldn't believe she had become a mother.

"How is your mother-in-law treating you?" Ma asked her.

"She is a little difficult sometimes, but I can manage."

"Are you happy?" I asked Anh.

"Yes, I am. I have my own family now, and it feels good."

Ma held the baby and sang him a lullaby. She seemed happy to be a grandma—a very young grandma. I knew she wished the situation would be different. Honestly, I thought Anh wouldn't have gotten married in a hurry if her father had not returned home. She would at least have waited until she graduated high school. I hoped her husband was nice to her, and I hoped she had found happiness in her new life.

***

While I was taking an order from a customer, a man in his late twenties was waiting for his turn. He kept staring at me, and it made me feel a little uncomfortable. As soon as I was done with the order, I turned to him and asked, "May I help you?"

"Hi, my name is Minh. I'm the owner of Quoc Toan Ink & Pen Company. I believe you're one of my retailers."

"That's right. We carry Quoc Toan Ink & Pen products. I don't think I ever met you before, though. Normally Hung was the one who delivered to us."

"He is my younger brother; he works for me. He doesn't feel well today, so here I am." He took something out of his wallet. "This is my business card."

I started to see the resemblance between them. Hung was tall, but Minh was even taller and more confident.

"Nice to meet you, Mr. Tran." I took out the order list "This is what we need for tomorrow."

"Please, call me Minh. What is your name?"

"My name is Lien."

"What a beautiful name."

"Thank you." I smiled.

A customer walked in, and I turned to help her.

"Nice to meet you, Lien. I'll make sure to get this in first thing tomorrow," Minh called out.

From then on Minh was the one who delivered instead of Hung. He stopped by almost every day, and I knew he liked me. Honestly, I didn't know what to think. I thought if I introduced someone to my family, he would turn around and run away as fast as he could. My parents wouldn't allow me to go out anyway, so I didn't show any interest. Then one day Minh showed up at the store when I wasn't busy.

"Hi, Lien. How's business?"

"Good, thanks," I answered.

"Do you need more ink bottles or pens?"

"I think we're good right now. I just placed an order yesterday."

"Would you like to come to my factory sometime to see how they're made?" He smiled. "I would love to show you."

"I would love to, but I can't seem to escape this store."

"Are you free in the evening, after the store closes down?" He was still trying to convince me.

"I really can't come to the factory at nighttime."

"Not the factory. I would like to take you out to dinner sometime, if you have a free evening."

I didn't know what to say. Yes, that sounded wonderful, but I knew I couldn't. How was I going to explain this to him?

"Don't tell me you're busy in the evening too." Minh paused. "I just want to take you to a nice dinner, that's all."

"I would love to, but my parents are very strict. They won't let me go out."

"Really? What if I go there and asked them for permission? Do you think that would work? I mean, your ma already knows who I am. I think she would trust me."

"Maybe you should ask her first." I thought, 'Good luck with that.'

"I'll ask her. I think she likes me." Minh nodded with confidence.

Surprisingly, for some reason, my parents allowed us to go out on a date. Maybe because Minh was a business owner and they trusted him. Minh took me to a nice restaurant. I was nervous because I'd never been to a nice restaurant before and certainly wasn't dressed for it; I hadn't had time to stop by Lan's for a makeover. He acted like he had been there before and seemed comfortable.

"Maxim used to be a French restaurant. It got shut down by the government and reopened after the new small business law." He was just trying to make conversation. "What do you think of this place?"

"A little too fancy for me, I think." I was too honest.

"You don't like it? We can go somewhere else."

"It's OK. I just don't know how to act properly in this place."

"You're doing fine. We don't have to come back here next time."

Next time? I thought, 'Be careful what you're asking for, Mr. Tran.'

***

Every time Minh and I went out on a date, he had to ask for permission. So after three months of dating, I told him I was ready to get married. I wanted to move out of the house, the sooner the better. I suggested, "Let's get married at the city hall."

He laughed. He thought I was joking.

My face turned tomato red with embarrassment. "No! I wasn't joking. I'm serious about it."

"What about your parents? I mean, they're really strict."

"You probably know he's my stepfather. I don't think he cares."

"I kind of figured that. You look half-American to me. Are you?"

"Yes, I am. Does that bother you?"

"No, not at all. I mean, you're very pretty. My question is, aren't you in the process of leaving the country?"

"It's a long story." I sighed.

"I have time." Minh looked at me patiently.

I told him I had failed the interview due to lack of

information about my American father, who had disappeared after he'd found out about Ma's pregnancy. I didn't want to tell him the rape story. It was just too painful.

"So I'm staying here for good." I paused. "Some of my friends already got married. My younger sister got married too. I just thought..."

"It's time." Minh finished my sentence.

"Yeah." I nodded my head slightly.

"If we're going to get married, I want to do it the right way. A wedding is a must, because I'm the oldest one in the family. First I have to take you home to introduce you to my family."

It sounded like an awfully long time before I could get out of my house, but at least he wanted to marry me. We went to his house the following week. Everybody was nice and welcoming. His family was bigger than mine. He had ten siblings. It scared me a little, to be honest. I had been hoping for a small family. How was I going to getting along with everyone? This was going to be a big task.

A month later Minh's parents came to meet my parents. They asked my parents for permission if Minh and I could get engaged. Then Minh's mother suggested a good day three months later; until then we weren't engaged yet. When the day came, we stood in front of both sides of our families. Minh gave me a pair of gold earrings—the Vietnamese custom— and we were engaged. His parents had already chosen the wedding day. It was nine months later.

***

I was in a good mood at the store, singing to myself a happy little song. I had a successful fiancé, and soon we would get married. Who wouldn't be happy? I was daydreaming when a woman walked into the store. I gave her a big welcoming smile.

"May I help you?"

"Are you Lien?" she asked me.

"Yes, I am. What can I do for you?"

"Do you know Minh? The owner of Quoc Toan Ink?"

"Yes, he's my fiancé." At first I thought she wanted to order some supplies from Minh. I was going to give her his business card.

"Do you really know him like I do?"

"I don't understand." I looked at her in confusion.

"Listen! Minh and I are in a relationship. We have a son together."

She took out a picture and showed it to me. There was Minh, holding a baby. The three of them looked happy in the picture. I froze. I didn't know how to respond to that. I kept staring at the picture, hoping it wasn't him. She snatched the picture back, said, "You know what to do," and quickly left the store. I felt tears running down my cheeks. She had come in for only a few minutes and taken all my happiness away.

I cried to Ma that night and begged her not to tell my stepfather.

"It's a red flag, Lien. You should break off the engagement, the sooner the better. I don't want people to start talking. It will ruin your chance to marry somebody else," Ma said.

"Why would it ruin my chance to marry somebody else, Ma? I didn't do anything wrong."

"Our culture is not very kind to women. People might think you and Minh already have a husband and wife kind of relationship. All men want to marry a virgin, do you know what I mean?"

I nodded.

"Don't wait too long to make a decision." Ma sighed.

I didn't know what to do. If I was breaking up with Minh, that meant I would be stuck in my family's house. Who knew when the next man would come along? I couldn't stand my stepfather any longer, but could I trust Minh to be faithful? Was the woman telling me the truth? Had they still been together when he'd met me? What about his parents? Did they know about this woman? Why would they ask my parents for us to get engaged if they knew Minh was with someone else? It didn't make sense to me. I needed to know the truth;

then I would make my decision.

The next day Minh came to pick me up for our wedding shopping trip. He could tell I wasn't happy. Instead of shopping, we went to a coffee shop nearby to talk. I told him about the woman and the picture.

"I can explain." Minh's face tensed up. "Yes, I did have a relationship with her, but it was over a while ago, before I met you."

"What about your family? Did they know about her?"

"I never brought her home. She was a widower and older than me. She wanted to have fun, and I made the mistake of sleeping with her. I wasn't in love with her, and when I stopped seeing her, she basically harassed me. I have no idea how she found you. I'm so sorry."

"What about the baby? Is he yours?"

"I don't know. We broke up, then she told me she was pregnant. I thought that was one of her games, so I tried to avoid her. One day I went to a friend's birthday party, and she was there. I had a few drinks, and I honestly don't know how I ended up in that picture."

I said nothing because I was still thinking. Minh reached out to hold my hands, but I didn't let him.

"Lien! I'm sorry if I caused you any pain or embarrassment. I was young and stupid. I promise I would never cheat on you. I want to marry you. I love you."

"How can I trust you after this?" I started to tear up.

"I will work hard to win your trust back. I'm older now, and I learned from my mistakes. It'll never happen again, I promise you."

"I need time to think." I wiped my tears and told him I wanted to walk home alone.

I made my decision on the way home: I would marry him. I made him wait a while to hear it, but I told Ma the wedding was on. I gave him a second chance. I wanted desperately to get out of the house, and this was my chance.

Chapter 17
1988

Our wedding was a blur to me. Since Minh's family paid for it, we had limited tables for my side of the family. Lan was my only bridesmaid, and only a few of my friends were invited. I felt a little awkward at my own wedding because I didn't know a lot of guests there. Most of them were Minh's family, his friends, and his clientele.

After the wedding we went home to his parents' house. Minh's mother wanted us to enter the house through the back door. Since our animal years weren't compatible according to her feng shui book—our culture was adapted to the Chinese lunar animal calendar—we had no choice but to obey her request. I thought, why bother with the wedding when I couldn't even walk through the front door like every other bride? Maybe it was because I was half-American, and she wasn't proud to show me to her friends and relatives. I reminded myself I had to be careful around my mother-in-law.

Minh's mother had set up our room. Her gift to us was a beautiful handmade armoire with a lock. The next day she told me I should be the one to keep the key. Since Minh was a spender, she wanted me to keep track of the money. It was the wife's job, she said. It turned out my mother-in-law was nicer than I had thought. I appreciated that she would want me to be in charge of her son's money. Minh wasn't happy about me keeping the key, but he gave it to me anyway, to make his mother happy.

I thought I had to cook, clean, and do laundry for everyone in the house, but I had to do only my husband's laundry. My mother-in-law told me stories about her difficult mother-in-law and said she wanted to be the opposite. I helped her cook only when I had nothing else to do. Four of Minh's siblings were working for him, so I didn't want to interfere in his business. Everything worked out better than I had thought it would. Of course I dreamt of having our own place, but I didn't ask Minh for it. Maybe a few years later I would; for now I was content.

Just shy of two months into our marriage, I started feeling nauseous and naively thought I had the flu. Minh decided to take me to the doctor, and it turned out I was pregnant. My husband was very happy about it.

"Do you think it's a boy?" he asked me.

"I don't know. It's too early to tell." I paused. "Promise me you will love your child whether it's a boy or girl."

"Of course! I just have a feeling it's going to be a boy. Do you want to go home to tell your ma about it? I'll take you."

Did I want to go home? Definitely not.

"I'd rather see her at Cho Lon," I said.

"OK, I'll bring you there tomorrow."

It was a little early to tell everyone, but I wanted to tell Ma. Maybe she would give me some advice about how to do things when expecting. What should I eat, and what should I avoid? I'd heard the first trimester is very important.

Minh dropped me off at Cho Lon. While he went around to pick up his orders, I went to see Ma. She smiled when she saw me.

"Hi, Lien, how is everything? How is your mother-in-law treating you?"

"Hi, Ma. She is nice to me. How is everybody at home?"

"Everybody is doing well. Ah! You got a letter yesterday from Thailand."

"Thailand? Are you sure?"

"Here." She took the letter out of a drawer. "I was going to ask Minh to give it to you."

My jaw dropped. The letter was in English, and it had come from the US embassy in Thailand. I quickly opened it. I couldn't believe my eyes! It was an appointment for an interview with the Americans in Saigon.

"Ma! We got a date for our interview."

"What interview?" she was confused.

"The interview—with the Americans."

"How?" She stared at me in shock. "We saw the officer put our file in the 'fail' box."

"I don't know, but we got it now." I was happy but wasn't sure if we would pass this time.

"Oh my God! You're married now. They won't let us come with you."

"They said to bring the whole family."

"What about your husband?"

"He'll come too. He's my family now."

"I wish you didn't marry him. Then we would be all right. What a mess!"

"Ma! I didn't know we would get this chance for another interview. We failed, remember?"

Ma was sad all of a sudden. I felt a little guilty that I had raised my voice, but I thought she knew why I had been in a rush to get married. I decided not to tell her about my pregnancy. It wasn't the right time.

"I'm sorry, Ma. We can't undo the past. Let's hope it all works out for the best."

"I want to ask you something, Lien. What if they make you choose between your family and your husband? What would you do? Are you going to pick him over us?"

"I don't know, Ma. What would you do? Would you leave your husband behind?"

Ma didn't answer my question. She turned her back to me like she was done with me. I sat down, waiting for Minh to come back. Ma didn't talk to me the rest of the time, pretending she was busy. I felt awkward and wanted to apologize to her, but Minh reappeared.

"Ready to go home?" He smiled then stopped suddenly, looking back and forth between Ma and me.

"Yeah," I nodded.

"Is everything OK?" Minh asked.

"I'll tell you later." I turned to Ma. "Bye, Ma."

"Bye." That was all she said. She didn't even look at us.

Minh detected something was wrong, so I told him about the surprise letter. He stayed quiet on the way home.

"So, what's going to happen? Are you going to the interview?" he asked finally.

"I think we should go and see what they say. I mean, we failed before; we might fail again."

"What about us? What would happen if you passed the

interview? Would you go without me?"

I took a long time to think before I answered. "It's my dream to go to America. I really don't know what to do."

"What about our baby? You can't take him away from me," Minh protested.

"The baby will have a better future in America, don't you think?"

"We will have a good future here too. I'll provide for both of you. My business is doing well. We'll be OK."

"Have you thought of the what ifs? What if the government changes their plan again, back to the way it was? What if you lose your business? We could lose everything overnight. They could come in and take everything." I paused. "How can you guarantee it won't happen again? It happened before. I saw it with my own eyes. What will happen to our child? No food to eat, no education. I don't see a safety net here in this country. I don't see it!"

Minh said nothing in return. In fact he didn't talk to me for a couple of days. I had to promise him we would either go to America together or stay in Vietnam together. We were newlyweds, and already we had a big disagreement. It was hard for us, especially when we lived with my in-laws. Everyone wanted to know what was going on, but we couldn't tell them yet. We had to wait for the interview, then we would tell them, pass or fail.

***

Minh and I went to the appointment an hour early and hoped my family would arrive on time. We waited in front of the building set up for the Americans. At the time there was no US embassy in Vietnam. Every morning a group of Americans flew to Saigon from the Thai US embassy for interviews and flew back the same day.

I watched people go into and out of the building. Some left with happiness on their faces; others seemed sad and disappointed. I could see who had passed and who had failed their interviews, and it made me really nervous.

There were many half-Americans waiting in line with their families. Some looked very American; others looked Vietnamese with lighter skin and hair. I couldn't believe there were so many of us out there. I prayed in my head, 'Please, God, let our family pass this time'.

We went in as soon as my family arrived. Everyone was there, including my stepfather, my sister Anh and her baby. A few minutes later, a man called my name. I raised my hand so he could see us in the crowded room. My heart started pumping faster.

"How many people in your family?" the interpreter asked.

I counted quickly. It was ten of us, plus Minh, my stepfather, and Anh's baby.

"There are thirteen of us," I answered.

"Wow! All of you can follow me." He led us to a big room.

A young American man sat at a desk watching us enter the room. He stared at my stepfather walking slowly with crutches, every step with a grunt and heave. The man asked the interpreter, "What happened to him?"

I understood the question but didn't want to jump in to answer. Ma might not like the result of this interview, and I didn't want to be responsible for it. My stepfather told the interpreter he had been a pilot and had lost his right leg during the war. Then the Communists put him in a reeducation camp with hard labor, and his joints had been painful and weak ever since.

I could see a sympathetic look on the interviewer's face. He opened our file, checking our names. He started to interview me finally.

"Are they your real family?" the interpreter translated.

"Yes, they are," I answered.

"How long have you been living with them?"

"My whole life," I lied, for good reason. "Until recently I got married."

"Do you have the marriage certificate with you?"

"Yes." I took out the certificate and held Minh's hand.

"This is my husband, Minh."

I looked over my shoulder and caught Ma's worried face. All my siblings were there staring at me. They were worried too. I loved them and wanted to take them with me.

The next thing that came out of my mouth was, "I'm expecting as well."

They all gasped. I couldn't tell if they were happy for me or shocked by the news.

"Sorry, Ma, I tried to tell you, but…" I choked up.

The room fell silent for a minute, then the interpreter told the American what was going on. He nodded his head, trying to understand the situation. He asked Anh a few questions about her husband's job. He wrote something down in our file then got up from the table.

"I'll be right back," the interviewer said and left the room.

Ma was still mad at me, I could tell. She thought I didn't care about the family. I had my own family now; what was I supposed to do? I had to tell them about the pregnancy, so there wouldn't be complications later on.

"Congratulations, sister Lien," Anh said quietly.

"Thank you." I reached out to hold my nephew's hand. "He is a good boy. He hasn't cried since we got here."

"He's an easy baby," Anh said with a smile.

My siblings started to play with the baby, but my parents kept their distance. Twenty minutes later the American came back in the room with his interpreter. He put down the thick file and said, "After carefully reviewing your case, I have determined all of you can go to America with Lien. However, Anh Luong is married, so she has to stay behind. Congratulations!" Then he left the room.

The interpreter gave me two forms to fill out regarding my husband's and my stepfather's additional information. I did it with shaking hands. It was unreal. We had passed the interview, but I felt so sad that Anh had to stay behind. I wished she could come with us. I looked at Anh's sad face and swallowed the bitterness in my throat.

"I'm so sorry, Anh," I managed to say to her.

She shook her head, unable to say anything. We walked out of there in a daze, with so many mixed emotions.

The next couple of months were really busy, with additional paperwork for my stepfather and Minh. Then we went to have many blood tests and health checkups. My stomach grew bigger and bigger. By the time the air tickets were ready for us, I was seven months pregnant. The government officials didn't let us leave, saying it was too risky for me to fly. We had no choice but to wait until the baby was born.

The lunar new year arrived. We call it Tet. This was my last Tet in the country, and I planned to visit all my friends with Minh. Tet is seriously important to the Vietnamese. All the schools and businesses closed down for days. People went home to the countryside to visit their families. Traditionally the first day of Tet was for visiting parents and grandparents. The second day was for visiting teachers, and the third was for friends. Tet was for relaxation, unwinding, and catching up with your family and friends. Everyone was in good mood or at least tried to be positive for the New Year.

On the first day of Tet, Minh wanted to visit my family. I didn't want to, but I didn't want my in-laws questioning my relationship with my family, so I agreed to go home with him. It was hard to describe my feelings. Of course I wanted to see Ma and my siblings, but my stepfather was there too. He could turn the house upside down the moment he wasn't happy about something. What if he didn't like the food Ma prepared for Tet? God forbid one of my siblings accidentally broke something on the New Year. I didn't want to witness the unpleasant scene.

I was surprised and glad to see my sister Anh at the house. It seemed my parents had forgiven her. Although her husband was uncomfortable around us, Anh did try to make amends with our parents. Then I noticed a young woman I hadn't seen before, talking to my stepfather.

"Who's that?" I asked Ma.

"Do you want to help me in the kitchen?" Ma said, changing the subject.

I followed her to the kitchen. When we were alone, she told me as she was preparing food. "That is your ba's long lost daughter. Her name is Loan," she whispered.

"Did he have her before he met you? Because she looks a lot younger than me."

"No, her ma used to be our nanny." Ma paused. "Loan is five years younger than you."

"I can't believe it. They were having an affair while she was working for you?" I hated him even more now.

"Part of it was my fault."

"How was it your fault? I don't understand." I shook my head in disbelief.

"My fault was trusting her. I trusted her to take care of my kids, so I could focus on the gas station. I was always treating her like a friend." Ma paused. "I fired her as soon as I found out."

"I don't know what to say. Did you know about her pregnancy?"

"Not at first. They were still seeing each other after I fired her. When he got injured, she dumped him and moved on."

"What is Loan doing here anyway? It's Tet." I was upset for Ma.

"It was the past. We're leaving the country soon, and I agreed she could come here to visit her ba. Her ma did the wrong thing, but Loan is innocent."

"I know why she's here."

Chi entered the kitchen. She had been eavesdropping. "She wants him to send her some money in the future. Maybe she wants this house too!"

"No, Chi. This house will belong to Anh. We already talked about that," Ma assured her.

"Did you see how he's so nice to her? He loves her more than the rest of us."

"It's just because she is a guest," Ma said.

"You're always defending him." Chi stomped out of the

kitchen.

I didn't want to stay any longer, so I said good-bye and left with Minh. I missed Vu; he wasn't there. Ma said he joined them only for the paperwork and health checkups. He stayed with his friend's family the rest of the time.

My first day of Tet wasn't so bad. My stepfather had been in a good mood because his long lost daughter was there. He had behaved better than I had expected.

The second day of Tet, I wanted to visit my English teacher, Mr. Loi, but I couldn't because Minh was in a bad mood. He had been gambling all night with his friends in the neighborhood and had lost a lot of money. My mother-in-law told me to hide the armoire's key so he wouldn't lose all of it. We kept the money in the armoire because there was no bank in Vietnam at the time, only the government's bank. Secondly, we didn't want the government to know how much money we had. If they knew you were rich, you were in trouble.

I was in our room after dinner, reading an English book. I tried to practice every night, so I wouldn't forget what I had learned. Minh came in and asked me for the armoire's key. He said he needed some money.

"What do you need money for at nighttime?" I asked him.

"I need money to play cards. I'll try to get back the money I lost last night."

"What if you lose some more tonight? It's Tet. You should stay home with the family."

"I'm with the family the whole day. I just want to have some fun with my friends. Come on, give me the key."

"Gambling is illegal, darling. What if you get caught? They can put you in jail for that. What am I supposed to do without you? I know nothing about running your business."

"Stop saying that. You're not supposed to say anything negative during Tet. We play cards only at night, and one of the players is a policeman."

"I really want you to stay home with me. Please," I begged him.

"No! You don't understand. I have to play. It's for the

business, so if I need a favor in the future, this group of people can help me. Now give me the key."

I didn't know what to do. If I gave him the key, he might lose all the money. Then my mother-in-law would be mad at me for not listening to her. We might lose the business; I couldn't take that chance. I stood up, pretending to look for the key. I lifted the pillows, checked under the bed, and went through the desk. I did all of this knowing the key wasn't in the room.

"I'm sorry, Minh, I don't remember where I put the key."

He tossed pillows through the air angrily. Then he moved to the desk and threw papers all over the floor. Out of frustration he kicked the chair to the corner and stomped out of the room. I let out a sigh and started gathering papers. I heard him downstairs borrowing his mother's money. Who was this man who turned into a beast in seconds? Were all husbands like this to their wives? Didn't he see I was nearly eight months pregnant?

I tried to stay calm. It was Tet, after all. After cleaning the room, I went back to reading. Hours later I heard Minh's voice, trying to borrow money from his mother again. This time she refused.

"I can't lend you any more money," she called out while he ran upstairs. "And leave your wife alone!"

I heard footsteps coming toward our room. Bang! The door burst open. Minh stepped in with a hammer in his hand. He looked angry, and I got so scared I jumped out of the bed. He went straight to the armoire and started to pound at the lock.

"Stop!" Minh's mother ran into the room screaming. "What are you doing?"

"It's my money! What I want to do with it is none of your business!"

"You're going to lose it all to gambling," my mother-in-law yelled at Minh. "You're going to be a father soon, so act like one!"

"I need to get back the money I lost. You can't stop me. I'm twenty-nine years old. I do what I want."

"I'm going tell your ba about this," Minh's mother said.

"Good luck! He's there right now gambling your money away. Why don't you try to stop him instead?"

I stood there dead silent and couldn't say a word. After Minh broke the armoire's door, he gathered all the money into a bag and left the house. Minh's mother wiped her tears as she walked out of the room and left me there alone with my own tears. I was shocked to see him destroy the armoire; it had been our wedding gift from his mother. He didn't have any respect for his mother at all. How could I trust him to respect me?

I felt frightened and worried. I had tried everything to escape my stepfather and took a chance on marrying Minh. Now he scared me too. I cried myself to sleep.

Minh didn't come home all night. It was better that way. I didn't know how I would feel sleeping next to him after that. I felt so alone. I missed Lan. I wished I could go to see her and tell her, "Don't get married. You will regret it."

On the third day of Tet, Minh came home empty handed. He had lost all his money to gambling. Needless to say, I was mad at him for being irresponsible. He apologized to me many times and tried to be sweet and caring. It took me a long time to forgive him. His parents lent him money to run the business again, and he promised he would give up gambling for good.

Chapter 18
1989

My son was born in my favorite season: Spring. This tiny little person had changed me. I experienced a different kind of love. The love was so great, so deep. It kept me up at night just staring at him. It was such a joy. Every time I looked at my baby, he took my pain away. Minh named the baby after his company, and I was OK with that. We started to apply for Toan's birth certificate right away, so we could add him to our paperwork. I couldn't wait to take my baby to America. The land of freedom, the land of opportunity.

Minh's family was very happy about the baby boy. His parents threw us a huge baby party. It's part of the Vietnamese culture to celebrate the baby turning a month old when the baby is strong enough to handle guests, and because we were leaving the country soon, a big party seemed appropriate. Toan was always the center of attention, and everybody loved him.

My sister-in-law Thuy played with the baby one day, and she had a slip of tongue. "You're my favorite nephew."

I thought, 'Minh said his family didn't know about the other woman.' Maybe he had lied to me. I had to find out.

"What are you talking about? He is your only nephew, isn't he?" I asked her.

"Oh, sorry, I shouldn't say that. My brother would kill me if he found out," Thuy said.

"Find out what? I already know about the other boy. Minh said the family didn't know about him."

"We knew. Minh was seventeen when he had him, so the boy should be around twelve years old now."

"What? I thought the boy is only three years old. I saw the picture."

"No! Minh's ex-girlfriend had the baby when they were still in high school. They were both seventeen. I remember vividly how mad Ba and Ma were when they found out."

So there were two of them out there. Minh had two other sons from two different women. One was twelve years old, and the other one was three. I felt cheated, betrayed by my dishonest husband, even though all of that had happened before he had met me. I loved him a little less, trusted him a little less, and respected him a lot less.

When I confronted him, he admitted it and apologized, saying he had wanted to tell me about it, but he was afraid it might upset me. He said he had been young and stupid.

"I swear I will never cheat on you," Minh said.

"I can't accept a cheating husband. I'm letting you know now, I won't stand for that."

I had to be strong. I couldn't be like my mother. My stepfather cheated on her, and she was still with him. I could not understand that, especially since she was the one putting food on the table. She didn't need him to take care of her or us. I wished she would divorce him for her own sake. I would rather be a single mom and happy than married to a cheater. Could I be that strong? Could I raise my son by myself? Provide for him and gave him a good life? I didn't know. I didn't have a job or a degree.

I gave Minh a chance to prove himself, to show he could be a good and faithful husband. He wasn't a perfect husband like my uncle was to my aunt Hai, but he didn't hit me, and he was a lot better than my stepfather. I decided to let it go. I promised myself I wouldn't think about his other sons and would not bring them up again in our conversations. I focused on my son and getting us ready to leave Vietnam.

***

Being a new mom was challenging. Besides taking care of the baby, I had to run back and forth to and from the immigration office quite often. I always took the baby with me because I was breastfeeding him, and I didn't trust anyone with him. I always felt my baby would be safer with me.

Then all of a sudden, Toan got sick. I wished I knew what I had done wrong. My four-month-old son had to be hospitalized. He was in intensive care for an internal infection. He had a fever, he didn't want to eat, and he got so skinny. I tried to breastfeed him, but he didn't want any milk, and it hurt me to see my baby crying. I cried a lot too and worried. Had I eaten something I was not supposed to eat? How come I was fine but he had gotten so sick?

I stayed in the hospital with the baby day and night. Minh went to visit after work every day. His family and mine took turns visiting us and offered to watch the baby for me, so I could go home to rest and shower. I refused. There was a public shower I used every day, and I was OK with that. I couldn't leave my baby there with anyone. I wanted to be with him all the time. The hospital didn't have good medicine. Even the doctor whispered in my ear, "Buy this medicine from the black market. It's imported." He scribbled something on a piece of paper and gave it to me.

"How do I know if it's real?" I asked the doctor.

"Just pray to God it is. Your son needs it."

Minh and I agreed we had to try this new medicine from the black market. Our baby had been in the hospital for three days, and he wasn't getting better. Minh went to buy the medicine, and I prayed he got the real one.

After a few days with the new medicine, Toan seemed better. He slept more and cried less. I played with him, and my heart lifted when I saw him smiling. He still didn't have an appetite yet, but the IV fluid was helping him.

Ma came to visit and asked me about the paperwork. Since my name was on the case, I was in charge of taking care of all the paperwork.

"Yes, Ma, everything is ready. We have to wait for the baby to get better first, then we'll go back to the air ticket office."

"Oh, OK. How is he?" Ma looked at her sleeping grandson.

"Better. Thank God the medicine is not fake."

"When will he be allowed to go home?"

"The doctor said as soon as he begins to eat, he can come home," I told Ma.

"Aunt Hai's family is leaving tomorrow for America," Ma said.

"Really? Who told you that?"

"Her oldest son, Phuc, came to our house yesterday and told us."

"Wow! That's great news. Do you know where in America?" I asked.

"Chicago." Ma paused. "I can't believe they kept the secret from us."

"Ma! Aunt Hai can't walk. Besides, she and Ba weren't talking, remember? I don't think they kept it secret from you. They just didn't have a chance to tell you until yesterday."

"You're right, are you coming to the airport tomorrow to say bye to your aunt's family?"

"Tell them I want to, but my son is still in the hospital. I can't leave him."

"OK, I'll tell them that." Ma said.

I was so happy for Aunt Hai's family and hoped to see them in America very soon.

Minh came to the hospital after Ma left. He was a little tipsy. I smelled alcohol on his breath. Really? How could he drink when his child was in the hospital fighting for his life? I was disappointed in Minh but didn't say anything.

"How are you doing, my boy?" Minh talked to our sleeping baby.

"Minh! Let him sleep. Why don't you go home?"

Minh stayed quiet for a while, sensing I was mad at him. We didn't talk; he didn't try to make any conversation.

"So you want me to go home?" he asked.

"Yeah, I don't want you to disturb the baby."

"All right." And he left.

I didn't like what I saw. It was hard enough that I had to deal with his previous women and sons, plus the gambling. Now drinking too? I had to let him know it bothered me.

A few days later, Toan was allowed to go home. The doctor gave Minh the prescription again. He said we would find it on the black market. After dropping me and the baby at home, Minh said he would go pick up the medicine. It was around eleven o'clock in the morning when he left. I started to get worried by three o'clock. What was taking him so long?

The baby needed the medicine, Minh knew that. Why didn't he come home?

By five I started to fear the worst. Was Minh hurt? Had there been a motorcycle accident? I was worried. My anxiety level was through the roof. I went to my mother-in-law and asked for help.

"Can somebody go out and look for Minh? He left this morning for the baby's medicine but hasn't come home yet. I'm worried."

"I didn't know he was supposed to pick up medicine. I'll send somebody to look for him. Don't worry."

They found Minh all right—in a bar, drinking with his friends. I cursed at him in my head. I was so, so angry. I wanted to scream. And that was what I did when I saw him walking in late at night.

"Where the fuck have you been? You were supposed to pick up the medicine for your son, and you just disappeared without even thinking about him!"

"I got the medicine." He was so drunk, he couldn't even stand. He flopped down on the floor and tried to search all his pockets for the medicine. "I bumped into a friend and ah…"

"So you care more about your friends than your own son? Our sick son waiting for that medicine? You're just so careless. I should have seen it. You have two sons out there you don't care about. Why was I so naive to marry you? This is a mistake, a fucking mistake!"

"Enough!" It was my father-in-law's voice, right outside our door. "You should not talk to your husband that way, even if he is drunk. Not in my house anyway."

"Leave them alone." I heard my mother-in-law's voice. "Your son was wrong. Let them work things out themselves."

"I will not let her scream and curse in my house."

The baby woke up and started crying. I tried to calm him, even though my head was pounding. Minh left the room, and his parents went back and forth arguing about us downstairs.

I felt awkward for the next couple of weeks whenever I bumped into my in-laws. I wanted to leave that place. There was no privacy in the house. I wanted to move out, but we couldn't because we would be leaving soon for America.

I regretted getting so angry. That was out of character for me. I hadn't known how to handle the situation, and it had gotten out of control. I asked my parents-in-law for forgiveness. I didn't want to leave their house on bad terms. I wished Minh would never drink again, and that was something he had to work on. They wished us good luck in the future, and they had a long talk with Minh. I could imagine how hard it was for them to part with their firstborn son for good.

Two months later Minh, the baby and I joined my side of the family at Tan Son Nhat Airport. We said good-bye to our family and friends. There was lots of crying on that day. My sister Anh couldn't hold back her tears. Lan and I gave each other a long hug and promised we would keep in touch, hoping we would see each other in America.

Ma had done a good job; all my siblings were dressed nicely. I gathered my whole family together, double checked our papers, and led them inside. We went through the small, humble airport filled with cranky, unhappy uniformed officers. They checked our papers and our luggage while yelling at us, "You can't take the coffee with you. No! No books either. Is that a radio? It has to stay." I thought they would like to keep all of the items they fancied for themselves. No one protested, though. "You like it?" we said. "Keep it."

There were more tears and waves to our family left behind as we walked to the airplane parked in the middle of an empty runway. The flight attendants were rushing us to get on the plane; the "fasten seatbelt" sign was already on. Everyone sat down in their seats so fast, like they all couldn't wait to get out of there. The jet engine started, and the plane moved faster and faster. I said my prayers, and the plane took off.

"Yeah!" People clapped their hands.

"Hallelujah," someone said, and the crowd burst into cheers.

I felt free. I was so happy. Finally I was there with my family on this plane to freedom. I whispered into my six-month-old son's ear, "Welcome to freedom, son. We did it."

Tears rolled down my cheeks, this time out of happiness. America, here I come.

Part 2

Chapter 19
1990
Oklahoma

We stepped out of the airplane after a long journey from the Philippines to Japan, then a stop in Los Angeles and now to the final stop, Oklahoma. More than thirty hours of being shuttled around. I was exhausted but excited. I couldn't wait to start the new chapter of my life here with our small family.

I tried to smooth out the wrinkles on my dress, the only dress I had left. We sold most of our things in the Philippines, and still I had less than one hundred dollars in my pocket. It was cold in the airport, and I had no stockings. I would have worn pants if they still fit me, but I was five months pregnant with my second child, so I sold them too. We needed the money for this journey.

My fifteen-month-old son was still asleep in my arms. Minh carried our two small bags behind me as we continued to follow all the passengers. We didn't know which direction to go and hoped our sponsor, a church, had sent someone there to pick our family up. We didn't even know the address of our destination, just Oklahoma City. Everyone in the Philippines refugee camp wanted to go to California, Texas, or Florida, where the weather was warm and there were already Vietnamese communities. No one was excited about Oklahoma.

We'd originally thought we'd be sent directly to America from Vietnam, but to our surprise we were led to a refugee camp in Bataan, Philippines instead. No one from the Vietnamese government had told us we would spend months in a camp. There we learned basic English, resume writing, and about American culture.

It was good I had learned a lot in the eight months living in Bataan, but it was hard to live next door to my stepfather.

Especially when he yelled at Ma or one of my siblings. The huts were so close to each other, with thin walls; there was almost no privacy. They were small and dark, with no real kitchen. The camp-style stove made my eyes sting every time I cooked, because of the smoke. There were dirty public bathrooms shared with hundreds of other people. Every day my husband waited in line to get buckets of water. Food was limited. I got really skinny because I nursed my son and didn't have enough food to eat.

I couldn't bear the thought of living near my stepfather in America, so I requested to be sponsored separately from my parents and siblings. I was grateful the church was able to sponsor just the three of us and happy I would be giving birth to my second baby on American soil. My uncle Thien would sponsor the rest of my family, and they would later settle in New Jersey.

At the airport, I saw two people who looked Vietnamese holding a board with my name on it. I headed in that direction with Minh.

"Welcome to America," the woman said.

"Thank you. I'm glad we're finally here. It was a long journey," I said.

"My name is Kim. I'm volunteering for the church. If you have any questions or requests, I'll do my best to help."

"Thank you," I said.

"I'm Nam. I work for social services. I handle the paperwork in general. This is my card. If you have questions, just call me."

"Let's get you home, so you can rest," Kim said.

We all got into a church van, and Kim showed me how to put my son in a car seat. He kept on sleeping; the poor baby was exhausted too. Kim climbed into the driver's seat. It was fascinating to see a woman driving a car. I hadn't seen that in Vietnam.

"Wow, you can drive?" I asked.

"Everyone drives here. You will too one day." Kim spoke softly.

I looked out the window and waited to see the city. So

far the scenery was basically faraway houses with generous lots and empty streets.

"Are we near the city?" I asked.

"We're in the city. Oklahoma City is pretty spread out," Kim said.

"This city is really quiet," I mumbled.

"You can't compare this city to Saigon. They're very different. You'll get used to it. I like it here. I'm sure you will too one day," Kim said.

Nam drove ahead of us in his own car. We turned into a small parking lot, and I saw the small duplex where we would live. It looked neglected, but I hoped the inside would be better.

"The one on the left is yours." Nam led the way and unlocked the door. "It's not much, but you can make it home."

We walked into the small living room, and I could see the entire apartment. A bedroom with no door—I would have to make a curtain for that later. There was a tiny galley kitchen that, I wouldn't be able to cook in if I got bigger later on. I turned on the faucet and smiled: water. I could live with this. Everything was old and a bit dirty, but I was OK with it. Much better than the hut in the refugee camp.

"We should let you rest, jet lag and all," Nam said, "I'll come back a couple of days from now to explain everything. How things work with welfare and stuff."

"Excuse me...what is welfare?" I asked him, wanting to know now.

"It's government assistance to help you start your life here in America."

"I'm still not following."

"The government is giving your family some assistance and food stamps. You should be able to find a job in a few months."

"Food stamps? What are they?"

"They're like checks, but only for buying food," Kim explained.

"How much is the rent for this apartment?" Minh asked.

"Two hundred dollars a month, plus gas and electricity.

Heat and water are included in the rent, so at least you don't have to worry about that."

"I brought some food for you." Kim brought in a box of instant noodles, a bag of white rice, and some vegetables and fruit.

"Thank you so much. You and the church for helping us," I said.

"I'll see you tomorrow. I have a couple of bags of used maternity clothes—they'll fit you—and clothes for your son too. I hope you like the furniture. It's all donations from the church."

After they left I put my son down on the bed and checked out the bathroom. It wasn't great, but at least my family didn't have to share with anyone else.

"Wow! The apartment is awful. The carpet, kitchen, and bathroom are so dirty," Minh said.

"I'll clean it up. It'll be home in no time," I told him.

I looked around. There was one old green sofa. A mattress was on the floor; it was old, but it was better than the wooden bed in the camp. There was a small table with three chairs in a corner against a wall and a television that had a wooden box frame, like a piece of furniture. I turned it on. It was color, but only one color: green.

***

Kim took my family to a supermarket. It was big and clean, with lots of different kinds of food. She introduced us to American food, like fresh milk, cereal, and apples—things we hadn't had in Vietnam.

"Your son can start drinking fresh milk now. It'll be good for him. It'll help him grow big and strong," Kim said.

"What does it taste like? Have you ever tried it?" I asked.

"Yes, I have. It tastes good. You should start drinking it too, Lien. It's recommended it for pregnant women."

"How long have you been here, Mrs. Kim?" I asked.

"I've been here fifteen years. We left in 1975, just before the fall of Saigon. My husband is American. We met and got married in Vietnam. After we heard the order to get out, we had no choice but to leave."

"Wow, you were lucky. You didn't have to experience the Communists," I said, without thinking.

"Yes, indeed." Kim nodded. "I try to help Vietnamese immigrants when I can. I know our people went through a lot."

"I still have bad dreams sometimes. I dream I'm still in Vietnam, struggling to get out of the country, but can't go anywhere. Sometimes I dream I'm already at the airport, but they don't let me get on the airplane. I'm so scared. Then I wake up relieved when I realize I'm already in America."

"It will get better slowly. One day you won't have those bad dreams anymore." Kim squeezed my hand.

Kim helped my family so much. She got the churchgoers to donate a lot of items for my son. We got a used crib for the baby, a car seat, and baby clothes. I was so grateful.

Kim also took me to see a gynecologist, to get me in the system for prenatal care. She introduced me to other Vietnamese mothers-to-be, and I couldn't have been happier. I didn't know there were a lot of Vietnamese who lived in Oklahoma City. Maybe not a big community like in California or Texas, but still a community existed. They even had a Little Saigon center, with one small supermarket, a phở restaurant, a bánh mì sandwich shop, and a clothing store. It was more than I could ever have imagined.

I froze at the fruit section "Grapes!" I remembered back in Vietnam, my mouth started watering every time I saw grapes in the high-end store. Only the rich people could afford them. I had tasted them before Saigon fell into Communist hands, before my family lost everything and became so poor. The exotic juicy fruit became so expensive that most Vietnamese couldn't even dream of having it.

"Would you like some grapes? They're inexpensive here," Kim said.

"How much are they per kilo?" I asked.

"They sell them by the pound, a dollar twenty-nine per pound. A pound is close to half a kilo."

I converted the amount of dollars to Vietnamese đồng in my head. It was expensive in đồng, but I bought some anyway. I bought some chicken too. Chicken was all cleaned and already cut here, unlike in Vietnam, where only live chickens were available for sale. We hadn't eaten a lot of chicken in Vietnam. It was a luxury thing as well, only for special occasions.

"How is the apartment? Are you all settled?" Kim yanked me out of my thoughts.

"Yeah, it's OK. The bedroom is small, and there is no room for the baby's crib. We might have to get rid of the couch so the crib can go there," I said.

"It is small for a family of four. I don't know why Nam picked that place. Do you want me to find another apartment for you? You need a two-bedroom apartment. Soon the baby will arrive, and you'll need more room."

"Do you think we can afford a two-bedroom apartment?" my husband asked. "I don't have a job yet."

"I will try my best to find you a job so you can afford a better apartment for your family."

"Thank you so much," I said.

A month later Kim found a job for Minh at a Vietnamese restaurant just outside of Oklahoma City. She also found a two-bedroom apartment close to the restaurant, so he could bike to work. It was a nice, freshly painted apartment with a real kitchen, and I was so happy.

Kim helped us so much. She even let me babysit her eight-month-old daughter, so I could earn a little extra money. Every morning Kim would drop off her daughter at our place before she went to work. I enjoyed watching the baby. Her name was Michelle. She was a cute little girl with blond hair and hazel eyes. She didn't look like Kim at all. Toan was happy too, because he had the baby to play with. Life was definitely better, I thought.

***

I stood in front of the mirror door of my closet. My wardrobe was sparse, of course. I tried to pick a good outfit for a special dinner. Kim had invited us over to meet her family. I had gotten a couple of maternity dresses from her, a blue one with flowers and a red one with stripes. I decided to go with the red one for good luck. Being seven months pregnant now, I was thankful Kim's dress still fit.

Minh couldn't come to Kim's house—he had to work. He didn't like his job very much, but he had to keep on working. Every night he came home cranky and complained about his boss. He worked twelve hours a day in a hot kitchen, with no breaks, and he often threatened to quit. I had to beg him to be patient, to hang on to his job for the family. I knew it was hard; everyone said it would be difficult in the beginning, new country, new language. I spoke some English, but Minh didn't. If he kept working long hours, he wouldn't be able to learn the language at all.

I had a plan. After having the baby, I would start looking for a job. That way my husband could work part time and go to school at night to learn English. That was the only way we could improve our life. At the time I could only hope Minh stayed at his job until the baby was born. We had bills to pay, and no one would hire a seven-months pregnant lady to work for them.

"Ma, I want to wear this one." Toan had started to speak in a cute little toddler's voice. He was holding a Superman shirt from the church's donations.

"You want to wear a Superman shirt?" I asked.

"Yeah, Superman."

I laughed. My son had never watched a Superman movie or heard of the story. How did he choose to wear this shirt out of the piles of his clothes? He would be an Americanized kid for sure. I helped him to put on the shirt and combed his fine baby hair. Then the doorbell rang, and Kim was at the front door waiting for us.

"Hi there. Are you ready?" she asked.

"Hi, Kim. Yes, we are." I held my son's hand, and we followed Kim to her car.

Kim's house was in the upper-class section of the town. All the houses there were big and new, with lustrous green yards. Her house was beautiful; it had a grand living room with a huge big-screen television. Kim's husband came to the door to greet us.

"This is my husband, Tom. Tom, this is Lien and her son, Toan."

"Nice to meet you," Tom said.

"Nice to meet you too." I bowed my head slightly, the Vietnamese way of greeting. Then I realized he was an American. I should have offered to shake his hand instead, something I'd learned in the Philippines.

"Make yourself at home," Tom said, and he went back to watching a football game.

Kim led us to the kitchen. It was big and very modern.

"Linda!" Kim called her teenage daughter. She had told me how difficult it was to raise a teenager in this country.

"Hi, Mom." Kim's son ran in the house and passed us. He looked half-American, half-Vietnamese. He was a very handsome ten-year-old boy.

"Tommy! Come here and say hello to Lien."

"Hi, Lien."

"Hi, Tommy, nice to meet you." I smiled.

"Dinner in half an hour, don't go anywhere," Kim said. "Linda!"

"Coming." Kim's sixteen-year-old daughter finally came downstairs. She was beautiful, very American, with light hair and fair skin.

"Say hello to Lien," Kim said.

"Chào, Lien, khõe không?" Linda spoke Vietnamese to me, saying, "Hi, how are you?"

"Wow! You speak very good Vietnamese," I said.

"Just so-so," Linda said.

"She understands Vietnamese a lot more than Tommy. I try to speak Vietnamese to them, but with a busy schedule it's hard," Kim explained.

Kim was making phở, I could tell. The whole house smelled like it. I offered to help, but she said she could handle it.

"Where is Michelle?" I asked Linda.

"She's taking a nap upstairs. She'll be up soon, I think."

"Let's eat now, before she gets up," Kim suggested. "Is the table ready, Linda?"

"Yes, Mom. I even put out the chopsticks."

What a good dinner it was. Kim had a perfect family, beautiful children, and they were well behaved. I thought Kim's husband was nice too, even though he was glued to his football game. Kim had what is called an American dream. I hoped one day I would have that dream too—a good job, a nice little house, with well-behaved children and a solid marriage. That was all I asked for.

* * *

I soon realized the English I had learned in Vietnam was British English, with a thick accent. The Americans in Oklahoma had trouble understanding me, and I got frustrated sometimes. I often had a pen and a piece of paper with me, so I could write the words down. My next-door neighbor was a woman, a single parent with an eight-year-old daughter, and I wanted to be friends with them. One weekend I went next door with my son. I let Toan ring the doorbell.

"Hi! I meant to come over when you just moved in, but then I got so busy," the neighbor said. "My name is Karen."

"Nice to meet you, Karen, my name is Lien."

"Say that again."

I wrote down my name on a piece of paper and showed it to Karen.

"Oh! I'm sorry. Nice to meet you, Lien. Come on in. This is my daughter, Kathy."

"Hello, Kathy. This is my son, Toan."

"Another difficult name to remember," Karen said.

"I know. In Vietnam we write the last name first, then the middle name, and the first name goes last. It's totally opposite here. They actually messed up my name on the greencard."

"Wow, it's more confusing than I thought," Karen said. "Anyway, would you like something to drink?"

"Water, please," I said.

Karen looked confused, so I wrote down "water" on the piece of paper.

"Oh, water." Karen said it with a D instead of a T. "Coming right up."

"How are you, Kathy?" I asked the girl after her mom went to the kitchen.

"Good."

"Do you want to play with Toan?"

"I only have girl toys. I don't think he would like them."

"We live right next door. You can come over anytime you want, OK?"

"OK."

Karen returned with the water. We chatted for a little bit. She said I could come over anytime, and I was glad. I could practice my American English now with Karen and Kathy.

***

I was in the kitchen feeding Kim's baby, Michelle, her food from a jar. Toan was by my side eating his cereal. He seemed to enjoy it, and he looked happy. Suddenly I felt the baby kicking strongly inside my tummy. "It's going to be a boy," I told myself, though deep down I wanted a girl. Like everybody else, I wanted one of each. I hoped Toan would be a good brother to his future brother or sister. The ultrasound couldn't tell me the sex of the baby. I would find out soon anyway; the baby was due in six weeks.

The sound of the key twirling in the lock yanked me out of my thoughts. Who could it be? Minh was supposed to be at work. I tried to get up, but the door opened before I could. Minh stepped in with his bicycle. He looked upset.

"What's wrong? Aren't you supposed to be working?" I asked.

"I quit." He went straight to the living room.

"What? Why? You can't quit." I followed him to the

living room. "We're going to have a baby soon. How are we going to pay the bills?"

"I can't take it anymore, OK?" he yelled. "You weren't there. You didn't see how they treated me. Besides the hard work, they were really mean to me."

I didn't know what to say. My husband was born wealthy. He had owned his own company in Vietnam, and he had treated his employees nicely and fairly. He had given up all of that and followed me here to this country, and he struggled. He didn't speak English, so jobs were limited for him. He had been unhappy since landing in Oklahoma.

"What are we going to do? Do you have any plan?" I asked.

"We can't afford to stay here. Besides, it's too far from everything. We need to move back to the Vietnamese area" he said. "I can learn English there in the evenings. The Little Saigon center is there. We'll be close to everything."

"Can we even afford an apartment in that area?"

"We can move back to the old place," he said.

"Back to the apartment you hated?"

"I didn't hate it. I was just surprised such an apartment existed in America. I didn't expect my house in Vietnam would look better."

"Kim worked so hard to get us here. How am I going to tell her? And the babysitting job. I won't have this job if we move back there," I protested.

"Look! We can't afford to stay here. Your babysitting job is not enough for us to stay. I know you like the place and you like Kim, but there is nothing for me here. No jobs, no night school. I can't stay here. We need to move back, and we need to do it soon, before the baby arrives."

"That means we have to move by the end of this month. How are we going to do that?"

"I'll call the old landlord, and if he is willing to help us to move back we'll do it, OK?"

"Let's hope it's still available," I mumbled.

Minh called the old Vietnamese landlord, and the apartment was still available. He was willing to help us move back at the end of the month. As difficult as it was, I had to tell Kim about my husband's decision. As I dialed her phone number, I hoped she would understand.

"Hello?" It was Kim's voice.

"Hi, Kim, how are you?"

"Hi, Lien. Are you all right? Do you need to go to the hospital?"

"No, I just want to talk to you about something."

"Yeah? What is it?" Kim sounded concerned.

"We need to move back to our old apartment."

"Why? Aren't you happy here?"

"I am, but my husband lost his job, and we can't afford to stay here."

"Really? I know the owners of that restaurant, nice couple. I can talk to them to give your husband the job back."

"No...Kim, he quit a couple of days ago." I felt something in my throat. I was about to cry. It was overwhelming.

"He did?" Kim sounded surprised.

"He wants to move back to the Vietnamese community so he can go to night school to learn English. Maybe he'll find a job there that would suit him better."

"I see." Kim paused. "Well, good luck with everything, Lien."

"Thank you for everything." I wanted to say more, but Kim quickly hung up the phone. She was mad at us, I could tell. Who wouldn't be? She had worked so hard to get us moved to a good neighborhood. She had found jobs for both of us, and we stayed for only two months. I felt guilty about it and wished we could stay. I loved the apartment; it was perfect for us. The baby kicked again, reminding me to get myself together. I wiped my tears and started to pack.

***

I tried to clean and fix up the old apartment, trying to make it feel like home. I didn't have a lot of time left; soon the baby would arrive. Minh had tried looking for a job nearby, but so far no luck. Even without a job, he rarely stayed home. He went out on his bike to Little Saigon center to make friends, saying that would lead to a job somehow. I hoped he was right.

He came home one day upset that dinner wasn't ready. I knew he was mad about something else, and he just poured everything out on me. Yes, dinner was a little later than usual because I was busy cleaning, and I lost track of time. Many times dinner was ready, but he arrived home late. Didn't he see how hard I worked?

"You're not going to die if you eat a little later." I was mad, slamming the pan on the stovetop.

"Why does dinner have to be late when you're home all day?" Minh yelled.

"Seriously? I'm due any day now, and still I work my butt off to make the apartment livable. What about you? What did you do?" I stir-fried the chicken that had been marinating. "You come and go whenever you please. You didn't tell me what time you were going to be home. How am I supposed to know when to cook?"

"I'm looking for a job!" he yelled. "You think jobs would come to our door?"

Toan, our twenty-month-old son, nervously looked at us back and forth.

"You don't care about your pregnant wife. You spend way too much time outside with your friends." I started to cry and slam things around.

Toan started to cry too. He didn't understand what was going on, but he cried because his parents were fighting. Whenever my baby cried, I had to pick him up. He would cry so hard until he choked and coughed uncontrollably. I ran to pick him up, and that was when I felt it. A pop! Something watery ran down my thighs.

My water just broke.

"I need to go to the hospital. Call somebody!" I screamed as my first contraction started. The pain.

Minh ran to the phone. He made a few calls. The first and second ones weren't answering.

"Call 911!" I yelled.

No! He wouldn't do it. He couldn't speak English, I realized. Luckily on the third call he tried, our neighbor was willing to help.

"She's on her way. What should I do?" Minh put the phone down.

"Turn the stove off! And I need a towel, ah!" A second contraction hit me.

Our neighbor Mrs. Doan came to the rescue. She ran toward me. "I'll take you to the hospital. Do you have a bag?" she asked.

"No, what bag?" I managed to ask.

"The baby items bag, clothes, diapers," Mrs. Doan said.

"There are some baby clothes in the drawer. Ah, it hurts," I groaned.

"Quick! Put some in a plastic bag," Mrs. Doan told my husband. "We have to go!"

Mrs. Doan led me to her car, and she started the engine. Minh ran out with a bag in one hand and a crying toddler in the other. We sped to the hospital.

The nurses admitted me to a room, telling me to change into a robe and get on the bed. They put IV fluid into my arm and connected me to other machines. I had no idea what they were for, but I felt safe. I'd had my first child in Vietnam, which had been much simpler. I hadn't gotten any medical equipment hooked up to me, no painkillers, not even IV fluid.

I felt the contractions come and couldn't wait to have the baby in my arms. I wanted it to be over quickly so I could go home, but it was not up to me.

"Can I see my son? Is he still here?" I asked the nurse.

"Your husband and your son are in the waiting room. I'll see what I can do."

A few minutes later, the nurse led them in. Toan cried as soon as he saw me. Minh tried to calm him.

"Are you OK?" my husband asked.

"Yes, the pain comes and goes."

"Ma." My son reached out to me.

"Toan, Ma is going to be OK. Don't cry. Come here, let me kiss you."

Minh lowered Toan down. I gave him a kiss on the forehead.

"Be a good boy, OK? I'll be home tomorrow. Good night, sweetie." I turned to my husband. "Take him home. I'll be OK. It's so late already. He needs to go to bed."

"OK. I'll come back tomorrow. Listen, I'm sorry about earlier." He seemed regretful.

"It's OK. Don't worry. I'll be all right," I said.

It was eleven o'clock by the time they left. It had been four hours since my water broke, but the baby still wasn't ready to come. The nurses came and checked on me periodically. I slept some and was jolted out of sleep because of the waves of pain. I was exhausted.

Finally, after hours in labor, I gave birth to a beautiful baby girl. I was tired but excited and surprised. Everyone had said I was going to have another boy. The baby, who I named Thao, was so precious. She brought joy to my world. I forgot about the pain, the hardship, and the poor conditions we were in. I couldn't stop smiling, wishing I had a camera to capture the moment. It was one of the happiest moments of my life.

I held my daughter's tiny hands and felt so blessed. I had a son and a daughter—a dream come true. It was hard to describe the love I had for my daughter. It was so precious and fulfilling, a no-boundaries kind of love. It was something only a new mom would understand. I put my daughter down next to me on the bed and stared at her until I drifted into a peaceful sleep.

Chapter 20
1991

My husband finally found a job in Cao Nguyen supermarket. It was a minimum wage job, but he didn't really have a choice. He worked during the day and went to school at night to learn English. He wanted to buy a used car, but he needed to have a driver's license first. I helped him to study for the written test. First I translated every word into Vietnamese so he learned its meaning. Then I asked questions, helping him to pick the right answers. Still, he failed twice. He said the second test was different from the first one.

The third time I went with him for emotional support. We took the bus there, and I waited outside with the children. Hours later he stepped out with frustration on his face, and I knew.

He had failed again.

I decided to take the test myself to see what was on it, so I could help him study. We swapped. He watched the children, and I took the test, passing it with ease. It wasn't planned, but I got a driver's permit before him. He was mad at me, at the motor vehicle administration office, and at the world.

We didn't talk on the way back home. I knew not to speak when he was in a bad mood; nothing good would come of it. As soon as we got home, he took his bike and left. He didn't even say anything to the children. Why are men like that? The ego?

I tried not to let it bother me too much. My children were more important than anything else. I didn't like to argue in front of them. The last time we argued, our son got scared and cried. My husband was a stubborn man. He smoked cigarettes inside the apartment, and we argued about it. He said it was too cold to smoke outside. I tried to explain to him the danger of secondhand smoke. It was all over the news. I wished he understood. He didn't believe that the children could get sick from it. He said cigarettes were the only thing left that kept him sane. I was strong when it came to the children. I told him to smoke outside or quit. Smoking with a window open was not an option.

After I fed and put the children down for a nap, I called my friend Vi. We had met in the Bataan refugee camp, and coincidentally we'd both ended up in Oklahoma City. Vi had left the Philippines two months before us, and we'd lost touch until recently, when I'd run into her at the supermarket. We had been friends ever since, and I was glad. We had the same background—half-American and didn't know who our fathers were. Vi was one of the only people I could share my true feelings with.

"Hey, Lien, what's going on?" Vi asked in a bubbly way.

"He failed his written test," I said.

"Again?" Vi laughed. "I'm sorry, it's not funny."

"I passed, but now he's mad at me." I sighed.

"Why would he be mad at you? Hey, at least one of you got the permit," Vi said.

"Remember when we were in the Philippines? He wasn't happy then, when they put him in the lower English class and I was in the higher class," I said.

"Yeah, I remember that."

"Why can't he just be proud of me?"

"I'm proud of you. Listen, You got your permit before me. I'm still depending on my husband, and when he's working I'm stuck. Maybe you'll give me a ride later on."

"Definitely! When I have my own car." I laughed.

"I'd love to talk more, but I have to go and pick up the kids from school. Congratulations, Lien! I'm proud of you."

"Thank you, Vi. Talk to you later."

I felt better after talking to Vi. I had lost Kim as a friend because of the move. I tried to call, leaving a couple messages, and still Kim didn't call back. Maybe she had never considered me a friend, just someone she wanted to help, and it had backfired when we'd moved back to Oklahoma City. I was sad about it at first, but not anymore. I had Vi now.

A couple of weeks later, I was feeding Thao her baby cereal when I heard someone banging on the door. My son ran to open it, but I stopped him.

"Toan! Wait! Let me look first. You can't open the door for strangers. Remember?"

I looked through the peephole. It was Vi's mom. I opened it right away.

"Bac! What's going on? Is everything OK?" I got a little concerned when I saw she was alone.

"My son-in-law and I had a fight. He kicked me out." Bac said as she was wiping her tears. "I walked here because I don't know where else to go."

"Come on in," I said.

"I know you are a good friend of Vi, and I need a shoulder to cry on." She was still crying.

"I am so sorry, Bac. Would you like some tea?"

"That would be nice, thank you."

I made two cups of tea and sat down with Bac, ready for her to let it all out.

"Vi's husband and I don't get along. I didn't like him from the beginning, but she didn't listen to me."

"How long have they been married?" I asked.

"Ten years, but Vi isn't happy. She's afraid of him. He is controlling and very jealous. He calls home multiple times a day. Like today, Vi went to school to pick up the children, and he called asking, how long ago did she leave? What was she wearing? Did she wear makeup? It's crazy…So I snapped. I told him to stop treating her like a prisoner." Bac paused. " He came home and told me to leave. He said he didn't want to see my face anymore."

"What did Vi say to him?" I asked.

"She didn't say anything, because she's afraid of him."

"Poor Vi. I had no idea."

"Vi is my only child, and it breaks my heart to see her suffer."

"I feel bad for Vi. When can I call her?"

"Wait until tomorrow. It's best to call when he's at work." Bac paused and asked, "Can I stay here tonight?"

"You can stay here if you don't mind the couch. As you can see, this is a very small apartment."

"Thank you, Lien. It won't be long. Vi still needs my help

with the children."

"You're welcome, Bac."

I called Vi the next day, letting her know her mom was OK. We had an emotional conversation about Vi feeling trapped in her marriage. She didn't know what to do.

A week passed by, and Vi's mom was still staying with us in our cramped apartment. To my surprise Minh didn't complain about it. Finally, after ten days, Vi and her husband came to pick up her mother. It was awkward even to say hi to him after I knew the story, but I had to.

"Hi, Hoang. How are you?"

"All right. We were in the neighborhood." He looked at Bac. "And maybe someone might need a ride home."

"Hoang! Apologize to her," Vi said. "She is my mother."

Hoang looked embarrassed. So I gathered the children into the bedroom to let him, Vi, and Bac have some privacy. I closed the curtain and paid attention to my kids. Vi came into the bedroom a moment later.

"Hey, thanks for everything. How is your husband?" she asked.

"He's good, working and studying." I studied my friend's face. "I'm glad you guys worked it out."

"Yeah, me too. Thanks again."

"Take care of yourself, OK, Vi? Call me if you need anything."

"I will. Bye, love." Vi squeezed my hand.

I hoped Hoang would be a better father for their kids' sake. I hoped somehow he would change, become a better husband, because Vi was a good mother and a good wife. She deserved to be happy.

***

Minh came home smiling, and I knew he got his permit.

"That's great! I knew you were going to pass this time," I said "You've been studying hard. You should be proud of yourself."

He waved his hand like it wasn't a big deal and pulled

out the Vietnamese newspaper to look at used car ads. Our budget was nine hundred dollars, and all the used cars in the paper cost a lot more. Frustrated, he slammed the newspaper on the table.

"I'm going out," he said.

"Why?" I looked at him. "You're off only one day a week. Don't you want to spend time with the children?"

"I need to talk to a friend, OK? To find out how to buy a used car and the insurance and stuff. What do you want me home for?" He pulled out a cigarette. "I'm not allowed to smoke in here. I'm not allowed to have beer in the fridge. How am I supposed to relax?"

"I'm just concerned about the children. When you have a family, you have to sacrifice."

"I'll be home for dinner." He took his bicycle and left.

I let him go. I couldn't stop him anyway. It did bother me that my husband was always out. I felt like this family was not important to him. I thought of Vi. Her husband was always home. Vi said Hoang watched her every move. Vi felt he was suffocating her. I wouldn't want that for myself, so I let it go. My marriage wasn't a romantic one like I'd imagined, but Minh was a better man than Hoang.

I was doing laundry in the bathtub when the phone rang. I ran to get it before my son would. He was so fast to open the door or pick up the phone.

"Hello," I answered.

"Hello, Lien, this is your landlord. I'm heading to your area in an hour. Do you think I can stop by to pick up the check for rent today?"

"Yes, Mr. Pham. You can come by anytime. I was going to mail it today."

"Don't bother to mail it. I'm heading in that direction anyway. I'll see you in a bit."

Mr. Pham was a retiree who had multiple properties for rent. He was a nice landlord and offered to help us occasionally. Mr. Pham stopped at the front yard while I was hanging the laundry on the line.

"Hello there," he said.

"Hi, Mr. Pham."

"You're doing laundry by hand? Why don't you bring that to the laundromat?"

"I have two little children, and we don't have a car. It's easier for me to do it by hand."

"Let me know if you need help to hook up a washer and dryer in the apartment."

"Thanks, Mr. Pham, but there isn't any room for them. Besides, we're looking to buy a car soon."

"Really? I have a used car for sale if you're interested. A Buick. It has eighty thousand miles, but it's in good condition."

"How much do you want for it?" I asked.

"Eleven hundred dollars. It's a very good car, but my wife wants a new one."

"It's a little more than we want to spend. Let me talk to my husband, then we'll call you. Is that all right?"

"Of course," the landlord said.

"Thank you, Mr. Pham." I handed him the envelope for the rent.

On his next day off, Minh went to see the car, and he liked it. After negotiating back and forth, the landlord agreed to sell us the car for a thousand dollars. He threw in a driving lesson as well. It felt so good to own a car. It wasn't just convenient; it was about fitting into American society as well. It made us feel less foreign.

After Minh got his driver's license, I told him I was ready to learn how to drive. Sometimes I needed to take the children to the doctor for checkups and shots, and I felt weird asking people for favors when we owned a car. He gave in.

Every Tuesday we dropped off the children at Vi's house. I practiced behind the wheel for an hour or two, with Minh in the passenger seat. Soon enough I got my driver's license as well, and Vi was envious.

"You have to talk to him, Vi. It would be better for you to have a license too," I said to her over the phone.

"I did, many times. He doesn't want me to touch his car. He doesn't want me to go to work either. My ma offered to take care of the children for me, but he refused."

"Talking about that, I'm looking for a job now. I hope I'll find something close to home," I said.

"Who's going to take care of the children for you?"

"I hope I can find a Vietnamese babysitter. I want my children to speak both languages. If I can't find one, then they will have to go to day care."

"I can watch them for you," Vi offered.

"No, Vi. You have four children of your own. I can't do that to you. Besides, your husband wouldn't be happy about it."

"Don't say that. Hoang likes you. Think about it, OK?"

"OK, I'll think about it. I have to go. Thao is crying." My daughter started to get fussy.

"All right. Bye, Lien."

Thao was a very easy baby. She rarely cried unless she was hungry or needed to be changed. I picked her up, and right away she stopped crying. I gave her a bath, fed her, then put her down—not even one peep. Thao was kicking her legs and babbling to herself while I gave my son a bath. The older Toan got, the easier he became. He had been a colicky baby and used to cry a lot, but not anymore. I thought, 'It's time to go to work.'

I called Minh's job and asked to speak to him. "Can you pick up a newspaper on the way home?" I asked.

"Why?"

"I want to look for a job, and a newspaper is a good start."

"All right! Bye." He hung up the phone.

Really? Sometimes I wished he wasn't so cranky all the time. People in Vietnam were dying to come here, but he wasn't happy. He didn't appreciate that his family lived in America, a free land. His children would have a good future; they would never have to look over their shoulders or be afraid to say what was on their mind. I knew he hated it here; he even said so once in a while. He used to own his own business in Vietnam. In America he had to work in a grocery store, stocking shelves, and he blamed me for it.

***

I got interviews for three possible jobs. One was taking care of a senior citizen lady who lived by herself, which I had no idea how to do. Another was a cashier job at a gas station. I thought it was kind of dangerous. The last one was for a custom-made curtains and drapes company. I liked this one best. I had known how to sew since taking a class in high school. I asked them to give me two weeks to find day care, and they accepted.

I called Vi and told her I had found a job and day care as well.

"Congratulations! I'm very happy for you. Are you sure about the day care? I can take care of them for you, you know," she said.

"Thanks, Vi, but you're so busy already. Maybe later, when the children are older."

"All right. I wish I could go to work with you. Wouldn't that be fun?"

"You should talk to him, Vi. Be strong about it. Two incomes would be better than one."

"I'm going to try to talk to him again tonight."

"Good luck, Vi. Call me tomorrow, OK?" I said.

"I will. Bye, Lien."

Later that night Bac knocked on my door. She was upset that her son-in-law had kicked her out again. She said Hoang and Vi had gotten into an argument. Something about Vi wanting to go to work, saying her mom would take care of the children. Hoang had gotten mad and twisted Vi's hand. Bac jumped in to stop him. He screamed at her to get out and told her never to come back.

"He hates me. I tried to stop her from marrying him years ago. He never forgave me for that. He didn't appreciate my help with the children. He says mean things to me all the time. He said I'm a burden to him." She wiped her tears. "I stayed this long because I love my grandkids."

"How is Vi? Should I call her?" I was worried about my

friend.

"I think we should wait until tomorrow to call her, while he's at work."

"I feel bad for Vi. She just wants to work, to have a job like everybody else," I said.

"I know. I just hope one day she'll be strong enough to divorce him."

I didn't know what to say, looking at an emotional grandmother worried about her only daughter and four grandkids. Bac looked tired.

"I feel bad about barging in on you like this, Lien. I'm so sorry. Can I stay a few nights until I figure things out?"

"Of course, Bac. You can stay as long as you need," I said. What could I say? She was my friend's mother.

I called Vi the next day. She sounded so sad on the phone. She was glad her mom was safe with us.

"Thank you for letting her stay with you," Vi said.

"You're welcome. Tell me what happened."

"Basically, he didn't want me to go to work, and we ended up arguing. My mother jumped in, of course, and he threw her out. He literally dragged her outside and shut the door." Vi sighed. "He did it on purpose, so I would have to stay home and take care of the kids."

"I'm so sorry, Vi."

"Thanks, Lien. Listen, my mother can babysit your kids. You can give her a little money if you want."

"I don't know, Vi. I wish we had an extra bedroom for her, but we don't. She's sleeping on the couch."

"I don't mind the couch," Bac jumped in.

"See? Give her something to do, Lien. Think about it."

"All right! I'll talk to my husband about it. Take care of yourself, OK? Call me if you need anything," I told my friend and gave the phone to Bac so they could talk.

Minh didn't mind Bac staying with us. She was really quiet anyway. She helped me with cooking and taking care of the children. She fed Thao and played with her. Bac was a little strict with Toan, because he was always jumping around, and she didn't want him to get hurt. I liked the idea of not taking the children out in the cold for day care. In the end Bac stayed and watched the children for us.

***

I liked my job. It was at a very small company owned by an American couple. They had a good warehouse, with a lot of different kinds of fabrics and materials. Sewing curtains was quite simple, and the bosses didn't rush us. They wanted their employees to do a good job. Apparently these custom-made curtains cost ten times more than curtains in a regular store. It took me only a month of training, then they let me handle some curtains by myself. The pay was not bad; at least it was above minimum wage, and the job was kind of relaxing. The funny part was when I tried to work faster, my coworkers told me to slow down.

I was glad I had a job. It felt good to earn money. Bac and I got along so well even in that tiny little apartment, although I still wanted to move to a two-bedroom apartment in the future, so Bac could have her own room. I tried to save as much as I could, trying not to take advantage of Bac's situation either. I paid her half of what day care would have cost. I thought it was fair for both of us. Bac could have some pocket money to spend on whatever she pleased, and I could save faster toward a new apartment.

I still shared the car with Minh. Every morning I dropped him off at his job then drove to mine. He worked longer hours, so I picked him up after giving the children their baths. He had been asking for a second car, but I said not yet. We needed to save money to move first, and he agreed.

One night the phone rang, and I had a feeling it was Vi. I picked it up. "Vi?"

"How did you know it's me?"

"Hey, I just knew. How are the kids?" I was relieved she sounded OK.

"They're fine. They miss their grandma, though."

"Are they home now? I can put her on the phone."

"We definitely will do that, but first I want to invite your family over for Thanksgiving dinner. I'll invite my mother too. The kids want to see her."

"Are you sure Hoang will be OK with that?" I said.

"Yeah, I already talked to him about it. It'll be fun," Vi assured me.

"All right! Thanksgiving it is."

"How's work?" Vi asked.

"It's good. Quite relaxing, actually. Nobody rushing around like I had imagined."

"Great! I'm happy for you."

"Thank you, Vi. Wait! Your mom wants to talk to you." I handed the phone over to Bac.

They spoke on the phone often. It was always Vi who made the calls, when her husband wasn't home. That was the only way Bac could check in on her daughter and the grandkids. After they hung up, I asked Bac her thoughts about going there for Thanksgiving.

"I miss my grandkids. I want to see them. Hopefully he'll start to let me visit them." Bac wiped her tears. "No grandma should go through what I'm going through."

"I'm so sorry, Bac. We'll see them soon."

I didn't celebrate Thanksgiving simply because we were new in the country. I had never eaten turkey in Vietnam and certainly didn't know how to cook it. Bac said she would make spring rolls to bring over to Vi's. She was excited to see her daughter and her grandkids.

Early on the morning of Thanksgiving, while my family was still sleeping, Bac got up to cook. I heard her in the kitchen cooking up a storm. I felt I had to get up and help. While Bac was steaming shrimp dumplings, I fried the spring rolls. We worked side by side until the children were up. I poured cereal for Toan and fed Thao, then cleaned and changed them into nicer outfits. Toan was very excited. He knew we were going somewhere. He loved car rides.

After all the food was cooked, we got into the car and drove to Vi's house. I rang the doorbell and heard Vi's children screaming with excitement. They knew their grandma had arrived. Vi opened the door and hugged Bac, with a big smile.

"Hi, Ma!"

"I missed you, Vi," Bac said with tears in her eyes.

"Grandma!" Her grandkids couldn't wait for their turn, hugging her tightly.

"Hi, guys. Come on in," Vi said, stepping aside for us to enter.

Hoang finally got up from the sofa. He came to shake Minh's hand and said hello to me. He ignored his mother-in-law. Bac and I carried the food into the kitchen while Vi was still cooking, but instead of turkey she was roasting two big chickens. She had green beans on the stove and boiled sweet potatoes draining in the sink.

"Do you need help?" I asked.

"No, I'm good. Sit down. We'll be eating soon," Vi said.

I kept an eye on the children, who were playing together nicely. I looked over to my husband. He was having a beer with Hoang. The two seemed to be getting along fine. Minh didn't really like Hoang; he was just being polite.

The food was delicious. Bac looked happy, and so were the children. Overall it was a nice holiday except that Hoang had too much to drink and insulted his wife and his mother-in-law a few times. I didn't want to stay long. After helping Vi and Bac clean up, I said good-bye to Vi and gathered the children to leave. Minh had drunk a few beers, so I offered to drive.

"I wouldn't let a woman drive me around. That's embarrassing," Hoang said.

"I can still drive," Minh said.

"No, you cannot. You've been drinking. I can't let you drive," I said.

We went outside to the car, and Bac helped Toan with his seatbelt. Minh walked over to the other side of the car, where I was putting Thao into her car seat.

"Let me drive just to the corner," Minh whispered in my ear. "Then you'll drive. It's a quiet street anyway."

I looked over to Hoang standing on the porch. He smirked at us.

"All right! Only to the corner," I told my husband.

We got in the car. Bac was in the backseat with the

children, and Minh put the car in reverse. He stepped on the gas pedal, thinking it was the brake, and the car sped backward into an electric pole. Bac and I were screaming. Toan and Thao started crying; they didn't know what was happening, but they were scared. Minh turned off the engine with his hand shaking. Thank God everyone had their seatbelt on.

My heart was beating so hard; I couldn't believe what had just happened. I was so mad at Minh, and most of all I was mad at myself for letting him drive. I yelled at him, saying he shouldn't have been drinking in the first place, and why on earth didn't he let me drive? His face was filled with regret and embarrassment. He stepped out of the car to check the damage. He had put a big dent in the corner of the car, and the brake light was smashed to pieces.

Vi ran to the car while Hoang stayed on the porch, a beer still in his hand.

"Is everybody OK?" Vi asked, then turned to her Mom. "Ma? Are you all right?"

"Thank God! We're all right," Bac said.

"Lien?" Vi walked over to me and gave me a hug. "Thank God it's just a fender bender."

"I'm so mad at my husband!" I said.

"It's OK, Lien, it's just a car. The most important thing is nobody was hurt."

I took a deep breath. Vi was right. I tried to calm myself down, looking at my children inside the car. I saw they had stopped crying.

"Are you OK to drive?" Vi asked.

"Yes."

"All right, drive carefully!" Vi put her hand on my shoulder.

"I will."

I asked my husband for the car keys. He handed them over without a word, and I drove us home in silence. I knew Minh was sorry for what had happened, he just never said "sorry." Staying silent was his way of saying it.

We had to take a chunk out of our savings to fix the car,

because we insured it only for liability. It was illegal to drive with the broken light. So the plan to move had to be delayed. Sometimes Minh took the bicycle to work to avoid sharing the car with me. He blamed America for giving women too much freedom and power. Slowly I had become more independent, gaining more confidence, and wanted to be treated equally in our marriage. It was not like the Vietnamese way, where the husband always had an upper hand. I was secretly happy about that.

Chapter 21
1992

I found a two-bedroom apartment not too far from where we lived. I took Minh and Bac there to take a look. They both liked it, so I called the landlord to put down a deposit. Since we didn't have a lot of furniture, the move was easy.

The children still shared a room with my husband and me. We had a full-size bed next to one wall, a twin-size bed for Toan next to the opposite wall, and Thao's crib in the middle. All had been donated by the church. We bought a bed for Bac from a flea market, and she was very happy that she finally had her own room.

Minh got a new job at the Golden Palace restaurant where they were willing to train him to become a chef. He worked hard to learn how to cook and hoped one day he would open his own restaurant. We bought another used car because we worked different hours, and one car wouldn't work anymore.

We were doing fine for a few months, then my job slowed down. I normally would make one curtain per day, but lately there weren't any to sew. I got laid off along with my coworkers. Three weeks later the owner called me back to work. They had gotten a new order, and this time everyone was working really slowly, hoping to make the job last. Still, after two months my company laid off everyone again.

I started to look for another job and got hired by a uniform company. This company was bigger, and they expected the employees to work quickly. I was always exhausted by the end of the day.

The children were always happy when their mom came home. Thao wanted to be held, and Toan asked me to play with him. I tried not to show them I was tired. Toan was very energetic, asking many questions about everything while he was jumping on the bed. I felt guilty that I was away from my children all day. I tried to give them some extra attention whenever I could.

"What did you do at work, Ma?" Toan asked.

"I sewed."

"What did you sew?" He was still jumping on the bed.

"I sewed karate uniforms today. Can you sit down?"

"I want to learn karate, Ma."

"When you're a little older. Can you stop jumping?"

"Why?"

"Because I don't want you to get hurt," I explained.

"I want to play. Bac made me sit in the corner all day."

I understood he needed to let his energy out.

"OK! Ten minutes. You can jump on the bed for ten minutes, then you have to stop so I can cook."

"OK. Watch, Ma. Watch me." Toan jumped with happiness.

I watched my son jump up and down on the bed, enjoying the little game he created, wishing I could be a stay-at-home mom. I would take them to the park every day to play.

"We can go to the zoo this weekend. Would you like that?" I asked.

"Yeah!" He jumped even more.

"OK, that's enough. Do you want to play in the living room or the kitchen? I have to cook dinner."

"Living room!"

I turned on cartoons for Toan, put Thao in her high chair, and went to the kitchen to start cooking. Bac was still napping. As soon as I came home, she would take her nap. She needed it, and I understood.

The phone rang. "Hello?" I answered.

"It's me," Minh replied. "The boss is looking for a waitress to work on the weekends. Are you interested?"

"Both days? I don't know. What about the children?"

"Bac will watch them. She's there anyway. You can pay her a little more. I don't think she would mind."

"I don't mind working lunchtime, but I don't want to work at dinner. I want to be home with the kids at night," I said.

"OK, I'll ask my boss. I have to go, they're calling me."

"OK, bye."

I looked at my children and felt guilty again. If I would take the waitress job, then how would I be able to take them to the park or the zoo? On the other hand, jobs were uncertain in those days. Two jobs were better than one. If I lost one job, I would still have the other.

A few days later, I went for an interview and got the waitress job. I would be working from ten o'clock in the morning to three on Saturday and Sunday. Before I started, I took the children to the zoo. I knew I wouldn't be able to do that later on.

***

The Golden Palace was nice, big and very busy. I liked all the waitresses I worked with. There were five of them in total, and they seemed to like me also. They showed me how to greet the customers and take orders. We worked together nicely, and the tips were generous on most tables. I was very happy to get this job.

The owner, Mrs. Dang, was a good businesswoman. A lot of customers seemed to know her by name. The restaurant had been in the newspapers before and had a good reputation. I was told Mrs. Dang had gone to college with one of the local television news anchors. Sometimes her old friend came in for a meal and a chat. This somehow brought more customers to her restaurant.

The kitchen staff was big as well. They worked really hard during lunch and dinner hours, when it was hectic and noisy. The good thing was that Mrs. Dang left them alone when the restaurant wasn't busy. Sometimes she saw them playing card games in the kitchen but didn't say anything. All the employees liked her; she really was a good boss.

I could tell my husband liked his job. He made some friends there whom he liked to talk about when he was home. He was interested in cooking, the pay was good, and he was finally happy. We worked hard to save up for a future restaurant, but deep down I wanted to buy a house instead.

My family's life started to improve. The children got new clothes to wear and new toys to play with. Eventually we bought a new television and a washer/dryer for the apartment, and I was content.

Vi's situation wasn't as good as mine. Hoang lost his job, and the unemployment checks weren't enough. Vi had been asking me to help her to get a job at the restaurant, but Mrs. Dang said she had enough waitresses at the moment. Vi was disappointed. She really wanted to work with me. After a couple of weeks, Vi called and told me she had gotten a waitress job somewhere else.

"Congratulations! Oh, I'm so happy for you," I said.

"Thank you. This is my first job in America. I'm so nervous."

"You'll be fine. I was a little nervous too for the first couple of days, but then you'll get used to it."

"It's going to be hard leaving the kids home with my husband. I hope he can handle it." Vi sounded worried.

"Don't worry. He'll get used to it. Maybe he'll start to appreciate you for all the hard work you do."

"You're right," Vi said. "Anyway, let me talk to my mother."

"Sure, hold on, let me get her. She's talking a nap."

"It's OK, let her sleep. Tell her I say hi."

"I will. Talk to you later, Vi."

I was really happy for her. It was about time for her to start a job and earn some confidence. Unfortunately, it soon became clear that Hoang couldn't handle the children on his own. Two weeks later Vi called and asked her mom to move back to help.

"I'm really sorry," Bac told me after our dinner together. "She needs help, and I'm her mother."

"I understand, Bac." Actually, I was somewhat disappointed that Vi hadn't talked to me about it.

"I told her to give you a couple of days to look for a new babysitter."

"Thank you for that."

I was asking everyone I knew to find a babysitter. I also went to a day care center to check out the price and schedule. The only problem with day care was they were closed on Saturday and Sunday. That meant I would have to quit the waitress job.

Luckily, a friend from work introduced me to a new babysitter. She was a nice Vietnamese lady, very calm, and I liked her right away. She lived not too far from us and was willing to watch the children at her place.

Hoang came to pick Bac up one Sunday afternoon, waiting outside in his car, without even coming in to say hello to me.

"Again, I'm so sorry, Lien. You know I like to stay with you, but they need me."

"I understand, Bac. No hard feelings," I said, not wanting her to feel guilty.

Bac hugged Thao good-bye and rubbed Toan's head. "Be a good boy for your mom, OK? Bye now."

"Bye," Toan said, waving his hand.

Vi didn't call me again after she had her mom back. It was sad that Vi all of a sudden avoided me altogether. Was she mad at me for not trying harder to get her that job? I called her multiple times, but I eventually stopped. I hadn't done anything wrong. I hoped she would come to her senses and would reach out when she was ready to have her friend back.

***

I moved the children's beds into the second bedroom and decorated a little bit to make them feel like that was where they belonged. Also, I liked the new babysitter, Mrs. Bui. The children seemed to love her, already calling her grandma. I assumed she loved them too and taught them to call her that. It was sweet.

My husband watched the children on his day off. Sometimes he drove them to his friends' house to hang out. It bothered me, because most of his friends were drinking and smoking. I smelled it on the children's hair and clothes.

"Can you not take the children to your friend's house today?" I asked Minh while getting ready for work.

"Why not? It's my day off," he said.

"I know it's your day off, but can you wait until I'm

home, then go by yourself?"

"Why? I don't want to be stuck at home all day."

"You're drinking and smoking around the children, and it's not good for them to see that," I said calmly.

"When we met, you knew I smoked and drank, and you married me anyway. Why is it bothering you now?"

"It was different in Vietnam. Doors and windows were always open to air out the house. Here it's closed up, and we have children now. We have to set a good example."

"So you want me to stop hanging out with my friends?" he asked in a cranky voice.

"I'm not asking you to stop hanging out with your friends. I'm just asking you not to let the children see you drinking and smoking. That's all." I picked up my bag. "I'm going to be late. I have to go."

I drove to work wondering why Minh had said that. Yes, I had seen him smoke, but I hadn't seen him drink before we were married. The first time I saw my husband drinking was at our wedding. I didn't say anything because that's what people do at weddings. After that he came home drunk lots of times. When I mentioned it, he always said he was socializing, he had to drink with clients. Here in America he had no clients. Why couldn't he stop?

I came home to an empty house after work and knew he and the children were at his friend's place again. I took a deep breath. How was I going to do this? He didn't listen to anything I said. I felt he didn't care at all about the children and our marriage. I dialed his friend's number—no answer. I called the next one—they didn't pick up the phone either. I just wanted to go there and pick the children up, to rescue them from the cigarette smoke.

I prepared dinner, hoping he would bring the children home in time for them to eat. It was seven o'clock, past the children's dinnertime, and they still weren't home yet. Pacing back and forth, I was trying to decide what to do. Then I heard a car door open and shut. They were finally home.

"Really? You know what time it is?" I asked Minh as soon as he stepped inside.

"They ate already!"

"What did you feed them?" I grabbed Thao from my husband's arms.

"Ramen noodles," he answered.

"Yeah! That's really good and healthy food for the children to eat."

"Stop being sarcastic! They said they were hungry, so my friend made noodles for them."

"Can you even smell your own breath? It's smells like beer. You were drinking, and I asked you not to drink around the children. Worse than that, you put their lives at risk. You don't even care!" I raised my voice.

"I had only two beers. I'm not drunk!" he yelled back.

"That's not the point. The point is I asked you this morning to wait for me to come home, so you could go by yourself. What part of don't take my kids out with your drinking buddies' don't you understand?"

"Who taught you to talk to your husband that way? Americans?"

I was done talking to him. I wouldn't argue, not when he was like this. My son was standing in the corner, confused and tired.

"Come on, Toan, let's take a bath." I took the children to my bedroom and locked the door.

I didn't talk to Minh for days. First of all I wanted to hear him say sorry for what he had done. Second, I hoped he would stop drinking and smoking for our children's sake, but he was still stubborn and deeply rooted in his masculine Vietnamese culture.

I worked in the restaurant on the weekends, and it was weird not talking to him at work. Thi, a full-time waitress knew something was going on.

"What's up with you two?" she asked me.

"What do you mean?"

"You and your husband. Something is up. I can tell. I'm married too, you know."

"I guess I didn't hide it well," I said. "It's small stuff anyway."

"Hey, If you need to let it out, I'll be your ear. I can keep a secret."

"There is no secret, really. I was mad at him for drinking in front of the children," I explained.

"They say the secret of a happy marriage is compromise. That's what we're doing in our marriage. We set agreements. It's working great for us," Thi said.

I thought, 'That's not a bad idea. I'll give it a try to see if it works.'

"Thanks for your advice, Thi. I hope it'll work for us too."

"I have confidence it will. It's going to be fine." Thi patted my shoulder.

Before I left work, I wrote a note to Minh saying we needed to talk later that night. I hoped Thi was right about compromising. What would I compromise on? I had to think about it.

I put the children to bed, made a cup of tea, then sat down to think it through. I wanted the marriage to work, wanted what was best for my children. I was so tired, I fell asleep on the couch. The sound of the door woke me up when Minh let himself in. He came home late, as usual.

"I couldn't get out early," he said.

"I know. We need to talk, and I'd rather do it sooner than later."

"All right." He sat down, waiting.

"You probably know what's worrying me," I started.

"I don't smoke inside anymore."

"But you're still drinking in front of the children. Worse than that, you drove them home after drinking. It's dangerous in so many ways. What if you get into a car accident? Could you imagine?"

He said nothing.

"I'm willing to compromise," I continued. "You can bring your friends here to drink, and I mean moderate drinking. Otherwise you have to get a babysitter if you decide to drink outside."

"You're letting me bring friends here?"

"On your day off I don't mind." I said "In return I'm

asking you to cut down slowly."

"It's totally socializing. You know I never drink by myself. I can cut down," he said.

"All right. We're good then?"

"Yeah, we're good" He nodded his head.

"I need to go to bed. I'm so tired." I yawned.

I was glad we had talked it out. From then on my husband brought friends home on his day off. I didn't really like to see beer bottles all over the living room, but that was what I was compromising on. I even tried to have some conversations with his friends too. I tried to be cool. I was trying to be a good wife.

***

I went to the mall after work to buy a dress. I hadn't gotten a new dress since coming to America. I had bought some clothes for work but didn't really want to spend money on myself. We needed to save for the future, and I was very frugal with money. But then Mrs. Dang invited all the restaurant's employees over to her house on Easter Sunday. All the women were always dressed so nicely, I thought I should look a little nicer for the party too.

I went to the women's department in JCPenney, hoping to find something on sale. While looking through a rack, I heard someone giggling. For some reason it sounded so familiar. Turning in that direction, I was shocked to see it was Vi. She wasn't alone; she was with an American man. As soon as Vi saw me, she froze. I didn't know what to do. Should I just run out of there or walk over to her? But then what? Say "hi, I miss you" or ask Vi frankly what was going on? Before I could finish my thought, Vi whispered something into the man's ear and walked toward me.

"Hi, Lien, how are you?" Vi was bubbly, like nothing had happened.

"Good! How are you? I called but couldn't get you," I said.

"Sorry, I've been busy working."

"How are Bac and the kids?"

"They are good." Vi paused. "Listen, can you not tell anyone about this?"

"Sure, I won't, I promise. Are you still with Hoang?"

"I'm working on leaving him. You know I'm not happy."

"I know," I said sympathetically.

"How are you doing? Still working two jobs?" Vi asked.

"Yes, I still am, seven days a week."

"Do you still live in the two-bedroom apartment?"

"Yes."

"I'm sorry you got the two bedrooms just so my mom could have her own room and then I needed her back."

"It's OK. My children needed their own bedroom anyway."

"You look good, Lien." Vi smiled genuinely.

"Thank you. So do you, Vi. I almost didn't recognize you."

"Look, I'd love to chat more, but I have to go. I'll call you, OK?"

"OK. My number is still the same."

Vi walked over to the corner of the store where the man was patiently waiting. She said something to him, then they both waved at me. I waved back, and they walked out of the store.

I drove home worrying about my friend. Vi was obviously dating someone while she was still married to Hoang. Wasn't that kind of dangerous? Did Bac know about it?

I stopped by the babysitter to pick the children up, and as soon as we got home I gave them some snacks and dialed Vi's number. I hadn't talked to Bac in a while. Maybe she would tell me more about what was going on.

"Hello." It was Bac.

"Hi, Bac, it's Lien." I was relieved it wasn't Hoang who answered.

"Hi Lien, how are you? How are Toan and Thao?"

"We are good. How about you?"

"I'm good but very busy because I'm taking care of the

grandkids by myself. Hoang and Vi are both working now," Bac said.

"Are they OK?" I asked nervously.

"Yeah, she's busy working, and he's driving us crazy, as usual."

I didn't know what else to ask. "Could you tell Vi to call me when she's free?"

"Of course. Take care, Lien. Say hello to your husband for me."

"I will. Bye, Bac."

I didn't think Bac knew about her daughter having an affair. I promised Vi not to tell anyone, so I wouldn't dare tell Bac. I had mixed feelings about this. I was happy for Vi but at the same time worried. What if Hoang find out? Only God knew what he might do.

I waited a few days for Vi's call, to tell me the details. How had they met? What was his name? What did she like most about him? I just wanted to hear Vi was happy, that she had a plan. I hoped everything would work out the way she planned.

Sadly, Vi never called me. I knew we couldn't talk about it when Hoang was home, but I didn't understand why we couldn't talk about something else. We had called each other every day before, and I missed that. Maybe he wouldn't allow Vi to have a friendship with me, or maybe it was Vi's choice. I didn't really know but hoped Vi would come around when her divorce was finalized. I would always be there for her and give her all the support she needed.

***

The restaurant was closed on Easter Sunday. I hoped the children would sleep in a little, so I could too. It was a rare treat to sleep an extra hour. Toan and Thao were so used to getting up early in the morning, it became their routine. Sometimes they got up even before me and started to make noises.

I was already awake but waited to hear that knock on

the door. So far there was nothing. I wished we could stay home and relax, but we had to go to Mrs. Dang's house. My boss was nice enough to invite us, considering we were fairly new employees.

Knock, knock. Bang! The door flew open. Toan climbed on the bed and crawled into my arms. I rubbed his back and said, "Next time, when you knock on the door, you must wait until we say you can come in. Then you open it."

"OK," Toan said sleepily.

"All right! Go back to sleep." I hoped Toan would fall back to sleep so I could enjoy the bed a little longer.

"I'm hungry," he said.

"Of course," I replied and dragged myself out of bed.

After giving Toan his cereal, I went to the kids' bedroom. Thao was already up, playing with toys by herself in the crib. I felt blessed with my easy toddler I picked her up and went to the kitchen. I could put Thao in the high chair as usual, but I didn't want to. I just wanted to hold her a little longer. It was a holiday, after all, and I felt like spoiling the kids a little bit. I peeled a banana and fed Thao piece by piece. It was nice not having to rush around in the morning.

"No coffee?" Minh asked as he entered the kitchen.

"Not yet. As you can see, I'm busy at the moment. Let me ask you something. What do you do when I'm at work? Who makes coffee for you?"

I tried to get him to help out a little around the house. It wasn't working; he refused to do any chores. I could make him coffee, but I wasn't going to, not until he was willing to share some of the work. He said nothing and started to boil the water for his coffee. He went outside to smoke while waiting for his coffee to slowly drip through the small stainless steel filter.

"Can we go to the zoo today?" Toan asked. Somehow he knew his mother had a day off.

"I think the zoo is closed today because it's a holiday, but we're going to a party today."

"Really? A birthday party?" Toan got excited instantly. He thought all parties were birthday parties, which made me feel bad that he hadn't had a birthday party yet. The apartment was too small to host a party for him, and we needed to save money. All he had gotten was one gift for each of his birthdays.

"No, it's not a birthday party. It's an Easter celebration at my boss's house. It'll be fun."

"Can we go now?" Toan asked.

"Not yet."

"Why?"

"Because the party won't start until noon."

"Can we go there early, Ma?"

"Nobody's there yet. There will be no food to eat and no one to play with, but we can go a little earlier if we're done with everything. How's that?"

"Yeah!" Toan jumped.

After breakfast I gave the children their baths and dressed them up nicely. I took a shower and dressed up for the first time since I had come to America. With the very little makeup I had, I managed to look decent.

We drove through a nice, fancy neighborhood, with big houses and manicured lawns. Mrs. Dang's house was the biggest one there, with a three-car garage and a very long driveway.

"Hello there!" Mrs. Dang said when she opened the door. "Come on in."

We walked into a grand living room nicely decorated with flowers and balloons. Some guests were already there.

"Happy Easter," I said.

"Who is this handsome young man?" Mrs. Dang lowered herself to face my son.

"My name is Toan. Do you have any toys?"

"I sure do."

"Can I play with them?" Toan asked Mrs. Dang.

"Don't you want to eat first? We have a lot of food," Mrs. Dang told him.

"Sorry, Mrs. Dang, he likes to talk," I said.

"Don't be. I love kids." She smiled. "We have four girls."

"We would love to meet them," I said.

Mrs. Dang introduced her husband and daughters to us. The girls spoke only English, although they seemed to understand Vietnamese when somebody spoke to them.

I followed Mrs. Dang to a big dining room, which she had set up for a buffet. There was a lot of food. People were hanging out, with either food or drinks in their hands. Minh joined his group of friends in the backyard. I took some food for Toan, and he ate really fast so he could play with the kids at the party.

The doorbell kept ringing. A lot more people came in. I chatted with some of the waitresses from work and learned Mrs. Dang actually had two restaurants, no wonder she could live in a house this big and send all her children to private school. Finally Thi came with her husband and son, who was the same age as Toan.

"Hey, Lien," Thi said and gave me a hug.

"Hi, Thi, long time no see," I joked. We had worked together just the previous day.

"This is my husband, Vinh," Thi said. "This is Lien. She works part time at the restaurant, and her husband just got promoted to chef."

"Nice to meet you," I said to Vinh.

"Nice to meet you too." He turned to Thi. "I'll let you girls chat. I'm going outside with the guys."

"OK, babe," Thi said.

"What took you so long?" I was being silly about Thi's late arrival.

"I know, my husband was on the phone with a client for a long time."

"He's working on Easter?"

"He's a realtor, and they call him at all odd hours."

"Wow, that's a good job, right?"

"Yeah, we're doing well. If you ever decide to buy a house, my husband can help you."

"Do you own a house?" I asked.

"Yes, we do. It's nice to have your own home. The mortgage is just a little more than rent, and you'll get the taxes back at the end of the year. It's a win-win."

"I don't even know how to start. What is the process, and how much money do we need in order to buy a house? I would love to buy one someday."

"It's easier than you think. My husband can explain it to you better than I," Thi said. "How's the food?"

"Very good. Try the clams with lemongrass sauce."

"Who cooked all of this?" Thi asked while she was putting some shrimp on her plate.

"Who else? Our executive chef, Mrs. Dang's brother," I said. "Did you see her kitchen? It's huge."

"I know. I've been here before."

After lunch Mrs. Dang took everyone to the big backyard, which had a pool in the middle, still covered since the weather wasn't warm enough to swim. Thank goodness! I felt it was safer for Toan to run around. There was a swing set with a slide, and the children were busy having fun on it.

"It's time for the egg hunt," Mrs. Dang announced. She gathered the children to line up on the patio. "Listen, children! There are a lot of Easter eggs hiding out there. Make sure to look in every corner. I don't want to give too many hints away, but I think you will like what you find inside the eggs."

Mrs. Dang gave each one of them a basket. "Ready…Get set…Go!"

There were about twenty children running around looking for the decorative eggs. Toan was among them, running and yelling with other kids excitedly. It was his first time; he didn't know what to do. Mrs. Dang helped him a couple of times, pointing out where the eggs were. In the end Toan got five eggs; some had candies, and some had money inside. He was sweaty, but his face lit up with happiness and joy.

Even though Thao didn't join the egg hunt, Mrs. Dang put some in her basket. Everyone had a good time. Toan talked nonstop on the way home. I was so glad our children had a chance to experience the American Easter that Mrs. Dang provided. In Vietnam we didn't have egg hunts as an Easter tradition.

I liked my boss and was glad to be part of her team. I

felt I could trust her and had confidence that my husband's job was secure. We worked hard, but I felt good and very positive about the future.

Chapter 22
1993

I had a love-hate relationship with the waitress job. I loved the people I worked with and made more money in two days at the restaurant than in five days at the uniform company. However, I had to work late sometimes when the restaurant hosted weddings or special events. It was hard to say no to my boss, especially since Mrs. Dang was nice and fair. The part I hated was picking up the children so late. They were either sleeping on Mrs. Bui's couch or really tired. I felt so guilty, and it wasn't fair for Mrs. Bui either. I tried my best to avoid the late hours.

Thi and the other waitresses liked to work the dinner hours because they made more money. It was easier for Thi, since her husband worked at home most of the time, so they didn't need a babysitter. I liked Thi the best of all the waitresses there because she was fun and trustworthy. Many times I wanted to pour my heart out to her, but I held back. I wanted to become Thi's friend very much, but I was still hurt from the way Kim and Vi had ended their friendships with me. Maybe it was best just to be work friends instead of best friends. That way if we parted, it wouldn't hurt so bad.

Thi told me a lot about herself. Her biological mother had abandoned her when she was a baby. It wasn't good to have a half-American baby in Vietnamese society, so Thi's mother put her unwanted child into an orphanage. Later, an older couple adopted Thi and raised her as their own daughter. Being half-American myself, I totally understood the pain Thi had gone through. It was unfortunate that most half-Americans like us didn't know our biological fathers. People in Vietnam looked down on us, like the innocent half-American children somehow stained their society.

Thi's adoptive parents were very old now and lived in Vietnam. They had other children and grandchildren, so they didn't want to come to America with Thi. She was a good daughter who sent money to Vietnam so her parents could live comfortably in their golden years.

"You know sometimes I wonder about my biological mother." Thi shared her deep emotions with me. "Did she ever think of me? Was she ever sorry about abandoning me? She must have regretted it after the government let all half-Americans go to America. She could have had this comfortable life if she didn't give me up."

"I'm so sorry, Thi." I didn't know what to say.

"It's all right. It was her loss." Thi bounced back quickly.

"That's right! Look how far you have come. You have your own family now, a good husband and a handsome son. That's all you need to focus on."

I was very happy for Thi. She had a husband who loved her. Vinh was a wonderful husband and a very good dad. He had a good job, and they both were doing so well. They owned a beautiful house together.

"If you ever want to tell me your story, you know and I can keep a secret," she told me.

"I know. Maybe another time." I wasn't ready to share my story yet. We hugged, a deep, long hug that almost made me cry.

"On a totally different subject, how did you train your husband to became such a hands-on dad?" I asked, wanting to cheer Thi up.

"He is so wonderful, isn't he?" Thi smiled.

"Seriously! Tell me your secrets. I can't get my husband to help out with my children."

"I didn't train him at all. When our son was little, Vinh was the one who got up in the middle of the night to feed him. He is such a good dad. He does everything with our son, from playing games to reading books. His job is working out great for our schedules too. Being a realtor, he works during the day while I'm home, and at night he takes care of our son while I go to work."

"You are so lucky. Many Vietnamese men think taking care of children is women's work."

"I know. Vinh is an orphan too. Maybe that's why he's such a good dad."

"How did you meet?" I asked.

"We met in the Philippines. I was by myself in the refugee camp, and he was alone too. His English was so much better than mine, so I asked him for help. Eventually our friendship turned romantic. He got sponsored to go to New York City, and he refused to go there. Can you believe he turned down a sponsor for me?"

"Wow! He really loves you."

"Then I got sponsored to go to Oklahoma City. He told me to go ahead, don't wait for him. I didn't want to leave him behind, but he pushed me to go. He said life in the refugee camp was harsh for a girl. He promised me he would find me, and he did. A few months after I left the Philippines, a nice American couple sponsored him to go to Texas. They actually drove him here. They said he drove them mad, talking about me day and night." Thi laughed.

I laughed so hard I cried.

"We got married soon after, and his sponsors were our witnesses."

"Your love story is incredibly romantic," I said.

"Vinh worked hard to put himself through college. It took him a long time to finish school, and in the end he chose to be a realtor. He's really good at it and has helped a lot of Vietnamese who live here to become homeowners."

"Oh, he's such a good man."

"Indeed," Thi said. "If you're interest in buying a house, he would be a perfect man for the job."

"Do you think he can help us?"

"Definitely! Come to my house and talk to him. He will help you."

"Thank you, Thi, for sharing your story."

"It feels good to talk it out sometimes." Thi smiled.

I admired Thi for being bubbly and happy all the time, even though she had deep wounds about her biological mother. I thought we had similar backgrounds and could become good friends. Maybe in the future I would share my story with her, but I had to take baby steps. Slowly, one step at a time.

I told my husband what Thi said. Buying a house wasn't that hard, and it would save us money in the end. Minh wasn't thrilled; he wanted a restaurant instead.

"I'm not trying to crush your dream, but we are never going to have enough money to start a restaurant," I said.

"We can start out with a small restaurant in Little Saigon center. Then we will sell it and buy a bigger one. That's how to start a business. It takes time." Minh continued, "And that's why I wanted you to work as a waitress, to learn how to run a restaurant."

"Do you have any idea how much it'll cost to open a small restaurant?"

"Fifty or sixty thousand dollars, maybe."

"We'll never be able to save that much money. On the other hand, if we buy a house, maybe we will get lucky in the future. When the house prices go up, we'll sell it and use that money to start a restaurant," I explained.

"It's not a bad idea. You think Thi's husband will help us?"

"Yes. Thi suggested we go to her house on your day off. Her husband will help us through the process. What do you think?"

"All right, we'll see what he says."

Thi invited our family to her house a few days later. Her husband, Vinh, had an office at home, and he wanted to talk to us about the process.

Thi opened the door for us. "Hello there! Come on in."

"Your house looks so nice," I said.

"Thank you. We bought a fixer-upper and turned it into this," Thi said proudly.

Vinh came out and invited us into his nicely decorated office. "Please, have a seat. Would you like something to drink?"

"No, we're good. Thank you for helping us," I said.

"It's my job. I have a list of houses to show you, but first I want to ask you both a few questions. Is that all right?"

"Of course," my husband said.

"How is your credit?" Vinh asked.

"What's credit?" Minh asked.

"Do you have a credit card?"

"No," we both answered.

"That's going to be hard. In order to buy a house, you must have good credit."

"How are we going to earn this good credit?" my husband asked.

"You have to buy something and make a payment every month, like a car loan or a piece of furniture. Make sure you pay it on time. That's how you build your credit."

"We did make payments on a used car and a washer and dryer. Does that count?" I asked.

"Well, that's a good start. Give me your information, and I'll check your credit score. If it's good, then we can apply for bank approval. Basically, they'll check both of your incomes and see how much mortgage you can afford."

"I hope everything will work out," I said.

"Good luck, guys. I'm going to start the paperwork as soon as possible."

A few months later, Vinh called and said we actually had a good credit score. I was so proud of myself for paying the bills on time. Vinh also told us we got the approval for a mortgage. We could buy a house with very little down payment. I was so happy. I couldn't believe my dream was close to coming true.

Vinh took us to see lots of houses. Some nice houses were in our budget, but they were too far away. Most houses in the city needed work.

"You remember my house? It was a fixer-upper," Vinh said.

"We don't have the money or the time to do it," my husband said.

"Yeah, it will have to be move-in ready," I added.

"All right. We just have to keep looking. I have confidence we'll find your future house," Vinh said.

"Thank you, Vinh," I said.

Vinh was very patient and helpful. He called me periodically to update us on the house search. He didn't give up or forget about us. Then one day I got the phone call I'd been waiting for. A move-in ready house in the city was just put on the market.

"We have to act fast, before somebody else jumps in," Vinh said.

"When should we see the house?" I asked him.

"Can you see it today?"

"Yes, but what about my husband? He works until eleven o'clock."

"Call him and see if he can get out of work for a few hours. It's rare to find a move-in ready house in the city."

Mrs. Dang was nice enough to let Minh take a few hours off to see the house. It had a big living room, three bedrooms, and one bath. Every room was spacious, including the kitchen. I liked it right away.

"What do you think?" I asked my husband.

"It looks good. Everything seems in order. I turned on the central air, and it works. That's a nice bonus."

"I know. For twenty-five thousand dollars, it's a good deal. I think we should put in an offer."

"What do you think guys?" Vinh stepped into the house with a smile.

"I love it," I said.

"It's a nice house. Obviously the owner has taken good care of it. I checked outside. The roof is fairly new, windows and doors are in good condition. Everything has been freshly painted inside and out, including the fence. Did you see the kitchen?"

"Yes, we did. It's lovely," I replied.

"And it's right in your budget."

"You did good, Vinh," my husband said.

"Do you want to put in an offer today? A house like this will get snatched up quickly."

"Yes, we want to put in an offer," I said.

"Great! Let me get the papers from the car for you both to sign," Vinh said and went to his car.

"I'm so nervous," I told my husband. "What if someone else puts in a better offer?"

"Then we'll keep on looking," Minh said.

Vinh prepared the contract for them. He suggested putting in an offer of $24,000 for the house. It gave room for negotiation without offending the seller. I crossed my fingers and hoped everything would go well. We took a risk on not paying for the inspection, since the house was in great shape. We didn't hire a lawyer either because Vinh said he would do all the work for us, so we could save money.

I couldn't sleep for a couple of days and was constantly thinking about the house. I was hoping, wishing, and praying we would get it. I imagined my children would be happy running around in all of the spacious rooms.

After a few days of negotiations back and forth, the seller agreed to sell us the house for $24,500. I couldn't have been happier. I called my husband to deliver the good news. I hung up the phone and danced a happy, silly dance like a fool. My dream had come true: I was a homeowner now, and I liked the sound of that.

***

Our family moved into the home as soon as we got the keys. The house looked so big and empty because we didn't have a lot of furniture. Toan and Thao had their own rooms now, and they seemed happy. I smiled a lot when I saw my children running around having fun. I even smiled when I cooked. How could I not? This was my own kitchen. I was happy every time I came home from work.

Soon afterward, credit card offers were automatically mailed to our house. Visa, MasterCard—"you're preapproved," it said on the envelopes. All we needed to do was sign the papers, and we would get multiple credit cards.

"It's good to have a lot of them," Minh said. "When the opportunity comes, we will be ready to open a restaurant."

We decided to buy furniture for the house. Why wait when we had credit cards? We bought a sofa set for the living room and a dinette set for the dining room. All three bedrooms would have to wait a little longer.

The house started to look warm and welcoming. People had been asking me when they would get invited to a housewarming party. The problem was I still worked seven days a week, so I couldn't do it unless there was a holiday.

I liked America very much, ever since I'd first set foot there. It felt good to have the freedom I had so craved back in Vietnam. I wasn't afraid of hard work and was thankful for the opportunity to own a house. My husband didn't feel the same way at first, but after we bought the house, I saw a change in him. He probably started to see the opportunity for the future, to be his own boss again someday. He finally stopped talking about wanting to go back to Vietnam.

Thi and I became closer and closer. We had lunches together at work and chatted when we were refilling the soy sauce. We laughed at each other's jokes.

"Tell me about your childhood," Thi said one day when we were folding napkins together, after lunch hour was over.

"What do you want to know?" I looked at my friend's hazel eyes.

"Did you stay in an orphanage?"

"No! I have a mother."

"That's good. Where is she?"

"She lives in New Jersey," I answered.

"How come she ended up there and you're here? Did you leave Vietnam together?"

"We did, but I didn't get along with my stepfather. So I didn't want to live near them. As soon as we got to the Philippines, I secretly went to the officials and asked them for a different sponsor. That's how I ended up here. My uncle lives in New Jersey, and he sponsored them."

"Do you miss her?" Thi asked.

"I do, but I would rather live far away."

"Oh, Lien, I'm so sorry."

"It's OK. I'm happy here."

I didn't feel like crying about the past and chose not to talk about it. I trusted Thi completely, but for some reason I didn't want to go through the details. There was no need to open an old wound.

"Look at the time. I've got to pick up the kids." I realized it was three o'clock.

"Go. I'll take care of the rest," Thi said.

"Thank you. I'll see you next week."

"Bye, Lien."

I hoped Thi didn't feel rejected. For some people, opening up about their past is therapeutic. For me it was painful, so I tried to avoid it. I loved my siblings and my mother, but I couldn't live close to them. My stepfather had been very abusive to the family when I was young. Even though he had stopped hitting us when we got older, he was still emotionally abusive to us, yelling and calling us names. It was hard for me to witness that. We had lived right next door in the Philippines, and I had heard him yell at my mother all the time. What was worse, my husband heard it too. It was embarrassing, especially when my stepfather had brought me up, the unwelcome half-American child, the thorn in his side.

That was the reason I'd wanted to live far away from my family. I had gone to the immigration office and asked to be moved somewhere else, the farther the better. Did I break my mother's heart? Or did I do her a favor? I didn't know. I liked to think my mother was probably relieved I was gone— one less burden for her.

I rarely contacted my family after I moved to Oklahoma. Long distance calls were expensive, and I had no time to write a letter. It was very hard for other people to understand my circumstances. That was why I didn't want to pour it all out to Thi. Maybe one day I would, but for now I just wanted to focus on the future.

***

I planned a birthday party for my daughter and a housewarming as well. Since Thao was born in mid-November, I thought Thanksgiving would be perfect for a combined party. I had already invited some people from the uniform company. When I invited the restaurant staff, they looked at me weirdly, and I had a feeling something was going on. I waited until the end of my shift to ask Thi about it.

"Do you know what's going on, Thi? I invited the kitchen staff to my housewarming, and they looked at me like I came from Mars or something."

"Well, there is something, but I can't tell you," Thi said.

"Is it about my husband?" I asked firmly.

Thi said nothing and looked really uncomfortable.

"Come on, Thi! We're friends, aren't we?"

"If I tell you…you have to promise you didn't hear it from me."

"OK, I promise."

"Your husband has been borrowing money from everyone here. Maybe that's why they looked at you that way."

"Are you sure?" I felt lightheaded.

"I heard he lost a lot of money on card games."

"Did he borrow money from you?"

Thi nodded.

"How much did he borrow from you?"

"I can't tell you. He asked me not to tell you about it, so let him handle it, OK? I don't need the money back right away."

I felt so embarrassed. How could he do this to me? How could I work there knowing my husband owed money to our coworkers?

"Thanks for telling me." I couldn't control my watery eyes.

"It's going to be all right. He'll learn his lesson," Thi said.

"I've got to go," I said, wiping my tears.

"Drive safely."

I drove home angry at my husband. We had just bought the house and needed to save every dollar, every dime to pay bills. How could he be so foolish as to borrow money from coworkers to gamble?

That night I put the children to bed and closed their bedroom doors. I didn't want them to hear the argument. I was mad at and disappointed in my husband, and he would hear about it. Life was hard already. Why did he have to put more stress on me? My chest had felt heavy all day, and nothing could make it go away.

I thought of a few times when I'd woken up in the middle of the night and found myself alone in bed. He worked late, I knew, but sometimes he came home really late, at two, three o'clock in the morning. A couple of times I thought, 'Is he having an affair?' No. I pushed that thought away. Now I knew the truth. He was gambling with his friends.

Minh stepped in the house late, as usual. He stopped abruptly when he saw me. I couldn't hide it. I was mad, and it showed. He had a guilty look on his face.

"I know you borrowed money from the people at work." I went straight in, not wanting to give him a chance to lie.

"Who told you? Thi?"

"It doesn't matter who!" I raised my voice. "Don't blame others for something you did."

"I just wanted to have the money to open the restaurant."

"By gambling?"

Silence.

"How could you do this to me? I work there too. It's embarrassing." I heard disappointment in my voice. He didn't respond. "We just bought the house. We have a lot of bills to pay. What were you thinking?"

"I didn't tell you, but I won a few thousand dollars before." He paused. "I set up a savings account to save up for the restaurant. My friends said I'm good at this, so I thought maybe I can open the restaurant a little sooner, so you don't have to work so hard."

"Don't even go there! Don't say you did it for me. I work hard, but I never complain."

"No! I'm not. I'm just saying I had a plan for a better future."

"That's the dumbest plan I ever heard! Did you ever meet anyone who got rich by gambling?"

He didn't answer.

"Do you still have that money?" I demanded.

"No." He shook his head lightly.

"You lost it all?"

"Yeah."

"Did you take any money from our account?"

"No, I didn't."

"How much total do you owe them?"

"Everyone?" he asked.

"Yes! Everyone."

"Why do you want to know?"

"I want to know your plan to pay them back."

"It's none of your business."

"It's none of my business? I work there too, remember?" I was so irritated.

"I'll pay them back whenever I can."

"How?"

"I'm going to talk to Mrs. Dang about letting me work seven days a week until I pay off those debts."

An awkward silence fell between us.

"I hope she will, and I hope you learn your lesson," I said.

"I will."

"I don't want to go through this again in the future." My tears started to fall. I had been so angry before, I couldn't cry, but now they came out uncontrollably.

"You won't. I promise," he said and tried to hug me.

"Don't!" I stopped him and went straight to the bedroom, locking the door behind me.

I tried to sleep but couldn't because of the crying. I was really worried about losing the house. I worried about the kitchen staff reporting my husband to Mrs. Dang. Would she still let him work there? What if she didn't want an employee like him creating problems at work? He could get fired, and we would lose everything. I was so mad at him, I decided he would be sleeping on the couch from then on. He totally deserved that.

It took us a long time to repay the debt. He worked seven days a week, and I took a third job at a Vietnamese clothing store. They let me bring the clothes home to sew, which was good because I could sew on my own time. Every day after work, I would sew while watching the children. Sometimes I would sew until late into the night to finish up before the deadline. There wasn't any time for fun activities, just sleeping, eating, and working.

Chapter 23
1994

I felt there was something going on at the uniform company. Half of my coworkers had been laid off a couple of months ago, and I'd been nervous ever since. This was my main job, providing health insurance for the family. I always had been a good employee, showing up on time and working as hard as I could. Lately I could tell the company's business was really slowing down. There weren't a lot of trucks outside the loading area, and inside the facility looked empty. I saw a lot of worried faces in the sewing department.

I got a basket of karate belts to sew and did them slowly, hoping I would get more things to do. Looking over to the empty sewing machine next to me, where Maria used to sit, I worried I would be next.

In the lunchroom, an older Vietnamese lady who had been working there for years sat down next to me. "You are new, right?" she asked.

"I've been here almost two years," I said.

"Well, that's fairly new. I've been here fifteen years, and we have never been this slow before."

I said nothing in return. I wasn't in a mood for chatting.

"You're lucky. A lot of people had been here a lot longer than you, and they got laid off before you."

"Have you ever been laid off before?" I asked her.

"Twice. They called me back, though, after a few months."

"A few months? How did you survive a few months with no job?"

"It wasn't easy."

With my mind still anxious, I went back to my sewing machine to finish up what was left in my basket. I worked slowly but steadily and still finished them before two o'clock. What was I going to do now? With nothing left to work on, I started to clean my sewing machine.

"Lien, can you come to the office please?" Nancy, my boss, called out.

I stepped into her office and closed the door behind me, as I was told. "Hi, Nancy." I nervously looked at my boss.

"Have a seat, Lien." Nancy waited for me to sit down. "I really like you, and I want to keep you here working for us, but unfortunately our company is going through a difficult time, and we won't be able to provide work for you any longer. I hope this is temporary, and we'll call you as soon as we get more business."

I said nothing. I didn't know what to say.

"Don't worry, Lien. You'll get unemployment, and you can still buy health insurance for your family through us."

"Do you know when I will get my job back?" I asked.

"I'm sorry, Lien, I don't really know, but I will call you as soon as we get something," Nancy said, handing me an envelope. "Take this home and read it. There's information about health insurance. All you have to do is fill out the form and mail it."

I drove home with thoughts spinning in my head and worry in my mind. At least I didn't cry like last time I was laid off from the curtain company. Thank goodness I still had the waitress job. I could get more clothes to sew from the Vietnamese clothing company, and everything would be all right, I told myself.

I picked up the children from Mrs. Bui. They were happy to see me as usual, but Mrs. Bui knew something wasn't right.

"You're picking them up early today. Is everything all right?" she asked.

"I got laid off. I was just about to tell you."

"Oh, I'm so sorry."

"I hope you understand that the children can come here only on Saturday and Sunday, when I work at the restaurant," I said sadly.

"It's all right. I understand. You'll find a new job soon," Mrs. Bui said.

"Thank you, Mrs. Bui. I'll see you on Saturday."

"Good luck, Lien. I'll see you soon."

I drove home in a daze. I was so worried about the

uncertainty of my family's future that I took a wrong turn. The area I drove into was very different from my part of town, and I soon realized I was lost, not sure how to find the way back. I kept driving deep into the bad section of the city. I got really nervous when I saw a lot of young hip-hop people hanging out in groups, with really loud music coming from their boom boxes. The buildings looked dirty and neglected. I drove slowly, trying to find the street's name. Then I saw some of the men staring at me. Their stares made me nervous, and I felt sweat beading on my forehead.

"When are we going to be home, Ma?" Toan asked.

"Soon, Toan, soon," I told my son.

I drove around nervously, the steering wheel wet from my sweat. I checked all the car doors; they were locked. I took a deep breath to calm myself down. Suddenly, I saw an older Asian woman walking slowly, carrying grocery bags. I slowed down, hoping this woman could show me the way out.

"Excuse me." I stopped the car and called out, "Are you Vietnamese?"

The woman turned around, and I was shocked to see it was Bac.

"Bac? Is that you?"

"Lien! What are you doing here?" She smiled in surprise.

"Get in the car, Bac!" I said, unlocking the car door.

"What a pleasant surprise," she said.

"Totally. I was lost. Thank goodness I saw you. Were you walking home from the store?"

"Someone has to go shopping. The kids need milk."

"I'll give you a ride home. Do you know the way out of here?" I asked.

"We live just around the corner, over there." Bac pointed to the building in front of us.

"You live here? When did you move?" I asked.

"A while ago. Hoang lost his job last year. Vi is the only one working, so we had to move to this housing complex."

"I'm so sorry. Is it safe here?"

"Well, they don't bother an old lady like me, but Vi and

the children have to be careful when they are outside. Sometimes we hear gunshots around here, and the police come around quite often." Bac let out a sigh.

"How is Vi? She doesn't call me anymore," I said sadly.

"She has a lot on her plate, between her husband, her kids, and her job. She's struggling to pull everything together. Give her time. She'll come around."

"Are they still together?" I was curious, remembering Vi saying she was working on leaving her husband.

"They're still living in the same apartment, but they argue all the time. He's constantly threatening to hurt her. She can't get rid of him because she's afraid of him, and she can't move on either."

"I feel bad for Vi and the children," I said.

"I know. The children deserve better than that." Bac paused. "I have to go in, and you have to get out of here. It's not safe."

Bac wrote down the directions for me. We exchanged our new phone numbers, and she got out of the car.

"Bye, Toan, Thao. Be good for your ma, OK?"

"Bye, Bac." I told my kids to wave good-bye.

I drove home and couldn't help thinking about Vi's family living in a housing complex with cheap rent. She had four children to support and a controlling husband who constantly treated her badly. Vi had to be stressed out all the time, but she never called me to borrow money. She had her pride, and I respected her for that. I hoped things would work out for her somehow and hoped one day we could be friends again.

***

Luckily I got more clothes to sew at home from the Vietnamese clothing company. My house was a mess, with loose threads all over the place, but I didn't care. I enjoyed working from home because I could spend more time with the children. The only problem was I barely made minimum wage and sometimes didn't have anything to work on for a week.

Our family lived within a very tight budget.

When I had nothing to sew, I went to see my friend Thi. Toan liked to play with Thi's son, and I was glad he had a friend to play with. I felt very lucky to have her as a friend. She was sweet and always looking out for my best interests. One day Thi came to hang out with us on her day off.

"I have good news," Thi said as soon as she sat down.

I stopped working and looked at her, waiting to hear the good news.

"Tammy is pregnant." She clapped her hands in excitement. Tammy was a waitress who had been working at the restaurant for a long time.

"I thought you were going to tell me you're pregnant," I said jokingly and went back to sewing.

"No, this is a good news for you," Thi said.

"How so?"

"Tammy works the lunch shift, and soon she'll be on maternity leave. Her spot will open for someone to fill in, Lien! You have to call Mrs. Dang now for that spot before anyone else. Tammy might not be coming back to work after the baby. Who knows?"

"How far along is she?"

"She's four months pregnant. That means you would be able to take her spot in a couple of months. She can't work as a waitress if her stomach gets in the way. She'll have to take an early maternity leave," Thi assured me.

"You're a genius. Thank you so much." I ran to hug her.

"The lunch shift is perfect for you, right?"

"Yes, it is. I couldn't ask for a better friend. You are the best."

"There's more," Thi said happily.

"More? What is it?" I asked.

"Mrs. Dang asked me if I know any good tailors. She's recently lost some weight and wants to have some of her dresses and gowns altered. I said you would be the perfect candidate for that."

"Oh, I don't know. I never did alterations before."

"Come on, how hard would it be? If you know how to

put all the pieces together to make the dresses, you certainly know how to make them a little smaller."

"All right!" I smiled. "I'll try my best."

"Good, now call her," Thi demanded.

"OK, boss." I joked.

"Do you want me to dial for you?" Thi picked up the phone and handed it over to me. I dialed the restaurant's number and asked for Mrs. Dang.

"Hi, Mrs. Dang, this is Lien. How are you?"

"Hi, Lien, I'm doing all right. What can I help you with?"

"Thi told me you're looking for someone to fix your clothes. If you would like, I could come to your house to measure and pick them up at your convenience."

"Oh, I appreciate that. How about tomorrow? Can you come by around four o'clock in the afternoon?" Mrs. Dang asked.

"Yes, I'll be there at four. Bye, Mrs. Dang."

"See you tomorrow. Bye, Lien."

As I put the phone down, Thi asked, "Why didn't you ask her about the waitress job?"

"I'll ask her tomorrow. I'm a little nervous about it."

"Don't be. She likes you, and I already put in a few good words. You're going to get it."

"Thank you, Thi."

The next day I dropped off the children at Mrs. Bui's and drove to my boss's house. Mrs. Dang led me into her big walk-in closet and showed me all the outfits that she would like fixed. There was enough to keep me busy for a while.

"Can you try them on, Mrs. Dang? I would like to take notes and measure them," I said.

"Of course," Mrs. Dang said.

"I heard Tammy is expecting a baby." I tried to start a conversation while measuring her.

"Yes, she is. She's been wanting a baby for a long time. I'm really happy for her."

"Soon she'll be on maternity leave. If you need someone to fill in for her, I'm available," I said nervously.

"I will put you on the list." Mrs. Dang smiled.

"The list?" I asked in confusion.

"It's a waiting list, and I'm happy to tell you that you are the first one on the list, meaning you'll get to fill in for Tammy when she's on maternity leave."

"Thank you, Mrs. Dang," I said happily.

"Thank you for doing this for me. I literally have no time to go to a tailor. How long do you think it will take?" Mrs. Dang asked.

"I'll try to finish them in a few days."

"Great. Thanks again, Lien."

A couple of months later, Tammy went on her maternity leave, and I got to fill in for her. I was very grateful that my friend Thi had gotten me the job. It had saved my family from slowly drowning in a financial crisis. I worked at the restaurant from ten to three, seven days a week, and continued to sew at home. I loved the waitress job because that was where I earned the most money. I was determined to save up as much as possible for rainy days, knowing full well they could come at any time.

I tried to show my boss I was trustworthy, hard worker. If there was a slow day, I would clean all the tables and chairs. I cleaned all the trays and the carts without asking. I knew Mrs. Dang was watching me and hoped she liked me enough to keep me there full time.

Then one day after a busy lunch hour, Mrs. Dang called me into her office and asked me to work permanently on the lunch shift. Tammy wanted to work only weekends, when her husband could look after the baby. It was perfect hours for me, so I was willing to trade with Tammy. Mrs. Dang insisted I should work the Saturday lunch shift too, if I wanted. Of course I happily accepted the offer and thanked Mrs. Dang for the opportunity.

I drove home so happy, knowing I would have every Sunday off. Maybe I would take the children to the park or the zoo again, when the weather was nice. It felt good to have some financial stability, but we still had to be careful with our money. I thought of buying health insurance for the family, but it was so expensive. We couldn't afford it now; maybe later, when we had more money in savings.

Being a planner, I was debating opening a separate savings account too, just in case. My husband had opened one without telling me, and it did bother me a lot. I felt like he was being sneaky, keeping money from me like I wasn't trustworthy. Even though he said all that money was from his gambling gains, he'd lost it all anyway and closed the account. Still, I didn't like it. Trust was the most important thing to me, especially in a marriage. Could I still trust Minh? That was another thing I was still working on, and I was feeling conflicted. He had been good; he'd stayed away from gambling for a while now. If I didn't like his secret account, why would I even think about opening one? The trust in our marriage would be crushed. He wouldn't respect me if he found out I secretly kept some money aside. No, I couldn't do that.

For better or for worse. I reminded myself of that and hoped he would never go back down that road again, for our children's sake.

***

I got emotional when I took my son shopping for school. It was a mother's pride, I guessed. Tears ran down my cheeks. I knew I should have saved it for his first day of school, but I couldn't help myself. He chose lots of dinosaur items, which made me smile. It seemed he could never have enough dinosaurs.

We didn't have the money to send him to pre-K, so he went straight to kindergarten. He struggled a little bit since we spoke only Vietnamese at home, but he was a smart boy, so he caught up quickly. I was very proud of him when he spoke English to me. My boss was nice enough to let me get out at two thirty on school days, so I could pick up my son.

"How was school today?" I asked Toan while we walked hand in hand to the car.

"It was scary," Toan said.

"Really? Do you want to tell me about it?"

"We had to pretend a tornado was coming, and there were a lot of loud voices on the speaker telling us we had to hide. I looked around, but I couldn't find any place to hide. Then the teacher pulled me to the corner and told me to get down! He yelled in my ear. It was scary, Mommy." Toan paused. "I'm tired."

"Sorry, baby. The teacher meant well. He wanted you to prepare just in case there is a tornado, so you'll know what to do."

"Have you ever seen a tornado, Mommy?" Toan had been calling me Mommy instead of Ma, probably learning it from the other kids. I didn't correct him. I liked the sound of it.

"No, I never saw one, but it's always good to prepare. You just taught me how."

"Really?" Toan asked.

"Yes. I wouldn't have known what to do if a tornado came, but I do now. See? You saved us already." I rubbed his head.

Toan looked confused for a moment, then he smiled. "Can I have some ice cream?"

"Yes. You were good today. You can have some when we get home, but first we have to pick up your sister."

"All right!" he shouted.

I gave the children some snacks and ice cream when we got home and went to the kitchen to put out some chicken for dinner. I washed the rice and put it in the rice cooker and went back to the dining room to turn on the sewing machine for work. I didn't allow myself to have any free time. All the while I tried to keep an eye on the children. Thank goodness they didn't like the same toys and rarely fought over anything.

My three-year-old daughter came over to the sewing machine and said, "I want school, Ma."

"Thao, you're still too young for school, and don't come too close to the sewing machine. It's not safe."

"I want school," Thao cried.

I stopped working, picked her up, and tried to calm her. I felt guilty about not putting her in pre-K, but it cost a lot more than Mrs. Bui. Thao probably felt lonely at Mrs. Bui's house without her brother.

"How about we go shopping for school first? Would you like that?"

"Yeah." Thao nodded her head.

"You look tired. Let's take a nap first. When you get up, we'll go shopping for school supplies. OK?" I wiped her tears.

"OK." Thao put her head on my shoulder.

I put my daughter down for a nap, and she fell asleep almost immediately. I went back to sewing and watching Toan too. He was still sitting on the couch, playing with his toys. Then the doorbell rang, and Toan ran to open it. I stopped him just in time. I looked through the window and saw a policeman waiting at the front door. What was going on?

"Is everything all right, officer?" I asked, surprised to see a policeman at the door.

"Is there an emergency here? Somebody dialed 911," he said.

"No, I didn't call 911. Are you sure it came from here?" I asked.

"Yes ma'am, somebody called and quickly hung up." The policeman looked at Toan. All of a sudden Toan turned and ran into his room.

"Sir, I apologize. I'll talk to him about it."

"I suggest you move the phone somewhere else, out of the children's reach."

"I will," I assured him.

"Have a good day," the officer said and walked back to his car, its lights still flashing.

When had Toan called 911? How had he picked up the phone without me seeing it? I went to Toan's room and found him in the closet.

"Toan, come out of there right now!" My voice came out a little louder than it should have.

He didn't move.

"Toan, come on, I need to talk to you. I need to ask you a question." I lowered my voice, realizing I had scared him.

He moved to the edge of the closet door but didn't say a word, which was not usual for a talkative child like him.

"Did you call 911?" I asked my five-year-old son.

"The teacher told us to dial 911 for an emergency," Toan finally answered.

"Do you know what an emergency means?" I asked, trying to stay calm.

"It's means somebody got hurt," Toan said after he took his time thinking about it.

"That's right. 911 is for when somebody gets hurt, and that's why the line needs to be free—for a real emergency. Do you understand?"

"I was just testing, to see if it works," he said softly.

"Now you know it works. No more testing, OK? Only if it's a real emergency."

"Yes ma'am." He gave me an innocent puppy face.

"Come on. Let's do your homework." I helped Toan get up.

I was the only one who disciplined the children, since my husband refused. If the children wanted soda, he would give them soda. If they wanted candy, they would get it without any negotiation. I would at least make them wait until they put their toys away or finished their meals before I rewarded them with treats. I knew I was strict sometimes, but wished it wouldn't always have to be me. Deep down I was proud of Toan for already knowing how to make a 911 call at age five, but I couldn't tell him that. I kept it inside my heart, knowing that if something ever happened to me, I could count on my little man.

***

A week later I took the children shopping for Thao's imaginary school. She got a backpack, a box of crayons, and a couple of children's coloring books. As soon as we got home, Thao wanted to do her homework. It was so cute to see Toan showing his little sister how to do it and teaching her the names of the colors.

The phone rang. "Hello," I answered.

"Lien! Oh God." Bac was crying frantically.

"Bac? Is everything OK?"

"No. Vi, she's in the hospital."

"Oh no, what's happened?"

"She was shot." Bac couldn't stop crying.

"Oh my God! Who shot her, a gangster?" I couldn't believe what I'd just heard.

"No, Hoang did...He shot her in the face." Bac was still bawling. "I can't believe it. That bastard shot my daughter."

"Oh, Bac, I'm so sorry. What hospital is she in? Can I see her?"

"Oklahoma Memorial Hospital. I'm not sure if they'll allow her to have visitors yet."

"OK. I'm coming to see you, Bac. You need somebody there with you, even for just a little bit."

"Thank you, Lien."

I called Mrs. Bui, asking her to watch the children for a couple of hours. Driving to the hospital, I couldn't wrap my mind around what had happened. Hoang had always been a controlling husband, but I thought he loved Vi. How could he shoot his wife in the face like that? Had he been drunk? Had Vi been aware of any red flags? Oh God, what about their children? Hoang was definitely going to jail. Their poor kids. I couldn't imagine what it would be like for the kids to live with that—Mom in the hospital and dad in jail. I felt bad for Bac too. Vi was her only child.

I parked the car and ran into the hospital. The receptionist stopped me, and I realized I had to stay calm for Bac's sake. I found her distraught in a chair, her eyes swollen from crying. We hugged, and Bac cried on my shoulder. My tears started to fall too. I couldn't stop them.

"How is Vi?" I finally asked.

"She's in the operating room. I'm praying for her to make it." Bac sniffed.

"Did the doctor tell you anything?"

"Not yet. I just hope she'll be OK." Bac paused. "Her children need her."

"Sit down, Bac." I led her to a bench. "Tell me what happened."

"Vi started dating someone. I haven't met him yet, but she told me about him. He's an American, a real gentleman, and she's in love with him. Meanwhile, she had been asking Hoang to move out, but he refused. He started harassing her, following her everywhere, to and from work."

"Are they still married?" I asked.

"Vi wanted a divorce, but he wouldn't give it to her. He threatened to hurt her numerous times. This morning he followed her to work and caught Vi meeting up with her boyfriend. When she came home from work, he was waiting for her in the bedroom with a gun. I heard them argue, then the gunshot. I ran to the bedroom and saw her covered in blood." Bac sobbed again. "I took the kids, ran outside, and asked the neighbor to call 911. We were all so scared of him."

"Thank God you were able to get out of there safely," I said.

"Ever since we moved there, I always felt unsafe and worried about stray bullets from the bad neighborhood. I never thought a bullet would come from my son-in-law's gun."

"Hoang will be in jail for the rest of his life. He will not get away with this." I tried to put Bac at ease.

"He's dead," Bac said frankly.

"He's dead? Did he kill himself?" I didn't know why I asked such a question.

"The police shot him."

"Did he shoot at the police too?"

"I didn't witness it, but the neighbor said Hoang was hiding under his car when the police arrived. They told him to drop the gun, but he didn't. Later the police told me they killed him because he started firing at the police car."

I didn't know what to say. It was impossible to imagine something like this happening in real life, let alone to somebody I knew. Bac looked exhausted. She had aged so much since I had seen her last.

"How are the children? Are they staying with someone you know?" I asked.

"They're staying with my friend who lives in the same building."

"Let me know if you need help with the children, OK?" I tapped Bac's hand.

"Thanks, Lien. You should go home to your children. I'll let you know when they allow visitors."

"Let me buy you something to eat before I go," I offered.

"I'm not hungry." Bac sighed.

"You need to eat something, Bac, so you have the strength to go on."

She didn't respond.

"How about some soup?"

"All right. Thank you, Lien. I really appreciate it."

I went home and hugged my kids until they didn't want to be held anymore. Instead of sewing I spent all evening with the children, playing with them and cherishing them. I gave them all the attention they wanted and more.

Bac called the next day to tell me Vi had made it through surgery. She was all bandaged up, but she had survived. I felt so relieved Vi was all right.

Vi finally agreed to see me on her last day in the hospital. I got emotional when I saw the bandages on one side of her face. She sat on her hospital bed, packing to go home.

"Hey, how are you doing?" I asked, trying to keep my voice neutral.

"I'm all right," Vi said sadly.

"I'm so sorry." I was trying to pick the right words to say.

"It's OK, Lien."

"I've been thinking about you, and I tried to call you a couple of times."

"I know. You've always been a good friend to me and my mother, and I pushed you away." Vi paused. "It's not that I don't want to be your friend, it's just that I was embarrassed about my situation."

"I would never judge you or anybody about their life," I said.

"I know. I guess I was a little insecure. Anyway, I just want to say I'm sorry for not being a good friend to you."

"Can I have a hug?" I asked.

"Come here." Vi opened her arms, and we shared a long, deep hug.

"How are the kids?" I asked.

"It's going to be tough for them for a while, but there's a social worker who will set up some therapy sessions for us."

"That's good. You guys went through so much."

"Life is hard, isn't it?" Vi said sadly.

"What about your boyfriend? Did he visit you?" I said, trying to cheer my friend up.

"He doesn't know what happened. I don't think I want to see him again, not like this." Vi teared up.

"It will heal." That was all I could manage to say while handing her a tissue box.

I was saddened to see my friend like that. I would do anything to bring back her smile. It would be a long road for Vi to be herself again. I knew it would take time, and I had to be patient instead of pushing her. I would give Vi time and as much space as she needed, hoping our friendship would grow again.

I called and checked up on Vi periodically. She was very depressed and often avoided me. When she did pick up the phone, she often complained about the scar on her face. Sometimes she blamed America for what had happened to her. Our conversations were often full of sadness, bitterness, and sometimes anger. We didn't laugh or joke anymore. It became clear our friendship couldn't go back to the way it was.

Eventually Bac and Vi moved far away, without giving me their new phone number. I understood Vi needed to do that. She needed to forget the past and focus on the future. It was a fresh start for her family as well. Her children didn't need to relive the trauma every day at the old school, where everyone knew their story. I prayed Vi would be strong for her children and hoped they would all eventually heal. I hoped we would see each other in the future, so she could tell me they were now happy and successful.

***

The restaurant got busier and busier during the lunch hours. Mrs. Dang brought in a new Mongolian grill, and it was a hit. Customers would pick their own raw meats, vegetables, and sauces. The waitresses would bring them to the grill bar, and the chef cooked everything right there in the middle of the restaurant, where customers could see.

On top of working nonstop at the restaurant, I had to rush to meet the deadlines at the clothing company. The Vietnamese work ethic had been drilled into my head.

I had been so busy; I was skipping meals, sometimes keeping going until I was exhausted. There were times I found myself falling asleep on the children's bed during their naptime. When I woke up, I was always mad at myself for wasting time sleeping. Then one day I could hardly drag myself out of bed. My head was so heavy, my nose was clogged, and my entire body ached. I probably had the flu but still kept on working. I told my husband about it, hoping he would help me a little with the chores. He told me to stay home. Stay home? Didn't he remember how hard it was for me to find this job? I had to go in. Then it would be up to Mrs. Dang to decide if I should go back home or not.

I went to work anyway, pushing myself to go on. I tried not to cough, but no matter how hard I tried, the coughing still came uncontrollably. Mrs. Dang heard me and told me to go home. I didn't think I needed to see a doctor; it was just the flu, and what I needed was some rest. Besides, we didn't have health insurance, so I didn't want to spend money on a doctor who probably would tell me to rest anyway. I set up the alarm clock so I could pick up the children, then flopped onto the bed.

I felt so drowsy when picking Toan up from school. When I arrived at Mrs. Bui's house for Thao, she was so concerned, she didn't want me to drive the children home.

"It's just a cold, Mrs. Bui. I'm fine," I protested.

"Lien, let me watch the children. I won't charge you for this. I'll feed them dinner and everything, so don't worry. Go home and rest. I'll call your husband to pick them up after work."

"Are you sure?"

"Yes. You look terrible. Go home," Mrs. Bui demanded.

"Let me ask the kids."

"They're watching a cartoon right now. Besides, you don't want them to catch your cold, right?"

"You're right. Thank you, Mrs. Bui."

I went home and buried myself in bed. I didn't remember anything until the next morning, when my husband woke me up and demanded I see a doctor. Minh drove me and the children to the Vietnamese doctor. His office was in the Little Saigon center, and I had forgotten it was Tet (Lunar New Year) until I saw a dragon dance in the street. I couldn't believe I'd forgotten to prepare for Tet. There was nothing in the house that said Tet. I hadn't even bought any gifts for the children. What a lousy mother I was!

Minh stopped the car in front of the doctor's office. "Are you OK to go in by yourself? I want to take the children to see the dragon dance."

"Yes," I said, even though my head felt very heavy.

"We'll be back in a bit."

"OK."

I went inside, and the receptionist asked if I had an appointment.

"No, but I don't feel well, and I really need to see the doctor today."

"OK. Sign your name here. You might have to wait for a while, because he's really busy. And I need to see your insurance card," she added.

"I don't have insurance," I said.

"OK, just fill these papers out, and have a seat in the waiting area."

"Thank you."

I took the papers and walked to the waiting area. My head felt so heavy, I almost slipped, and I grasped a chair. I waited for my balance to return then started to fill out the paperwork. I managed only to write down my name, then everything got blurry; then it went black. I hit the floor. I could hear people screaming something like "get the doctor!" and then I was out.

I woke up in an ambulance, an IV drip connected to my arm.

"No, no, I don't want to go the hospital. I don't have any insurance," I told the young technician, worried about the hospital bill.

"Ma'am, stay still. You need medical care."

I realized I was still very weak. Closing my eyes, I prayed I'd be all right. Who was going to take care of the children if something bad happened to me? I said a prayer over and over.

As they admitted me to the hospital, a young female doctor came to my bed and asked about my symptoms. "When did you start feeling sick?"

"About a week ago," I answered.

"Did you ever lose consciousness before?"

"Once, a long time ago, when I was seventeen."

"What happened that time?"

"A panic attack, I think." I let out a sigh.

"Did you seek medical care at that time?"

"No."

"Why not?"

"I was OK after I woke up."

"And your family medical history?" The doctor wrote down something in my file.

"My mother is healthy." I felt ashamed to say that. I hadn't talked to her for years.

"What about your father?"

"My father?" I hesitated.

"Yes, your dad, how is his health?"

"I don't have one...I never met him, so I don't know."

The young doctor looked at me gently. "We're going to run some tests on you, OK? First we're going to check your heart."

"OK," I said.

They ran an EKG test on me, and it came back normal—my heart was fine. They checked my blood, then did more tests.

My husband finally arrived with Toan and Thao. "What happened? I went back to the doctor's office, and they said you fainted, told me to come here. Are you all right?"

Thao started crying as soon as she saw me. She leaned down toward her mom and wanted to be held. Toan looked at me with concern.

"Mommy, are you OK?" Toan asked.

"I'm fine, honey, I'm just a little tired."

"Did they say what's wrong?" Minh asked.

"They're still running some tests."

The nurse came back to the room, saying a bubbly hello to the children and my husband. She then turned to me and said, "We need to take you for an X-ray, OK?"

"OK." I turned to Minh. "Take the children home. They're probably hungry and tired."

"That's a good idea. Your wife needs rest too," the nurse said.

"OK. I'll come back later."

The nurse wheeled me away, and Thao started screeching.

After the X-ray, they told me I had pneumonia. They gave me antibiotics and wanted to keep me overnight. I didn't sleep well, worrying about the children and the bills.

The next morning Thi came to visit me. "Hi, Lien. I just heard. How are you feeling?"

"Hi, Thi. I feel a bit better. They told me I can go home today."

"What happened?" Thi put her hand on my forehead, checking my temperature.

"I had flulike symptoms, and I thought it would go away on its own, but it got worse. Minh took me to the doctor, and I passed out in the office, so they called 911, and I ended up here, in the hospital, without insurance. I can't imagine what the bills will be like."

"Don't worry. You only stayed one night."

"They ran so many tests on me."

"Did they find out what's wrong?"

"My flu turned into pneumonia."

"I'm sorry, Lien. At least it's treatable. I'm sure they have some kind of payment plan for you. I'll ask my husband to find out for you. Don't worry too much. You need to get better first."

"You're right," I admitted.

"I heard hospital food is horrible, so I made you some rice soup. Eat some, then I'll take you home."

"Oh, thanks, Thi."

Thi was a godsend. She took me home and bought soup and medicine. Then Thi sat next to my bed, keeping me company until it was time for her to go to work.

"Thank you, Thi, for everything," I told her.

"No problem. Call me if you need anything else, and don't rush back to work too soon, OK?"

"Yes ma'am."

"Happy New Year." Thi smiled.

"Happy New Year to you too, love."

I slept for a long time, until my husband brought the children home. Toan and Thao wanted to spend time with me, but I asked Minh to keep them away so they wouldn't get sick.

I stayed home for the next five days, resting, eating, and slowly getting my strength back. During this time I was constantly thinking about my mother and siblings, wishing they lived closer to us. For the first time since leaving the Philippines, I missed them. There were times I wanted to call my mother, but was afraid my stepfather would pick up the phone. I didn't want to even hear his voice, so I waited and wished Ma would call me instead. I once had a dream about our reunion during Tet, and it felt good, like I was loved. I wished one day it would become reality.

I eventually went back to work and was now very careful about my health. I asked Mrs. Dang to let me work in the nonsmoking section only. I ate healthier and tried not to rush around so much. I was still sewing but a lot less than before. I had learned my lesson; I had to be strong and healthy for my kids.

***

I tried my best to live a stress-free lifestyle, with no worries and no arguments. Now I didn't mind that my husband wanted to spend his whole day off out with his friends. I didn't even want to know how much money we had in the bank. It used to make me worry. We both were working, so as long as we had enough to pay bills, I shouldn't be worried about it. The stress-free life was sadly short lived.

One day I got a letter from the bank saying the check I had written to pay the mortgage had bounced. How could it be? I was very sure we had more than $800 in there, and the mortgage was $225. I decided to go to the bank to find out.

"Good afternoon, how can I help you?" The bank teller smiled and greeted me.

"I got this letter saying my check bounced. I'm very certain we have more than eight hundred dollars in the checking account."

"Let me take a look." Her face became more serious as she started typing on the computer. "There it is, eight hundred dollars withdrawn last week, so you have only forty-two dollars left in your checking account."

"I didn't make any withdrawal last week."

"I suggest you ask your husband about it."

Could it have been him? How could he take the money out without telling me? What was it for? I thought for a second and decided to take care of the mortgage bill first.

"Can I make a transfer from the savings account to my checking?" I asked.

"Sure. What is your account number?"

I gave the bank teller the account number, and her face changed again. She looked at me with a sigh.

"I'm sorry, the account has been closed."

"When?" I was shocked.

"Yesterday. Is there anything else I can help you with?"

I couldn't answer, feeling embarrassed and disappointed in my husband. I gathered the children and walked out of there.

How could he do this to his family? Was he gambling again? Had somebody else stolen our money? I called the restaurant as soon as I got home. They said he was cooking, and he would call me back. I waited for hours; he didn't call back. I put the children down for a nap and dialed Thi's number. I needed to talk to somebody.

"Hello." Thi picked up.

"Thi, I'm in trouble," I cried.

"Lien, are you all right?"

"I tried to pay the mortgage, but the check bounced, so I went to the bank and found out we have no money left. Somebody emptied our bank accounts. We had more than a thousand dollars in savings and eight hundred in checking, and it's all gone." I sobbed.

"Oh, Lien, I'm so sorry."

"I called my husband, but he didn't call me back. I think it's him. He's probably gambling again."

"Lien, I'm coming right over. I have something to tell you."

Ten minutes later Thi walked in, embraced me, and gave me a shoulder to cry on. Many tissues later, we sat down on the sofa, and Thi told me what she had come there for.

"I heard a rumor that your husband went to an illegal casino with his new friend. They both lost a lot of money."

"How long has he been going there?" I asked.

"Probably about a month, but I just heard it last week. I was going to tell you, but I wasn't sure if the story was true."

"Where is this illegal casino? Do you know?"

"I don't know. What is your plan?" Thi asked me.

"Maybe I'll go there to confront him or call the police to shut it down. I just want to do something about it." I was thinking out loud.

"Lien, they won't let you in, only somebody they know."

"How did my husband get in?" I asked.

"His new friend is a regular customer there. He vouched for your husband. Besides, they can be dangerous people. Promise me you won't go there."

"What am I going to do?"

Thi said nothing.

"What would you do if you were me?" I asked.

"I don't want to tell you what to do, but if my husband had a gambling problem I would leave him. I couldn't stand it. Thank God Vinh isn't a gambler. That would drive me crazy."

"I'm not going to lie, part of me thought about that, but the children are so young, and how would I pay all the bills by myself?" I wiped my tears.

"I know, it's easy for me to say, since I'm not in your shoes," Thi said.

"I don't know what to do," I said, looking at my friend for answers.

"I would open my own bank account if I were you, to make sure there is food on the table and a roof over the children's heads."

"You're right. I can't trust him anymore."

"Do you need money? I can lend you some." Thi pulled out her checkbook.

"I don't know. God knows I need money, but I don't want to ruin our friendship, and money can do that."

"What are you talking about? Lien, I'm offering to help my best friend in a time of need. Why would it ruin our friendship?"

"I have so many bills, I don't even know which one I should pay first, and I don't know when I can pay you back. That's why I'm worried."

"Let him worry about it." Thi put the checkbook away and opened her wallet. She took out a hundred-dollar bill and put it into my hand. "Buy food for the children."

"No, Thi."

"Keep it. I insist."

"Thank you. I'll pay you back as soon as I can," I said.

"Don't worry about it. I know you would do the same for me."

After Thi left, I sat down and planned what to do when Minh got home. We would have a talk—yes, a talk. I didn't want to yell or scream. I would ask him to come clean, to admit he had a gambling problem and seek help. I would ask him to choose either his family or gambling; he couldn't have both. Then I would tell him I wanted to keep a separate bank account, and we would split the bills. I would tell him I couldn't trust him with the money anymore. He would have to quit gambling, and it might take me a long time to trust him again.

He didn't come home that night. He was avoiding me or probably was continuing his gambling, I didn't know. I cried myself to sleep. This wasn't the marriage I had signed up for. This wasn't a happy home for my children to grow up in.

The next morning I got the children up to prepare Toan for school and to get Thao to the babysitter as usual. I went to work at the restaurant and found my husband already there. I didn't ask him where he was the previous night, not while we were at work. He didn't look at me, not even when I placed the customer orders. Was that what he wanted? A cold war? I didn't deserve it. I felt he owed me an apology and should beg for forgiveness. Instead he was ignoring me.

I went home, moved the children's belongings into the master bedroom, and went on about my day, cooking and taking care of them. We all settled in my bedroom and played. When it was time for bed, I locked the door and cuddled with my children until they fell asleep.

The next morning, while I was preparing breakfast, the children were playing with each other as usual, and Thao said, "I saw Daddy."

"Where?"

"He's sleeping on the couch," Thao said.

"Mommy, why is Dad sleeping on the couch?" Toan asked me.

"Oh, he didn't feel well. That's why he's sleeping there," I lied.

"Why? You slept in the bed when you were sick."

"Well, he doesn't want us to get his germs."

"What is germs?" Toan was curious.

"Now that is a science question you can ask your teacher today. Hurry up and finish your breakfast, or you're going to be late for school."

Toan went back to eating. I didn't know how long I

could hide it from the children. They were smart, and soon they would know their parents weren't talking.

A few days later, the Visa card bill came in, and I was shocked when I opened it. Minh had maxed it out for cash—ten thousand dollars. I was numb. How could we pay for that? Both of our names were on the card, but he hadn't even bothered to tell me. Then the MasterCard statement came the next day—another eight thousand dollars. I felt humiliated and betrayed by my own husband. I shouldn't have listened to him and agreed to apply for those credit cards.

The following week all the other credit card bills started to pour in one by one. The debt total was over forty thousand dollars. I was devastated. It was double the amount of our mortgage. I was emotionally exhausted, feeling like my world had crashed down before my very eyes. I walked around the house filled with bitterness. Soon it would belong to somebody else. I sat down at the kitchen table and pulled out the yellow pages. I looked for a divorce attorney, and my tears rained down. I didn't even have money for a divorce. That would have to wait.

I stared at the phone, debating what to do. Should I call my mother to ask for help? My situation was beyond help, but I was desperate. With a shaking hand, I dialed Ma's number in New Jersey. It rang. What if my stepfather was the one to pick up the phone? I put the phone down abruptly. My heart was pumping fast.

I went back to the living room, where the children were playing. I looked at my innocent children and felt tremendously guilty. They didn't know it yet, but their lives were about to change. I thought if I didn't want them to end up sleeping on the street, I had to make that phone call. I went back to the phone, and this time I had the courage to do it. Taking a deep breath, I dialed my mother's number.

"Hello." It was Ma's voice. Thank goodness.

"Hi, Ma."

"Lien? Is that you?"

"Yes, it's me, and I need your help. I want to move to New Jersey." And I started to sob.

Part 3

Chapter 24
1995
New Jersey

The flight from Oklahoma to New Jersey seemed so long. We had to stop in Houston, Texas, before heading to New Jersey. Along the way the children kept asking about their dad. I told them we were going to visit their grandparents, and their dad would join us later. I lied.

As soon as I got the air tickets, I secretly packed our belongings. I didn't tell my husband anything because we still weren't talking at that point. I left him a note on the coffee table the day we left. It said, "We're going to be in New Jersey, not sure when we'll be back."

I didn't plan to come back.

I wasn't sure if New Jersey was going to work out, but I had to give it a try. Ma said the family would help me. She wanted us to stay with her, rent free, until I got on my feet. The problem was my stepfather. I didn't like to be near him, especially with my children. I was afraid he might say things he shouldn't say in front of them. What if he got drunk? He was an ugly drunk, swearing at everyone in sight. I promised myself that as soon as I got a job, I would move out immediately.

We landed at Newark Airport. I asked Toan to hold his sister's hand and follow me while I carried two big carry-on bags.

"Toan, Thao do you still see me?" I turned back to them. "Hold on to each other's hands, and keep following me, OK?"

"Yes, Mommy," they both said nervously.

We kept walking, and then I saw them. Ma and all my siblings were there to greet us. They looked good, all grown up and somewhat Americanized in the way they dressed. We hugged each other, and I saw some tears on my mother's cheeks. They all turned to my children and asked a lot of questions. Toan and Thao weren't used to getting so much attention. Thao clamped on to me and refused to talk to her aunts and uncles.

"Hi, Lien. Welcome to New Jersey," my sister Chi said.

"Thank you," I replied.

"How was your flight?" Ma asked.

"Good. Thanks, Ma...for everything."

"You're welcome."

"Toan, say hello to Grandma," I told him.

"Hello." That was all he said.

"Toan, Thao, say hello to Aunt Chi, Uncle Vu, Aunt Truc, Mai, Lieu, and—"

"It's OK. There are too many of us. They can't possibly remember everyone's name right away," Ma said.

After we went to get my luggage, we all got into two mini vans and headed home. Jersey City was a busy city with a lot of narrow streets. House next to house, people walking in a hurry—the city seemed hectic to me. How was I going to survive here?

We turned down our one-way street, and I saw cars parked on both sides. Nobody parked on the street in Oklahoma City. There was no grass anywhere here in Jersey City, and no one had a front yard. It reminded me of Saigon, except Saigon was prettier, in my opinion.

My brother Vu double-parked the van so we could unload the luggage. Ma took us inside her four-bedroom apartment. Every room was tiny, including the living room and kitchen. She settled us in the small room next to the kitchen. It had a queen-size bed—thank goodness, because that was where my children and I were going to sleep. At least it fit all three of us. There wasn't any furniture, but it had a small closet. Everything was going to be OK, I told myself.

Ma made a delicious dinner for the whole family, and everyone was there. My stepfather came out for his dinner, then he went back to his room. I was nervous, but nothing bad happened. We talked until late, making up for the lost time.

Chi still didn't get along with my stepfather. They had argued a lot when they'd just arrived here, and he had kicked her out of the house. Luckily enough, her new boyfriend at the time lived alone, so he asked her to move in with him. They got married a year later and had a daughter.

My brother Vu was a cabinetmaker. He worked for a good company and had good benefits; he seemed to like his job. He had a group of friends he hung out with most of the time. He was rarely home.

My other sister, Truc, was the only girl still living at home. Mai lived with her boyfriend. Lieu was about to get married in a couple of months, and she lived with her future husband. Trang, whose nickname was still Little, also lived with her boyfriend. She'd just had a baby boy, and she was only eighteen years old.

I could see the pattern here: all the girls didn't want to live with my parents. That meant their father was still unbearable. I was worried for myself. Had I made a mistake in moving here?

Last but not least, my youngest brother, Nha— nickname Be—was still in high school. Be was the center of the family; he was kind and got along with everybody. He put up with my difficult stepfather, and the family loved him.

All my sisters had become manicurists. They had come to New Jersey when the nail industry was booming. Apparently people paid big bucks for fake nails. They wanted me to start school right away, so I could become a manicurist too. Maybe we could open a nail salon together, they said.

It was almost midnight, and I was tired. I was about to say good night, then the phone rang.

"Who's calling at this hour?" Ma was annoyed, but she picked it up. She covered the phone and whispered, "It's Minh, your husband."

"I don't want to talk to him," I told Ma.

"I'm sorry, Minh, she's sleeping…Yes, yes they got here OK. They're sleeping right now. I'll tell her you called."

Minh kept calling, and I refused to talk to him every time. I let the children talk to him, but I was done with his apologizing and broken promises. I wanted to move on with my life. Sometimes Ma was on the phone with him for a long time. I told her to hang up on him many times, but she never did.

"Maybe you should give him a second chance," Ma told me one day after a long conversation with him.

"Ma! I did. I gave him three chances already, and he kept going back to gambling. It got worse each time."

"Minh told me he really regrets it this time."

"He told me that every time, Ma."

"You have to think for your children, Lien!" Ma said.

"I am, and that's why I need to move on."

I went to apply for a waitress job at a couple of restaurants nearby. I didn't have a car yet, so I couldn't go too far, but I was learning about public transportation. I also registered Toan in school near Chi's house and used her address as ours, because there was a better school system there.

Chi and her husband had bought a two-family house on a nice, quiet street. Her parents-in-law used to live upstairs, but they had moved out recently. She offered me cheap rent to live upstairs if I was interested. It had three small bedrooms and an eat-in kitchen. I liked it, but I didn't have a job yet.

My sister Truc came home one day and told me her boss was looking for a manicurist. I knew nothing about nails. She insisted it was very easy to learn—in fact she could teach me. We went to talk to the owner, and she said she would hire me if I was enrolled in beauty school.

For the next couple of days, I ran around to fill out the paperwork. I had to translate my high school diploma into English in order to be admitted to school. That was where the trouble with my name began. My first name originally was Lien, and my middle name was Mỹ, but the immigration officials in the Philippines had mistakenly swapped them. I had used Mỹ as my first name for five years in Oklahoma, but here in New Jersey they wanted me to correct it. I didn't have the money for the legal fees. Most lawyers wanted at least a thousand dollars for the process. I realized the cost of living in New Jersey was a lot higher than in Oklahoma, and I couldn't get a job because my name was messed up. I tried to get a New Jersey driver's license, and I couldn't for the same reason. I was frustrated.

Chi told me to apply for citizenship. If I passed I would be able to change my name for no additional cost. It was a brilliant idea. Since I had been living in America for five years, I was eligible, but the process took time. I started to study American history right away, even though I had to wait for the test. What else could I do in my free time?

Ma had babysat for a nearby Vietnamese family for years. The couple had a sister who owned a hair salon in New York City. Somehow in conversation Ma got me an interview appointment at their house. I wasn't sure about it, since I knew nothing about hair, but I went to meet them anyway.

The couple was really nice, and they loved Ma. Their younger sister, Chin, interviewed me. She had a salon/bridal shop, and she was willing to train me.

"Don't I need a license to do hair?"

"Well, I normally hire licensed hairdressers only, but your mom said you're a quick learner, and you're planning to start beauty school. So we'll give it a try, right?"

"Thank you." I said with relief.

"Any more questions?" Chin asked.

"When should I start?"

"How about this Saturday?"

"Thanks again, Mrs. Chin."

"Call me Chin. Come here on Saturday, and I'll show you how to get to the salon."

My siblings took turns watching Thao and picked up Toan for me from school. It was one of the benefits of having a big family, and I couldn't thank them enough.

I had to take a bus from where we lived to Newport, then transfer to a PATH train to the World Trade Center in New York City. From there I walked about six blocks to Chin's salon. Her shop was big; one side was a full-service salon and the other side was for bridal rentals.

"If the state board officer comes in, you run to the bridal side, OK? If they ask you what your job is, you tell them you are the cashier," Chin said.

"OK."

"I want you to learn everything, because in the wedding season we will be busy every Saturday doing bridal parties' hair and makeup. Plus the salon will be busy."

"Yes ma'am."

"Don't call me ma'am, just Chin, please! We're practically the same age."

I smiled. Chin was nice. She taught me how to do hair. I shampooed the customers. She cut, then I blow-dried their hair. While she cut, she made sure I watched her every step. She mixed color, then let me apply it on customers' hair. I learned a lot from her and realized I would really like to become a hairdresser. With that in mind, I decided I would start school for cosmetology as soon as I passed the citizenship test.

***

I packed all of our clothes into three suitcases and stuffed all our belongings into a couple of shopping bags. We were moving to Chi's house. My brother Be would help me with the move. I was very excited about it; after three months living with Ma, it was time to have our own space.

My stepfather stayed in his room most of the time. Thank God I worked; it kept me from being around him. But this was my last day there, and I had to thank him before we left. I wished I could just leave without having to face him, but I couldn't do that to Ma. She probably begged him to let me stay there, so I had to be nice to him for Ma's sake.

I had to say he had gotten a lot better than he had been back in Vietnam. He didn't drink every day like he used to, but he was still drinking on the weekends, when his friends stopped by. Yes, he still badmouthed my mother and Chi to his friends when he was drunk. I felt so uncomfortable every time his friends came to the house. I had to move out even though I wasn't financially ready.

I knocked on his bedroom door.

"Who is it?" he asked in a cranky voice, like always.

"It's Lien." I was hoping I could tell him quickly from the outside. "I'm moving out today and just want to thank you for letting us stay here."

"Come in!" he ordered.

'Oh crap,' I thought. 'What should I do, run?' Instead I opened the door. His room smelled heavily of cigarette smoke. I held my breath and stepped in. He was playing a video game with a cigarette in his mouth.

"You probably heard I'm moving out today. I just want to thank you," I said really quickly, hoping that was it, so I could go.

"Where are you moving to?" He put out the cigarette and paused the game.

"Where?" I didn't think he cared. It was so unexpected that he asked me.

"Yeah! Where?"

"I'm renting Chi's upstairs apartment," I said.

"Why hers?"

"She's giving me a discount, and she's family," I said.

"Family my ass. She cares only about herself."

Did he really hate her that much? And why would it bother him that I was going to live there?

"Mommy? Mommy?" Toan and Thao were calling me from the kitchen.

"I'm in here, but don't come in," I yelled out.

"Why can't they come in?" my stepfather asked.

I paused and said, "It's very smoky in here. I don't want them to breathe it in."

He stared at me, and I couldn't figure out if he was surprised or angry. I realized that was the first time I was standing up for myself.

"Get out!" he yelled.

I stepped out of his room, gathered my children from the kitchen, and ran outside. Be was waiting in the car.

"What's wrong?" he asked.

"Nothing. Ready to go?" I asked calmly.

"Grandpa yelled at Mommy," Toan jumped in the car

and told Be.

"I'm scared," Thao said.

"It's OK. Mommy is right here." I hugged her. "Come on, let's get in the car so we can go to our new place."

Be didn't ask again about what had happened. He could tell by the look on my face.

It was a quick drive, since Chi didn't live too far from Ma. As soon as Be stopped the car, Toan unbuckled his seatbelt and was anxious to get out.

"I want to see my room," he said.

I understood he was excited to have his own little space. I just hoped he wouldn't be too disappointed, because it wasn't much. His room was small and without any furniture, just a mattress on the floor.

Chi had some old furniture I could use for the time being—an old sofa in the living room and a table with mismatched chairs in the kitchen. I bought two mattresses, one full size for Thao and me to share and a twin mattress for Toan. There was a small spare room for Thao to use later, when I had enough money to set it up.

"Welcome to your new apartment." Chi came up from downstairs.

"Thank you," I said.

"What do you think?"

"It's great. Close to school, close to you."

"I have some old pots and pans. Do you want them?"

"Yes, that'll be great. Do you have any old plates and utensils too?"

"I do. Let me go get them for you. If you need anything, don't hesitate to ask. I'm right downstairs."

"Thanks, Chi."

Chi and I hadn't been close when we were little. She had a strong personality and was a little stubborn like her dad, but now she opened her door for me and my children. That said a lot. I just had to make sure to pay the rent on time, and we would be fine.

I found a babysitter right across the street from the school—a Filipino lady who spoke some English. She wanted the children to call her Tita. Every morning I walked Toan to school, with him holding on to one hand and Thao on the other. After I dropped Toan off, I crossed the street to drop Thao off at the babysitter's, then I walked to the bus stop. It took me about an hour to commute to New York City and back on a regular day, so my day was usually long.

Tita picked Toan up from school for me, and the children stayed with her until I got back. I picked them up around eight or eight thirty at night and walked home in the dark. I felt guilty feeding the children their dinner late, but I didn't have a choice. I checked Toan's homework while we were eating and talked about school a little bit. I gave them baths every night and put them to bed around ten. After they went to bed, I would prepare dinner for the next night and after-school snacks for the children for the next day. I am not going to lie—being a single mom was hard, especially when I worked and lived in two different cities.

I found Toan's graduation note in his book bag one day and thought I read it wrong. Was there such a thing? Kindergarten graduation? Two days from then? We didn't have that in Vietnam. We had only high school graduation.

I asked Chin for that day off, and she totally understood. I couldn't buy Toan a new outfit because I got out of work so late, all the stores were closed by the time I got home. I looked through our luggage the night before Toan's graduation, hoping I could find a decent outfit for him. I found a long-sleeve shirt and a pair of pants I had bought for him in Oklahoma. That would do, I told myself. I ran downstairs to borrow an iron from Chi and smoothed out all the wrinkles.

The next morning Toan got up very excited about his last day of school. After breakfast I helped him to put on his outfit. It looked great, except it was a little too short for him. He had grown. Oh, I wished I'd had time to buy him a new outfit.

"What do you think, Toan? Do you like it?" I asked, feeling guilty about it.

"Yeah! Can we go now?" He ran to the door.

"In a minute. Let me get your sister ready."

We walked to school an hour later than usual, following

the directions from the principal's letter. The weather was nice; that meant the ceremony was going to be outside. After the teachers gathered all the kindergarteners inside, they opened the gate to let the parents in. I found a seat in the second row and sat down with my daughter. A while later the children walked out in line. They were all so cute.

"Mommy! There's Toan." Thao pointed him out.

"Yes, that's right. It's your brother."

People started clicking their cameras. At that point I realized I didn't have a camera to take pictures of my son. This was an important day in his life. How was I going to capture this precious moment for him? What if he asked me about it later on?

I felt tears on my cheeks. Other moms cried too, but they were crying out of happiness. I cried because I couldn't give my son a perfect graduation day like the rest of his schoolmates.

I waved at Toan. He smiled back, and then he started to sing the national anthem with the rest of the group. It was an uplifting song, with meaningful lyrics. I felt lucky to be in this country. My children would have better educations than I did. They would have opportunities to go to college and have better futures. All of a sudden, I felt better. Yes, life was hard right now, but it would improve. I felt good thinking about my children's futures and promised to do anything in my power to make their lives better than mine.

***

I put the children to bed after their baths, as usual. While I was preparing food for the next day, the phone rang. I had a feeling it was Ma. I hadn't called her since we'd moved out—partly because I was busy, but the main reason was to avoid my stepfather.

I picked up the phone. "Hello?"

"Lien." It was Ma. "Guess who is here."

"Who?" I wasn't in the mood for guessing. It was late.

"Minh, your husband. He just arrived," Ma whispered.

"What? How does he know where you live? Did somebody pick him up from the airport?"

"No, he drove here by himself from Oklahoma, and he wants to see the children."

"They're sleeping right now, and I don't want to see him."

"What do you want me to do?" Ma asked.

"Can you tell him to go back to Oklahoma? Tell him I want a divorce, and I want to move on with my life."

"I can't do that, Lien. You have to talk to him yourself." Ma paused. "Besides, he is the father of your children, and how would he visit them if he lives in Oklahoma?"

"He didn't care about them when he was gambling. He didn't even care if the children had a roof over their heads. Why would he care now?"

"I know you're upset right now, but he told me he regrets the gambling, and he misses the kids."

"I have to get back to my chores Ma. It's late."

"All right. Think about the children, OK? Good night, Lien."

"Good night, Ma."

I tried to sleep, but I couldn't. What should I do about this situation? I couldn't keep the children from seeing their father, but every time I thought about Minh I just got so upset. I blamed him for putting us through this. He had made our life harder, and it was difficult for me to forgive him.

I went to work not as my normal self. I was quiet, and people knew something was bothering me. I didn't talk about it, though; I didn't feel like sharing my story because I knew it would make me cry.

The next day the children and I were surprised to see their dad waiting at the front door as we were about to leave for school. Toan and Thao were so happy, they ran to hug him. I thought, 'Really, Ma? Did you have to give Minh the address?'

"Who wants a ride to school?" he asked.

"I do," both children said in unison.

"OK, let's get in the car." He opened the car door, and

the children jumped in. "Don't forget to buckle your seatbelts."

"Hi." He turned to me and asked, "Do you want to get in?"

"Why are you doing this?" I asked him.

"Doing what? Seeing my children? Or giving them a ride to school?"

"You can't just show up like this. It needs to be arranged ahead of time."

"I don't understand. They are my children," Minh said.

"I know they are, but we need to arrange which day is your day and which day is mine to take them to school."

"We can arrange later if you want, but they need to go to school now, don't they? And I don't know where the school is, so you have to get in the car and show me how to get there."

I got in the car angry but tried not to show it in front of the children.

"So tell me, what grade are you in?" Minh asked the children.

"I'm in kindergarten," Thao said. "And I didn't cry."

"Good job! How about you, Toan?"

"I'm a first grader," Toan said.

"Where have you been, Daddy?" Thao asked.

"I have been working far away, but now I'm here."

"I don't see your stuff in the house. Are you going to live with us?" Toan asked.

I couldn't believe the children asked those questions.

"Mommy and I are working on some stuff, but I will be home soon," Minh said.

"There's the school. Can you drop us right up here?" I said.

"All right. Have a good day, and I'll pick you two up later." Minh turned to me. "What time are they getting out?"

"The babysitter will pick them up. Come on, kids, let's go."

Minh stayed with my parents. It made me feel very uncomfortable. Ma said she wanted to help him until he got on his feet. It was nice of her, but it wasn't helping me. I felt Ma didn't support my decision. I felt she was on his side instead of mine.

Minh wanted to pick up the children after school, and I let him. It was easier for me, but it was good and bad. It was good that the children could be home earlier; it was bad that Minh just showed up unannounced most of the time.

"Happy Anniversary." He showed up once on my day off, with a dozen red roses. We had never celebrated anniversaries before. I didn't move and kept my eyes on the children doing their homework. "Where do you want them?"

"I don't want them," I said abruptly. "What are you doing here?"

"I owe you an apology." Minh looked over to the children. "Can they go watch television or something? We need to talk."

The children looked at us nervously.

"Go watch television for a little bit," I told them. They got up and walked to the living room.

"Look, I know I messed up. I'm sorry," Minh said.

"I don't know, Minh. We've been through this before, and you keep going back to gambling. This time you really put us through hell, and I'm done." I couldn't believe how strong my voice sounded. I had never talked like that before.

"I wanted to own a restaurant so badly, I messed up. It won't happen again, I promise. I learned my lesson."

"What's happened with the house?" I asked.

"I had to sell it. I sold your car too. I'm sorry. I sold everything to come here."

"I loved that house," I mumbled.

"I have four thousand dollars with me from selling our stuff." Minh reached in his pocket and took out a stack of money. "Here, you keep it."

I took the money. God knew we needed it.

"What about the credit card debt?" I asked him.

"I filed bankruptcy," Minh said.

"You mean you don't have to pay them?"

"No. We're going to have bad credit for a long time, but we don't have to pay them back. My lawyer took care of it for us."

"Us? My credit will be bad too? I did nothing wrong. Why didn't you tell the lawyer you acted alone?" I said angrily.

"I did. He said that because both of our names were on the credit cards, we both will have bad credit."

"You have to clear my name," I told him.

"It's impossible. I'm sorry."

"I can't forgive you until my name is cleared."

"You're being unreasonable!" Minh raised his voice.

"Am I? You know what? Get out!"

"You took the money, then you kick me out?"

"It's my money too, and you know it." My blood was boiling! "Do you want it back? Here, take it and get out of my life!"

I threw the money back in his face. He dodged it, and the money flew into the wall, scattering all over the kitchen floor. He stared at me in shock. He couldn't believe what I had just done. I had changed from a dutiful wife to an independent, strong woman, and he hadn't been expecting that.

He didn't pick up the money. After a long pause, he walked to the living room to say bye to the children, and then he left.

I saw the looks on the children's faces—worried and terrified looks. They knew now their family was broken, and it broke my heart to see them like that. I couldn't hold back my angry tears. I wiped them quickly because I didn't want the kids to see. I kneeled down to pick up the money from the kitchen floor and got ready to cook dinner. "We will get through this," I told myself, "and the children will be all right."

I used some of the money to find myself a lawyer for the divorce. A few weeks later, Ma called to tell me Minh got a job at a Vietnamese restaurant downtown. I asked her when he would be moving out, and she said he didn't have to. She was happy to let him stay there, because he paid his part of the rent. I was annoyed. Why did Ma have to be so friendly with him?

Minh had a different day off from mine, so we took turns taking care of the kids. The children seemed happy spending time with their dad. Hopefully we could all move on.

Then came winter. Bitterly cold, with the wind cutting through your skin. I agreed to let Minh drive the children to school because I still didn't have a car. One wet, snowy day, I waited at the bus stop for a long time, and the bus didn't come. All of a sudden, Minh's car appeared right in front of me. He rolled down the window.

"Get in. I'll give you a ride to the PATH station," he said.

"It's OK. The bus will be here in minutes," I said.

"It won't be running on schedule today. Come on, get in."

I hesitated. I really didn't want to get in that car, but it was snowing heavily, and I was already late for work. I opened the car door and got in.

We stayed quiet for a while, then he started a conversation.

"I work downtown, not too far from the PATH station. I can give you a ride there every morning after dropping off the children."

"It's OK, I manage," I said.

"Why don't you buy a car with that money I gave you?"

"I work in the city. I don't need a car."

"Then let me give you a ride, especially in the bad weather."

I said nothing, neither agreeing nor disagreeing. Of course it was easier with the ride when the weather was bad, but I felt awkward. Somehow Minh always showed up for the bad weather and even when the weather wasn't bad. I resisted at first, but then I just accepted the ride because it was easier.

One day Minh told me about his opportunity to become the boss. Apparently the owner of Miss Saigon Restaurant was tired of running the place. He wanted Minh to take over. I was surprised because Minh had worked there only about six months.

"This is my dream, Lien. And my parents will help me financially, but they want to talk to you." Minh was excited about it.

"Why me?"

"They want you to be my business partner. They trust you."

"But I don't want to be your partner," I protested.

"You don't have to do anything, just say OK, so they send money for me to take over the restaurant."

"Do they know about our situation?"

"No, I didn't tell them. It would break their hearts if they found out," Minh said.

"I don't want any part of it, Minh. I already filed for divorce."

"You did?" he asked in a panic.

"Yes! I told you I want to move on."

"Lien! Please cancel it. I gambled because I wanted to have the money to open a restaurant. Now this is my chance to have one. I would never ever gamble again. Besides, running a restaurant will take up all my time. You'll see."

I said nothing, still thinking about the news. Would he actually quit gambling for good now that he had this opportunity? Should I trust him again? I remembered the look on my children's faces when they found out their parents were going to split up. I felt torn, not knowing what to do.

"You don't have to work anymore," Minh continued. "You can be the boss with me, but I'll do all the work. You can stay home with the kids if you like."

"I have to think about it," I said finally.

"OK. They'll call again next week. Please forgive me for my mistakes. I swear it won't happen again, I swear to you."

Minh begged for forgiveness again and again, and in the end I gave in. I talked to his parents about the restaurant for him. They sent the money, and Minh became the new boss. He turned a slow, empty restaurant around. Minh was a good chef, and soon enough the restaurant got busy with Vietnamese and American customers. He worked seven days a week, but he liked it, and I was happy for him.

When Minh was served the divorce papers, he was upset. He neglected the new restaurant, leaving the work to his employees, and followed me everywhere, begging me to take him back. He said he was a new man now, with a new business, and he could take care of me. He bought me gifts— a gold necklace and a Movado watch. It touched me; I thought he really loved me, especially when he had almost lost me for good.

I told him I wanted to start beauty school, and he said he supported me. So I took him back and canceled the divorce. The children were so happy when we announced that their dad was moving back in.

We were a family of four again, but my heart wasn't full of happiness. Like the old and wise saying, you can try to mend a broken heart, but the scar will always be there. I gave up my job to be a stay-at-home mom for the first time. I attended beauty school in the mornings, while the children were in school. I studied hard. I wanted to learn everything about hair so I could be a good hairdresser and maybe open a salon one day. That was my dream. Minh had his, and I had mine.

Chapter 25
1996

Finally, I got the letter for my citizenship test, and I was so excited. I took out my American history book and studied it again. This was such an important test for me. I was half-American, so technically there was American blood in me, and I couldn't wait to become an American officially. True, I didn't know who my father was, but since I was a little girl I had always been longing to come here. I wanted to learn about this country that I felt so much connection with.

I was also happy because finally I could correct my name. People outside of the family called me Mỹ, but that was my middle name. My first name was Lien. It got mixed up during the immigration process. I was thinking about what my new name would be. Definitely not Mỹ; it was already confusing. I wanted an American name just to fit in. Something close to my old first name. I thought of a whole bunch of names, including Lily and Lynn, but ended up not liking any of them. In the end I chose to add an A in front of Mỹ and was happy with the sound of it. Amy Lien was going to be my new name when I became an American citizen, and I couldn't wait for that day to come.

It was bad enough that I didn't know my real birthday because my mother couldn't get a birth certificate for me until a year later. She simply forgot the date. Could you imagine what it's like not to know your real birthday? Imagine when someone threw you a birthday party and in your head you knew it wasn't yours. I had been a sad little girl because of my unsure identity, but I was a mom now. I knew there were more important things in life. I wasn't sad about that anymore, and hey, I got a year younger on paper.

I did well on the test, passing it with ease, and was so proud of myself. I held the certificate of citizenship with my new name on it and felt very much American in my heart. I was proud to be part of this country. I felt this was where I belonged; this was my country, my home.

I believed hard work would pay off and taught my children that as well. My children were the most important thing to me. I loved them with all my heart, but I was a strict mom. Like one of those tiger moms from Asia, pushing the children to be their best. Toan's and Thao's report cards were excellent. I was the one who disciplined them and gave them more homework to do on the weekends. I made them read more in their free time and limited game and television time. If they did badly in school, I would take away their favorite toys or games for weeks. I wasn't proud of what I did, but I was a young mother and didn't really know the new culture yet. So I used the old one on them. I admit raising kids using Vietnamese culture in America wasn't easy. I just tried the best I could and hoped they would become nice, kind, and educated people when they grew up.

I also got A's on every test in beauty school because I studied every day. I became the best student and ended up graduating as valedictorian at the end of 1996. It was just a beauty school, but I was so proud of myself. My sister Chi went to my graduation instead of Minh. He was busy with the restaurant, and I preferred having my sister with me anyway.

"Wow! I can't believe you're valedictorian. Good for you," Chi said. She didn't give out compliments easily, so it meant a lot to me. We hugged; it made up for the old times. Chi and I got along so well now. We had been like oil and water when we were young, but ever since I moved to New Jersey our relationship had changed. I had gotten my sister back. My niece came upstairs to my apartment every day to play with my children, and I loved her. Chi and I were carpooling and took turns watching the children. I didn't see her as my landlord; she was my sister, and I was happy to stay in her house.

***

I got a job at Mara salon on Westside Avenue. I picked this one simply because it was two blocks from where we lived, and it was near the children's school. I thought it was convenient so I could run to the school when they needed me. It was a very small salon, only three hairstylists: Maria, Sonia, and me. Maria, who was also the manager, hired me on the spot even though she knew I was brand new. She saw the issue date on my license. I would get paid by commission and was happy about it. Later on I learned I was the only licensed hairdresser there. Apparently Maria had bought the hair salon from the previous owner and rented the cosmetology license from someone else.

Maria and Sonia were nice to me, but the problem was most of the customers there were Spanish, and a lot of them didn't speak English. They didn't give me a chance to touch their hair; they wanted only Maria or Sonia. Occasionally I got customers who weren't Spanish but Filipino and sometimes Caucasian. I didn't see any Vietnamese customers when I worked there. I lasted only six months because my paychecks were too small for me to stay.

During that time Minh caught a waitress stealing money from the register, and he fired her. He wanted me to step in and be the waitress at the restaurant so other waiters and waitresses wouldn't do anything to hurt his restaurant. I helped him for a short time but found out it was hard for us to work together. We had different opinions on how to run the place. In the end we both agreed on hiring my brother Be to be a waiter instead of me. Be was a senior in high school—a little young, but he was eager to work. I trained him; he was a fast learner, and soon enough he became a good waiter just like everyone else. We both trusted Be, as he had proven to us he was indeed good at his job.

I went on job hunting and found a cute upscale salon in Hoboken named Rovile. It was small, but everything in Hoboken was miniature. The salon had only four chairs, but the design was very modern, and the staff looked very stylish. I didn't think I would get a job there, but to my surprise they hired me.

This salon was very different from the other salon I had worked for. It opened short hours, 1:00 to 9:00 p.m., and was closed on Sundays. The owner, Vivian, ran it well. She was calm and very easy to talk to. She made sure we always had red and white wine to offer customers as soon as they sat down. The music was carefully chosen, and it really helped people to relax. It was a perfect match for Hoboken.

Vivian taught me everything from basic details to more advanced techniques. She sent me to all classes that were available, like coloring, cutting, and styling, to improve my skills. She gave me new customers to work on, and she did it so professionally that none of them were aware I was new at it. She watched me handle the customers without interfering, then whispered to me later, "Next time this is what you should do."

The other two hairstylists, Stan and Alissa, were also incredibly friendly to me. Stan was a great colorist and was really nice when I came to him for help with colors. Alissa's cutting technique was way above my knowledge. I watched her all the time when I was free and hoped one day I could get to her level. I learned a lot from that place and was very happy to be part of such a great team. I began dressing more professionally and invested in my appearance, so I could feel confident enough to work there.

I sat Minh down one day and finally told him I wanted us to have separate bank accounts. We would share the bills for the apartment, but I didn't want any part of his restaurant. His parents sent him the money for it, and it was always his, not mine. I made decent money at my job. Honestly, after we lost our house to his gambling I didn't want to keep our money together anymore.

We became a modern American couple. He kept his money, and I kept mine. God forbid he ever got into trouble with money again; at least I had money to take care of the children. Here and there he would say he wished I would quit my job and help him at the restaurant, but it sounded like he was doing well, and I was very happy for him.

Chapter 26
1998

Vivian called me one morning and asked if I could come to work an hour earlier, at noon. She said it was for an important meeting. She needed to talk to us. We'd never had a meeting before because the staff was so small. If she needed to talk to us, she would tell us right there in the back room. Vivian said she didn't like to be a slave to money, and that was why our salon was a unique one. We were lucky to have a boss like her. Nothing made her upset.

I walked into the salon after Vivian unlocked the door. It was strange not hearing any music. Music was Vivian's air. Everybody knew that.

"Hi, Amy, how are the children?" Vivian always asked about my children, but this time her voice seemed different.

"They're good, thank you. Is everyone here?"

"Stan and Alissa are on their way."

"Do you need me to do anything?" I asked.

"No, it's going to be a brief meeting."

Alissa walked in, so stylish in her nice outfit. She took off her sunglasses and kissed us on the cheeks—she liked to do both cheeks, European style—then sat down on her chair to fix her hair.

Stan came in next. "Sorry, ladies, I shouldn't be the last one to arrive, but I couldn't find a parking space. I had to park so far away," he said.

"No problem, Stan. Have a seat," Vivian said.

"So what is the meeting about?" Stan asked casually.

"Well, I have some news." Vivian choked up, continuing after she cleared her throat. "Did I tell you my partner and I own this salon together?"

"Yes, you did tell me that when I just started," Alissa said. Stan nodded his head in agreement. I was the only one who hadn't known.

"Well, Rossana and I are no longer together, and she wants to put the salon on the market," Vivian said sadly.

We all looked at each other in shock.

"She can't do that! The salon is yours," Stan said.

"I own only half of it, and she isn't interested in keeping it going." Vivian sounded miffed.

"Why don't you buy her out?" Alissa asked.

"I don't have enough money. She wants market value for it, and properties in Hoboken have gone up tremendously."

"That's just not right. You're the one doing all the work, and she wants to take half of it and walk out without thinking about you or us," Stan said.

Nobody said anything. We all agreed with Stan. I'd met Rossana only twice in the two years I'd worked at Rovile.

"What will happen to us if someone else buys the salon?" Alissa asked.

"I will try to find a new owner who would accept you guys as a package deal, so you could all stay," Vivian said.

"What about you? Are you going to stay too?" I asked Vivian.

"I'm not sure. I'm still trying to figure it out."

We were all sad and nervous from that day forward. Who was going to be the new owner? Would she or he be nice like Vivian? Stan even said something optimistic, like he would try his best to find the money to buy Rossana out. We all hoped he could, but in the end he didn't.

For the next couple of months, buyers came and went. They checked the salon out carefully, even when we had customers. It just felt weird every time they stared at us like we were objects that belonged to the salon.

Alissa pulled me to the side one day and asked me if I could be her model. She had found a job in another salon nearby, and they asked her to perform a haircut.

"Sure," I said. "As long as it's not too short."

"Don't worry, it's just a basic shoulder-length haircut, and I'll return the favor when you need a model for an interview."

"Seriously? You trust me with your hair?" I was surprised to hear that.

"Amy! You're a good hairdresser, and I completely trust you with my hair."

"Oh, Alissa, thank you." We hugged, and I almost cried.

"Don't tell anyone about my interview," she told me. "I don't want to hurt Vivian's feelings, but I have to have a backup plan."

"I won't," I promised her.

Alissa picked me up from my apartment on the way to Hoboken for her interview, before our workday started. The new salon had an upscale look but more edgy, and like Rovile, it was small. Her interview went well. The owner, who was bald with a bleached blond goatee, liked the haircut she gave me. Apparently one chair had just opened up in his salon because one of his hairstylists moved out of town. I knew it wasn't easy to find a hairdresser job in Hoboken. Alissa was lucky this time, just like I had been two years before. I wasn't so sure about this time around for myself.

Three months after Rovile was put on the market, Vivian announced to us that the salon had been sold to a new owner who had her own staff, and she wouldn't be needing any of us. We had thirty days to tell our clientele about it. I had been looking for a job in every salon in Hoboken, but I couldn't find anything available. All of a sudden, I was out of work again. Hoboken had no place for me.

***

After a few months of actively looking, I found a job at Newport Mall in Jersey City. It was a big salon, with about twenty hairstylists, and it was a busy place. Newport was an up-and-coming neighborhood. It had a view of New York City across the Hudson River, and a lot of New Yorkers relocated to Newport. Restaurants and businesses were starting to open up in this area more and more. The mall was packed on weekends, and so was our salon.

I blended into the new environment and worked hard, determined to keep this job. Soon enough I started to have repeat clients who requested me. My weekends were booked up quickly. The manager was happy, and so was I.

While I was focusing on my new job, Minh was acting

suspiciously. He used to come home right after the restaurant closed, but lately he had been sneaking in after the children and I were already in bed.

"Why are you home so late?" I asked him one time.

"Plumbing problems at work."

"Again? Didn't you get it fixed last week?"

"I'm tired. Can I just go to sleep?" he said crankily.

We never had a chance to talk about it after that. He worked seven days a week, coming home late a lot. Then one day while I was cleaning, I found unpaid bills in his nightstand. It wasn't a good sign.

I called the restaurant, but he wasn't there. My brother Be had no idea where Minh was. I thought maybe he had gone to get supplies for the restaurant. I asked Be to tell him to call me back. I waited all day, but Minh didn't call.

That night I waited for him. He came home a little after one o'clock.

"Where have you been? The restaurant closed at eleven," I said to him.

"I went to shoot some pool with a friend, no big deal," he said.

"Really? No big deal? You neglect your family. Your children aren't a big deal to you?"

"Even if I came home at eleven, they would be in bed anyway. Sometimes I just need to hang out with friends to relax. You know, running a restaurant is very stressful."

Maybe he was right.

"Did Be tell you to call me?" I asked him.

"He did. I forgot, sorry. What was it about?"

"I found the overdue electric bill, gas bill, and phone bill in your drawer. Why don't you pay them? They can cut off the services at the restaurant, and it would be bad for business. Have you thought of that?"

"I will pay them. I'm just a little busy, that's all."

Why couldn't he be more organized? He always wanted to be the boss, the business owner, but never seemed to get it together. I let it go. He wasn't a child, and I couldn't always worry about him.

A few days later, when I was shopping in the supermarket, a Vietnamese woman I had met only once at the restaurant stopped me abruptly.

"Hi. You're Minh's wife, aren't you?" she said.

"Yes." I recognized her but forgot her name.

"How is the restaurant?" she asked.

"Good," I said politely, trying to remember her name, but I was still drawing a blank.

"Interesting. Your husband borrowed five thousand dollars from my husband, saying he would pay us back in two weeks. It's been over two months now, and every time we call he's not there."

I could feel the heat on my cheeks. It was so embarrassing and upsetting at the same time.

"When do you think you can pay us back the money?" she asked.

"Excuse me, I don't know you, and you don't know me. I know nothing about the loan. Why don't you ask Minh? He was the one who borrowed from you, not me. How dare you embarrass me in public?" I was so upset.

I left the food in the cart and walked out of the store as quickly as I could. How could he do this to me? I drove home crying from humiliation. I had never felt so embarrassed in my life. I had tried to forgive him and forget about the past, but again he made me remember all the bad things he had done back in Vietnam and Oklahoma City.

I was still angry by the time I got home. My son was playing a video game when I got in the house, and I asked the children if they'd finished their homework. Thao had, but Toan had not. I yelled at him, yanking his Nintendo out of the cabinet and throwing it out the window. It broke into pieces. Toan was terrified.

I regretted it later, of course. I shouldn't have done that to my nine-year-old son. I was so stressed out about their father, I snapped and lost my self-control. I should have calmed down first. I was their mother, the one who was supposed to love and protect them, not scare them.

As soon as he got home, I confronted Minh about the

loan. He admitted borrowing five thousand dollars from the couple to pay bills for the restaurant. He said the business was slow in the winter, and he was behind on paying the bills. I understood winter was tough on every business, and that was why he should have saved every penny when business was good. Why did he have to go out after work for drinks or to play pool?

I didn't understand why that couple had lent Minh the money. What was in it for them? I wouldn't lend five thousand dollars to someone who's not a family member. Somehow he knew how to sweet talk people into trusting him. The restaurant, the loans—he had often borrowed money from people in the past, but I didn't understand that at all. It seemed Minh always had secrets, and that bothered me. I was tired of his secrets.

***

Chi told me she had overheard someone saying they had seen Minh gambling in Atlantic City. I was stunned. Hadn't he learned anything from the past? How could he go back down that road again? Who was managing the restaurant for him while he was in Atlantic City? I decided to go to the restaurant to ask him about it. I wanted to see if it was true.

Minh wasn't at the restaurant.

Nobody knew where he was. His employees told me he had opened the restaurant and then left. They weren't sure when he would be back. I decided to wait for him. The restaurant was empty, only a few customers. It was lunch hour; it should have been really busy. I waited for a couple of hours, but he didn't return. If he'd gone to get supplies, he should have been back by then. Where the hell was Minh? Was he neglecting his restaurant to go gambling in Atlantic City? I couldn't forgive him this time if he indeed was gambling again.

I asked Minh about it that night. He swore it wasn't him in Atlantic City. He said he was running errands when I came to the restaurant, and he was stuck in traffic. He told me I was paranoid and listened to the wrong people saying bad things about him.

A couple of days later, while I was cleaning up after dinner, the phone rang. I almost didn't want to pick it up, but I did, and as soon as I heard the voice, I froze. It was my stepfather. He had never called before—ever.

"Hello, hello," he yelled.

"Yes, I'm listening. Is Ma OK?" I thought it was an emergency.

"She's fine. I called to tell you your husband borrowed money from me months ago, and I want it back. Tell him I want my money back immediately." He hung up.

Minh had borrowed money from my stepfather? Minh knew my stepfather and I didn't get along, and he did it anyway? Why did Minh keep borrowing from people? I had told him many times not to. It bothered me that he didn't talk to me about it first. He did it secretly. Why?

I called Be to ask him if he knew anything about Minh's gambling situation. Be said he didn't know anything about it. And if he knew, he couldn't tell me. Minh was his boss, after all. I called my sisters to see if they knew. No one seemed to know anything.

Resigned, I went back to my chores. I sat down to go through the mail I hadn't had time to look through earlier, and there it was. An invitation from a casino in Atlantic City with Minh's name on it. They wanted him to come back soon. My biggest fear had come true: Minh was indeed gambling again.

I cried alone in the kitchen, not wanting to confront Minh anymore. It had been foolish of me to believe he would change. He had lied to me again, and I couldn't take it anymore. I wanted to be free from this toxic marriage and the embarrassment he repeatedly put me through. He might not care about his reputation, but I cared about mine. I couldn't let him drag me down into a deeper hole, so I had to be strong and put a stop to the disaster I saw coming.

I told him that night I would file for divorce as soon as the sun rose. We were shouting at each other so loudly, we woke up the children. Toan and Thao appeared, staring at us like they knew something really bad was happening. We stopped fighting when we realized the children were scared. I told Toan to go back to bed and took Thao back to her bedroom. I cuddled with my daughter in her tiny bed, and she went back to sleep after a while. I couldn't sleep at all; I was too worried about my son. I wanted to go to Toan's room to check on him, but his father was in the living room. I was afraid we might start arguing again, because it was still raw, and I was still upset.

Minh slept on the sofa after that, and we argued almost every day. It wasn't fair for our children. They deserved good parenting, so they could have a normal childhood. I couldn't be a good mother if I was still married to Minh. I was bitter and easily upset.

I finally refused to talk to him, because every time we talked, it would end up in an argument. I filed for divorce and asked Minh to move out, but he didn't make an effort to do so.

A few weeks later, while I was home on my day off, the phone rang. I picked up, and there was a man's voice asking if this was Minh's phone number. I hung up on him, since he refused to tell me who he was. My heart was pumping fast; I was so scared. Who was this guy? A loan shark? I didn't pick up the phone again for days.

I bought a newspaper to try to find a new apartment. Minh had no intention to move out, so I had to. I had to keep my children safe. God forbid a loan shark would come looking for Minh at our apartment. I was on the phone with a possible new landlord when Minh walked in.

"Are you really moving out?" he asked after I hung up the phone.

"You think I'm joking?" I snapped at him.

"Where to?"

"I don't know yet. Wherever I can afford."

"You don't have to move. I'll move."

"When?"

"When do you want me to?"

"As soon as possible. If you don't move out by next month, I will!"

"All right!"

I was counting the days until the end of the month. I came home from work a week later, and his stuff was gone. I felt so relieved. I knew it wasn't over between us, but at least the arguments would no longer be in front of the kids. I looked forward to again being a good mother to my children. I wanted to have a calm environment in my home, no anxiety or stress, so I could be myself again.

I learned later that Minh had moved into my parents' house. I was a little annoyed about it. What was he doing living in my parents' home? At least this time Ma didn't tell me to give him another chance. She didn't interfere at all. I guess she finally understood.

Chapter 27
1999

Life was hard as a single mother, but I tried my best to move on. The separation was hard on my children as well. Toan didn't want to talk about it, but his report card showed he was struggling during that time. Thao cried a lot, but thank goodness she was still an excellent student.

I asked Minh to pick the children up from school every day and drop them at Chi's. I thought it was good; that way the children could spend some time alone with their father.

Minh and I weren't on good terms. Every time he saw me, he would beg me to take him back, beg me to forgive him, but I was done. I told him I didn't want to be with him anymore. Then he would get upset, and we would end up arguing. He said I must have been seeing someone else, that I probably had an affair, which wasn't true. What made me upset the most was that he questioned the children about it. "Did you ever see Mom with a man? Did any man call her at the house?" It confused my children, and I hated him for that. It was hard enough for them to see their parents separated; why would he hurt them even more?

I stopped talking to Minh and hung up the phone on him when he called. When he came to pick up the children, I stayed upstairs and looked down through the window. I avoided him as much as I could.

I was at work one day, and I saw Minh right outside of the salon. He just stood there watching me, and it made me very uncomfortable. After a while I went outside and told him to leave.

"I can't work if you're watching me like that. You have to leave, or I'll call security," I said quietly.

"I want to know who your boyfriend is," Minh said.

"I don't have a boyfriend." I was annoyed by his accusation.

"If you do, I will take custody of the kids."

"You have to leave. Now!" I couldn't take it anymore.

He didn't move, so I went back inside looking for my

manager. By the time I found her, my soon to be ex was gone.

My manager, Shona, wanted to know the whole story, so I told her as much as I thought she needed to know. Minh showed up again at my job, and this time Shona called security on him. She called me later that night at home to see if I was OK. I thought that was very nice of her.

I thought Minh finally got the message and would leave me alone, but I saw him again following me to and from work. I didn't know what else to do. Shona advised me to get a restraining order against him, so I went to court and applied for one. After waiting for a while, they sent me a letter for a hearing.

"Did your husband ever hit you or your children?" the judge asked.

"No, Your Honor, he did not, but he keeps following me to and from work."

"Did he disturb you at work?"

"He just sat there watching me from the outside," I answered honestly.

"Does he still do that?"

"No, Your Honor, he stopped after my boss called security."

"Does he still see the children?" The judge looked at me.

"Yes, Your Honor, he picks them up from school every day."

"Mrs. Luong, I don't think your husband is dangerous; otherwise you wouldn't let him pick up the children every day, right? People go through divorce all the time, and it's best if you both be kind to each other for the children's sake."

I was going to tell her more, but the judge ended our conversation.

"The restraining order you requested is denied." She pounded her gavel, and it was over. I walked out of the courthouse feeling lost and disappointed.

One day I found a caller ID device hidden behind my nightstand. Minh must have secretly installed it. I felt violated.

Who gave him the right to watch my every move like that? I had to watch over my shoulder all the time when I was driving or walking to the stores. Now he wanted to know who I was talking to? He was stalking me repeatedly. I disconnected the caller ID and called Shona.

"How did he get into the house?" Shona asked.

"He still has a key. I asked him to return it, but he never did," I said in frustration.

"Amy, you need to change the lock. I can't believe you haven't done it yet."

"You're right. I will," I said.

"Get it done today. You're working tomorrow, and you don't want to wait till next week."

"Thanks, Shona. I'm looking in the yellow pages for a locksmith right now. I'll see you tomorrow."

"Bye, Amy."

I had the locks changed that day and felt safer. He wouldn't be able to come in and disturb me anymore, or so I thought.

Barely a week later, I was home with the children, and Minh banged on the door. I realized then that he still had the key for the main front door, and now he was upstairs banging on the door of our apartment.

"Open the door!" He sounded drunk.

"What are you doing here? You don't live here anymore," I yelled back at him.

"I want to see my children!" He was yelling and pounding on the door.

"Not when you are like this."

"Like what? I should be calm when you're going out with another man?" Minh was out of control.

"There is no other man. Are you out of your mind?" I yelled.

"So why didn't you forgive me like you did before?"

"No! Been there, done that. It didn't work. I'm done."

"You're not done with me! You hear me?" Minh yelled. "Open the damn door, or I'm going to break it."

"No!" I said.

Minh pounded the door with something heavy. What if he broke it down and came inside? Would he do anything to harm the kids? I didn't think so, but he was angry at me; he might do something to hurt me. Just then I thought of my old friend Vi from Oklahoma. Her husband had shot her out of jealousy. Minh sounded very jealous right now. I had to do something. I picked up the phone and dialed 911.

I gathered the children into my bedroom and locked the door. I was running back and forth to the window, praying for the police to come before Minh got in. Suddenly I heard the door bang into the wall, and I jumped. He was inside now. What should I do? Then I saw a police car stop right in front. I called my sister downstairs to let the cops in. Thank God they arrived just in time. Minh was arrested. The children cried when they saw their father being handcuffed by a policeman. The police asked me to tell them what had happened, so I told them everything.

"Do you want to press charges, ma'am?" one of the policemen asked me.

I looked at the badly damaged door and said, "Yes, I do."

After they took Minh away, I sat down and hugged my children. We were still shaken by the incident. When had Minh become so violent? I felt bad for our children; this image would stay with them for a long time. Chi came upstairs finally and wasn't happy when she saw the broken door.

"Wow! Look at the door. My husband is going to be mad."

"I'm sorry. I'll pay for it," I said.

"I wanted to come up earlier, but I was worried for my daughter's safety." Chi paused. "I'm glad you and the kids are all right."

I cried. It was still too raw to talk about. Chi stayed for a little while, saying she would ask her husband to change the lock, and hopefully that would keep Minh away.

The court finally gave me the restraining order. Minh wasn't allowed to be near me anymore. I felt a little safer but not necessarily better. I would rather have a friendly relationship with Minh, but he just wasn't cooperative. I hoped he would obey the law and leave me alone from then on.

Chapter 28
2000

There was a lot of talk about the year 2000. People said all the computers would shut down, and we would have a blackout for a long time, if not forever. There would be shortages of food and supplies. Money in the bank would be gone, since it would be erased by computers. People talked about all kinds of crazy things that would happen, including the end of the world.

Ma and I went out and bought a lot of rice and canned food, just to be safe. We stocked up bottled water and candles in case we had no power. My whole family was panicked about this. Chi stocked her supplies down in the basement until it was half full.

New Year's Day came and went quietly; nothing happened. There was no blackout, all the computers worked normally, and money was still in the bank. Chi and I looked at each other and laughed. It was funny. We really believed it would happen! Chi's supplies would last her at least half of the year, if not more.

My sister Lieu lived in the suburbs, about a forty-minute drive from Jersey City. Her house was big and beautiful, in a nice neighborhood with good schools for her two children. Lieu used to be so shy and cried easily when she was little, but she was a strong woman now. She was a successful business owner, and I was so proud of her.

Lieu hosted a lot of holiday gatherings for our family, which my stepfather rarely went to. We always had a good time at Lieu's, everyone together under one roof. We laughed at good jokes and cried at old memories. Sometimes I looked at my siblings and felt we were incredibly lucky. Despite our difficult childhood, we all turned out OK. Everyone was normal; no one had a drinking problem or depression.

Vu was always joking around, making people laugh. We all said he should be a stand-up comedian instead of a carpenter. Chi, Truc, Mai, Lieu, and Trang were all doing well. They all married and had children. The family continued to grow larger over the years. My youngest brother, Be—I should call him his real name, Nha, by now—still lived with our parents, and he took on the role of caretaker.

I missed my sister Anh most on those holidays. She was still stuck in Vietnam, divorced and alone. She had a really hard life there. Her husband had forced her to sell the house Ma had left for her. He cheated on her and physically abused her, and they ended up divorcing. Anh got custody of her two sons, and they lived in a small studio apartment in Saigon. She worked two jobs and still didn't make enough to provide for her family. My other siblings and I took turns helping her, sending money here and there.

Ma tried to sponsor Anh and her two sons to come over to America, and it had been more than ten years of waiting without success. We were still hoping Anh and her sons would be there with us one day. That's all we could do: hope and pray.

***

By the springtime I got a hearing letter to finalize my divorce. 'It couldn't be better timing,' I thought. A fresh start for the new millennium.

I went to court expecting a fierce fight from Minh, but he didn't show. With all of the harassment and threats, spending all his parents' money to take custody of the kids, why didn't he show up in court? This was one of his games, wanting to prolong the process. I was nervous, thinking the judge would postpone the hearing, but to my surprise she proceeded. She granted me the divorce with full custody of my children. I walked out of the court feeling light as a feather, a ton of weight lifted off my shoulders. I was a free woman finally.

A couple of weeks later, I was about to drive the children to school as usual. When we got outside, my daughter pointed at the car.

"Mom, we have a flat tire."

"Oh no." I hoped Thao was joking, but she wasn't. I squatted down and looked at the tire. A huge nail was embedded in it. Had I driven through a construction site? I didn't think so. If I had driven over a nail the previous night, I would have known right away.

"Looks like we have to walk to school, guys," I told the children.

"Oh man," Toan complained.

"Remember the time when we used to walk to school every day? We had a lot of fun."

"Not really," he said.

The children and I half walked, half ran to school. They were late for class, of course, but at least the school still let them in. I called my boss when I got back home to say I would come in as soon as the tire was fixed. She wasn't happy about having to go in early and open the store. She grunted on the phone.

While I was waiting for AAA to come, the phone rang. "Hello," I answered, expecting the AAA guy on the other end.

"Hi, it's me." It was Minh's voice.

"What do you want?" I asked crankily, because he had really caught me on a bad day.

"I'm just wondering if you need help with the tire," Minh said.

"What?" I was stunned. "How do you know I have a flat tire?"

He didn't answer me.

"You put a nail in my tire, didn't you?"

Silence.

"You are such a jerk!" I said.

Minh hung up the phone abruptly. I was so upset. Our divorce was finalized, and he still wouldn't leave me alone. How could he go poke my tire and expect me to let him fix it? What was he hoping to get out of it? Reconciliation? He was out of his mind. What else could I say to him to get him to accept that our marriage was over? It had been over a long time ago. Maybe I should get myself a boyfriend, I thought, so he would see I had moved on.

I'd been asked out for dates before, a couple of times. They were all nice guys, but I kept saying no. I didn't have any luck with men in my life. I didn't have a real father, my stepfather physically abused me, and my ex-husband was a gambler. I had a trust issue with men.

I finally went on a first date with a guy who happened to be a client. He was always kind of flirting with me every time he came in for a haircut. Then one day he asked me out to dinner, and I said yes.

We went to a restaurant nearby. The meal and the date were nothing memorable. In the end he offered to give me a ride to the parking lot, so I could pick up my car. I took the offer, since it would be faster than walking, and my children were waiting for me. I thanked him for the meal when he stopped his car, and he leaned in, expecting a good night kiss. I was still debating if I should or shouldn't when out of nowhere, I heard someone yelling in the distance. It was Minh, yelling and running toward us.

"Go!" I told my date.

"Who is that guy?"

"My ex-husband," I told him, and I got out of his car.

My date's face suddenly turned cold, and he sped out of the parking lot with screeching tires. I ran to my car with Minh chasing after me. I felt so scared. What was he doing following me around? We were divorced! Did he want to hurt me?

"You're supposed to be home with the children, but you went out, having fun like a teenager," he was yelling behind me.

"The children are with my sister, and you are violating the restraining order," I yelled back. "You're not supposed to be near me."

"You promised me you're not going to have a boyfriend!" he said angrily.

"I did not promise you anything!"

I jumped in my car and drove in disbelief about what had just happened. I was shaking with fear. He wouldn't leave me alone, even with a restraining order. I had to report this to the police, but where were the police when I needed them?

Besides the embarrassment Minh put me through, I was afraid he might do unthinkable things to me. I was scared for my life and my children's lives. You think you know someone—until you don't.

"I have to move out of here," I told myself.

I called my best friend, Lan, for advice. Lan was my childhood friend from Vietnam; she lived in California now, along with her sister, Diep. Lan told me to move closer to her, saying she would help me. What a great idea! I would love to move to California.

I made a plan, hoping we could move as soon as the children finished their school year. I went to the Child Support Department, asking them to send future checks to San Jose, California. That was when they told me I wasn't allowed to take the children out of New Jersey. That would be kidnapping, they told me. Unbelievable! I was so disappointed that my plan didn't work out.

My sister Lieu suggested I move to her town. It was far enough away that it might help to stop Minh from harassing me. I was allowed to move anywhere in New Jersey as long as I didn't take the children across the state line. She said they had a good school system there, and it would be perfect for my children.

Lieu offered to let us to move in with her until we felt safe to be on our own. After thinking it through, I accepted her offer. I had to try something. Maybe moving a little farther away from Jersey City would help, and thankfully it did. Minh stopped harassing me after we moved. We lived with Lieu's family for six months and later on got a place of our own.

I loved our area in the suburbs. It was green and so quiet, totally the opposite of all the cities I had lived in. Finally my life had calmed down. I still worked hard, but I slept better. I enjoyed the fresh air in my backyard and watched my children grow. Thank God they too turned out OK. I was so blessed to have them in my life. They gave me strength and courage; without them I'm not sure I could have become a strong, independent woman.

Slowly I learned to forgive and forget. I forgave my stepfather and forgot the darkness of the past. I let all the negatives go and focused on the positives, and it helped to heal me. I stopped having nightmares. I enjoyed the quiet ordinary life there in the quiet little town. I was content and happy—finally.

Chapter 29
2006

Maui, Hawaii

I woke up to birds singing right outside my window. I felt like they were singing to me. They didn't want me to miss the sunrise, especially on my wedding day. I had to take it all in, enjoy every moment of it. I opened the door, stepped out onto the balcony, and breathed in the fresh air. The sun was rising beautifully over the blue ocean; it was so gorgeous in Hawaii.

My fiancé, Don, had found this beautiful vacation beach house for rent online, and we had loved it at first sight. It had five bedrooms, a big living room, and a view of the ocean from every room. It also had a pool and a small secluded beach. It was perfect for our families.

"This is where I want to marry you," Don had said, pointing at the beach on his computer.

"It's so beautiful. Can we afford it?" I asked.

"Let's find out."

My fiancé was good with this stuff. He sat with me and searched online to find a wedding planner, and now there we were in this paradise, getting married. I couldn't believe it; I should have pinched myself.

We had met two years earlier, and right from the beginning we just clicked. It felt right. I felt safe with him. He was so good to my children, and I trusted him completely. We were both calm people, we liked to read and travel, and we both liked to cook. Don was a chemist, a very kind and smart man, and I was very lucky to find him. I was the one who actually asked him out on a date, and we had been together ever since.

"Good morning, Em." Don liked to call me Em—it means "sweetheart" in Vietnamese.

"Good morning, honey. Come here to enjoy the sunrise with me." I reached out for his hand and pulled him closer to me. "So, are you excited? Today is our big day."

"Of course I am, but do you know who's even more excited than us?"

"Who?"

"My parents. They told me last night that they love you, and they can't wait for you to become their daughter-in-law."

I admired Don's relationship with his parents. They were so close, even though his parents lived far away.

"Oh, they're so sweet. I love them too." I really admired his parents' love for each other. I was in awe whenever I saw them holding hands. "How long have they been married?"

"Forty-seven years, and I never heard them argue, not even once," Don said.

"Wow, you have good parents," I said.

"Yeah, they're great."

"I have to thank them later when I have a chance," I said.

"What for?"

"For giving me you. I love you."

"Anh yêu Em," Don said. It means "I love you" in Vietnamese.

He was wonderful like that, learning and accepting my culture. He pulled me into his arms. I leaned my head on his shoulder, and we just stood there watching the sunrise.

After breakfast and some laughs with my in-laws, my daughter and I went back to the master bedroom to get ready. I curled our hair, and she helped me to put on my gown. It was so nice of Thao to stay there with me, talking and chatting, so I wouldn't be alone. It was a perfect time for mother-daughter bonding and to express our love for each other.

The wedding planner, Kelly, came into the room and told Thao to go to the beach and put her flower lei on. Kelly put a flower lei on my head, and she showed me how to walk and what to do for the ceremony.

"When Pastor Vince asks you to put the flower lei on Don, you put it on slowly, half hanging in the front and half in the back. Do not put it on like a necklace, like most tourists do."

"Got it. Half front, half back."

"It's time. Everybody is at the beach now. Pastor Vince is ready. Are you ready?"

"Yes! I am."

"I'm going there now to make sure everyone is ready. I will call you, then you'll take your walk. Don't forget to smile."

I walked down to the beach slowly, with a bouquet in my hands. Hawaiian music filled the air; it came from the huge conch shell Pastor Vince was playing—a nice surprise. Don was standing in a circle of purple flowers, waiting for me to join him. His parents stood nearby, with big smiles on their faces. Next to them were his brother's family. My two children, Toan and Thao stood next to my friends Jamie and Syida. Everyone had flower leis on; they looked beautiful. The scenery was gorgeous, the white sand beach next to the crystal-clear blue ocean. I couldn't have asked for a better place to get married.

The music stopped just as I entered the flower circle. Pastor Vince welcomed our guests with some Hawaiian greetings and started the ceremony with Hawaiian prayers. Pastor Vince told Don to put a flower lei on me as a symbol of love and honor. Then it was my turn to put a flower lei on Don while Pastor Vince said prayers and blessings in Hawaiian to us. It was beautiful and magical, with the ocean waves washing in gently.

The second ceremony was a Christian one. Pastor Vince said prayers, this time in English. He asked God to protect us and help us in the future. He told us how to value each other as we merged our two lives into one.

"Donald, do you take Amy to be your wife and promise to love and to protect her for better or for worse, as long as you both shall live?"

"I do," Don said while he put the ring on my finger.

Pastor Vince asked me the same thing as I put the ring onto Don's hand.

I looked into Don's beautiful blue eyes and said, "I do."

"Under the power of God, I pronounce you husband and wife. You can kiss the bride."

We kissed as our family clapped their hands. I looked

at my husband and was grateful for the love and support he gave me. I looked over to my two children, and they were smiling, genuinely happy for their mom.

My in-laws wiped their tears as they walked forward to us. I realized they had been crying during the ceremony. It touched me deeply, as they accepted my two children and me with open hearts. They congratulated us; we hugged and talked about how beautiful the ceremony was.

"Thank you, Mom and Dad, for being here. It means a lot to us," I said.

"We wouldn't miss it for the world. We're so happy for you," my father-in-law said.

Don's brother, Kevin, his wife, and his daughter walked up and hugged us.

"Congratulations!" they all said.

"Welcome to the family, Amy," Kevin said.

"Thank you," I said happily.

My friends Jamie and Syida embraced us, wishing us a happy future.

Last but not least, my two children joined us for a group hug as we started our new life together as a family.

"You look so pretty today, Thao," I said, since she had put an effort into looking nice for me today. Thao wasn't like other teenagers; she wasn't into makeup or dressing up. Her focus was school—that was it, nothing else.

"You look pretty too, Mom," Thao said, smiling.

"Congratulations, Mom," Toan said.

"Thank you, son, and thank you for taking the pictures."

"You're welcome." Toan raised his camera and clicked some more jokingly.

After Don and I cut the cake, we all hung out at the pool area eating and bonding. Both sides of the families got to know each other a little more. There was joking and laughing in the air while the breeze flowed through the palm trees. Everything turned out the way we had imagined it: a small, cozy wedding where the focus was family.

We went to the Old Lahaina luau for dinner. It was a

beautiful outdoor restaurant next to the ocean with a view of the sunset. The food was delicious, and the show was amazing. After dinner the host asked the newlyweds to go out to the dance floor. They played a beautiful Hawaiian song, and we danced our first dance there as husband and wife. I wished the song would last forever.

I wanted my whole family to be there, and they had all been invited, of course, but my siblings were married with children. Tickets to Hawaii plus a hotel was a lot of money for them. I understood. I offered to buy a ticket for Ma to come with us, but she didn't want to leave her handicapped husband behind. She had her responsibilities, and I understood that too. My family was happy for me from afar.

We stayed in Maui for ten sweet days on our "family-moon." My in-laws stayed only five; the last five days were just Don and I and the kids. We explored the island, seeing rainforests and waterfalls. Don and I relaxed on the beaches while the children snorkeled with colorful fishes. We all enjoyed the beach house and Hawaiian food. It was the best trip I'd ever had, and for me it was a happy ending.

Chapter 30
2016

Vietnam

My husband and I landed in Ho Chi Minh City—I still called it Saigon—after a long flight. I was excited and nervous at the same time. I had to take a deep breath to calm myself down. Having lived in Vietnam for the first twenty-three years of my life, there were a lot of good and bad memories there. I couldn't help the emotions stirring inside of me. I got even more nervous when we were in line for customs. Not that I had done anything wrong, but Vietnam was still a Communist country, and I had trust issues with them.

Ma had told me to put a fifty-dollar bill in my passport, so the Customs agent wouldn't give us a hard time. But I was an American now, and I refused to pay a bribe. My husband agreed with me, so we waited on line like everybody else. The line was long; it took more than two hours to get through. The Vietnamese official stared at me, then my husband. It was an intimidating game. I told myself not to worry, even though I was so nervous inside. After a few questions, he let us through. I felt relieved as soon as we got our luggage and moved forward to the exit door.

Ma was waiting for us outside. She'd gotten to Saigon a week before, and it was nice of her to pick us up at the airport. When Ma heard we were going to Vietnam with Thao, she immediately booked her ticket so she could spend some time with us. She was so excited about this trip. It was the first time three generations were traveling together in Vietnam. She couldn't wait to take us and my daughter to see our relatives. She wanted us to go straight there.

"Hi, Ma!"

"Where is Thao?" Ma asked.

"She's on her way. She'll be here in a few hours," I said.

"Why didn't she come with you?"

"Ma, she's a PhD student. She's very busy. She had to

fly here from her school, but don't worry—her boyfriend is with her. They'll be here soon."

"All right. We'll go to your cousin's later, then," Ma said, sounding disappointed.

I knew Ma wouldn't like the idea of my daughter traveling with her boyfriend like that. She was still old-fashioned and followed Vietnamese culture, like most older generations, and probably didn't want to hear my cousins' questions about it. It didn't matter that my daughter and her boyfriend had been together for more than three years and Thao's boyfriend was an educated man (he was a postdoc). She would rather Thao traveled with us alone, without her boyfriend.

I had tried to raise my children in the Vietnamese culture. It was all right when they were young, but we argued a lot in their teenage years. Slowly I adapted to the new culture and accepted that my children are in fact Americans, so I let them be. I just wanted my daughter to be happy and didn't care if the Vietnamese approved of our lifestyles or not.

"Thao is an American, Ma. It's normal for an American to travel with a boyfriend. You know that, don't you?"

"I didn't say anything," Ma said. But I could tell she wished I had raised my children the strict Vietnamese way. I could almost hear the voice in her head: Children have to listen to their parents no matter if they're right or wrong. Girls are not supposed to travel with boyfriends, postdoc or not.

I was very proud of my daughter for working so hard in school and achieving so much at her age. She had been given a lot of opportunities, and one of them was traveling. This time the university had sent her to Hong Kong for a conference. Thao wanted to see Vietnam too, so she asked her boyfriend and Don and I to go with her; that was how this trip had started.

It was so hot and humid, there was no way we could wait for Thao at the airport. We climbed in a taxi and drove through the crazy traffic of Saigon. The city had changed so much; all the streets were filled with scooters and cars. I thought we would get into accidents a couple of times, but the taxi driver seemed to know what he was doing.

Tall buildings had popped up everywhere. It wasn't the Saigon I remembered at all. When I left, this city was filled with bicycles and cyclos. They had been replaced with motor vehicles instead. Occasionally we saw an American fast food chain, like Popeye's, Burger King, or Starbucks. Starbucks? That really surprised me. Vietnamese people are very particular about their coffee. How could Starbucks compete with Vietnamese coffee? But I was so wrong; it was packed with customers. Where was my old Saigon?

The taxi dropped us off at our hotel. I had picked it because it was right in the center of District One. We could walk everywhere from there. Ma waited for Don and I to check in, then we went to Ben Thanh market for lunch. We passed Nguyen Hue street, and I saw a lot of tourists around. Hotel next to hotel, and restaurants and high-end boutiques were everywhere. My best friend, Lan, used to take me to this area when we were teenagers. We would come to this upscale street to drink coffee and socialize. There were still some local coffee shops hanging in, but the one Lan and I went to was no longer there.

"Do you need to change some money?" Ma asked.

"Yes. We need to find a bank," I said.

"No, you can exchange it right here." Ma pointed at a jewelry store.

"In the jewelry store? Are you serious? They don't have a sign saying 'money exchange.'"

"Trust me, you'll get more Vietnamese đồng in a jewelry store than at the bank."

"Let's try it," my husband said.

Sure enough, they gave us more than the bank or the airport. Apparently all the small business owners loved to have US dollars. They were easy to keep and held their value. I traded a hundred-dollar bill for 2.2 million đồng. That was a lot of bills to carry around. Ma joked that everyone was a millionaire in Vietnam, even the poor. It made me think of my poor sister Anh.

"Where is Anh? How is she doing?" I asked Ma. Honestly, I was kind of surprised she hadn't been at the airport with Ma.

"She's working. I asked her to take a couple of days off, but she's afraid of losing her job."

"What does she do for a living?" Don asked Ma.

"She works as a nanny, and she cleans houses," Ma said sadly.

"Wait a minute. She isn't a hairdresser anymore?" I asked.

"No. Anh didn't say anything, but Di Hue told me the other day, Anh isn't a hairdresser anymore." Ma sighed.

I translated our conversation into English for my husband.

"Do you remember my best friend, Di Hue?" Ma asked.

"Of course I remember Di Hue. Does she still live in our old neighborhood?"

"Yes, she still lives in the same house. I stayed there a couple of days when I first arrived."

"We should visit her sometime soon."

"She would love that. We could arrange something on Anh's day off, so we can go there together," Ma said happily.

Anh was the only one who was stuck behind in Vietnam. She had been married at the time we'd left the country, then later she divorced. She had two sons who also struggled to hold on to jobs. Every time I talked to Anh, either one of her sons or both were unemployed. It looked like the city was thriving, so why was my sister's family struggling? It was sad, and I felt really bad for her. She had been apart from us for twenty-seven years.

After we ate lunch, Ma went to visit her friend, and Don and I went back to our hotel room to cool off. Saigon was really hot in the midday, and this was January. I couldn't even imagine what it was like in July. It hadn't felt this hot when I was younger. Maybe it was because the population had grown so much since I left. More people, more cars, and more scooters giving off more heat.

Anh called me saying she would come to our hotel as

soon as she was done with work. She said she couldn't wait to see me, but jobs were hard to find, especially at her age. She didn't want to ask her boss for time off, afraid it would cost her the job. I told her not to worry, we would meet up for dinner and catch up then.

I was hoping my daughter and her boyfriend would join us for dinner, but they were so jet-lagged they went straight to bed. Anh also came alone, saying her two boys were busy working.

"I'm sorry, Lien. They'll see you on Sunday," Anh said.

We hugged each other for a long time, and we went to a restaurant nearby for dinner. My sister looked skinny and sad. I could tell her life was hard. Anh cried a couple of times during dinner, saying she missed everybody. I showed her some pictures of the family members on my phone, and that put a smile back on her face.

"Tell me, Anh, what happened with your hairdresser job? Ma told me you're a nanny now," I said.

"It happened a few years ago. I went to work as usual, and the boss just told me to pack up my stuff and leave."

"Why? Did he give you a reason?"

"He said I was too old for the job. They want only young and pretty hairdressers now."

"But you aren't old. You're only forty-seven."

"Unfortunately, to them I am old. I looked for jobs at many salons and got rejected by all of them. I still do hair in my spare time, though, for my friends and neighbors," Anh said.

"It's just so wrong." I was upset at the crude society for Anh.

I gave Anh and her sons some money, hoping that would help them for a little while. I was very happy to see the smile on her face when she held US dollar bills in her hand.

***

We took a seven-seat taxi to our old neighborhood. I sat next to Anh so I could talk to her, making up for lost time. It was Sunday, but the traffic didn't seem any better. Thao and her boyfriend were fascinated with all the scooters snaking through traffic with ease. Some of them carried huge amounts of merchandise on the backseats. We saw people on the scooters carrying boxes, plants, chairs, and mirrors. It looked so dangerous, but this was normal everyday life to the Vietnamese. Things needed to be delivered, and this was the only way they knew how.

"At least everyone is wearing helmets, though, so that's good," Thao said while she was taking pictures.

"Are there a lot of scooters in America?" my nephew asked.

"Mostly cars. We have winter, and it's really cold, so cars are more practical," Thao said.

I was so proud of her speaking Vietnamese to her cousin. She spoke with a thick American accent, but they understood her, and Thao understood even more Vietnamese than she could speak.

We got closer to my old neighborhood, but I didn't recognize it at all. The area used to be so green, with houses and big properties. It had become busy blocks of businesses, and houses were built more narrow and tall, as land was so expensive. None of the houses had yards anymore. Anh pointed out our old school when we passed by; it looked so different now. It used to be more spread out, like a California campus. Now it was one tall building with a tiny little front yard. Ma pointed out a couple of houses where our old neighbors' still lived. The rest had moved away.

The taxi dropped us right in front of Di Hue's house. We got out, and Ma started to get emotional as we stood there staring across the street. Our old house was gone. Six new houses had been built on our old property. The water spinach pond was gone too, replaced by a couple more houses. My sister had made a mistake in listening to her ex, and she'd sold the house when real estate prices were low. Right after she sold it, the government opened the door to doing business with foreigners. That was when the prices of houses and land shot up dramatically. Ma was still bitter about it sometimes, saying Anh could be so rich if she hadn't listened to her ex-husband.

I understood Ma's feelings; it was the house she had risked her life for, fighting with those soldiers. To me it was a sad house of darkness, and I was glad it was gone. Maybe my sister felt the same way and didn't hesitate to sell it.

"Ma, let's go inside. Di Hue is waiting," I said, pulling her away from staring across the street.

We rang the bell, and a woman came to open the gate for us. She said hi to Ma, then ran upstairs to get Di Hue.

"Who is that, Ma? Her daughter?" I asked.

"That's Di Hue's maid. Her daughter is a doctor; she'll show you her picture."

Di Hue came to us smiling, so happy to see us. She looked a lot older, of course, but I still recognized her. We hugged; it was so emotional for us because we hadn't seen each other for twenty-seven years. I introduced her to my husband and my daughter. Ma was happy to see us catching up, asking each other about our families and lives.

Di Hue had retired. Her only daughter, the doctor, couldn't be there with us due to her duties at the hospital. Her daughter was married to a doctor as well, and they had two sons.

"I can tell you're so proud of your daughter," I told her.

"You too. Both of your children are going to college, and look at your daughter. She's doing a PhD in physics. That's incredible," Di Hue said.

"Thank you," Thao said humbly.

"Thank you for helping us in the past, Di Hue. You saved us so many times," I said.

"You're welcome," she said, looking over at Ma.

Ma didn't like to talk about the past. My stepfather had passed away two years earlier, and she was still sensitive about it, so we moved on. We talked about Saigon and how it had changed so much. We showed each other pictures of our families, and it was good to see Ma and her best friend reminiscing and having a good time.

***

My daughter mentioned to me that she wanted to visit the grandparents on her dad's side. I didn't know what to do. I couldn't say no to her, but I didn't know how her grandparents felt about me. My ex and I had divorced sixteen years earlier, and we weren't on good terms. I told my daughter I would drop her off and pick her up, but I didn't want to go in.

Thao said she was very nervous about going there alone. She was afraid her Vietnamese was not good enough to communicate with her grandparents. My daughter needed me to translate for her, because none of them spoke English. I thought about it. She was my daughter; I would do anything for her, especially when she needed me.

"All right, I'll go with you, but if they start to blame me for the divorce, I'm going to leave right away. I'm not going to sit there and let them say anything bad about me."

"If that happens, I'll leave with you. We'll leave together right away," Thao said.

I talked to my husband about it, and he understood that I had to do this for my daughter. Don was a good sport; he told me not to worry about him, that he could get lunch by himself. I was a little worried, because he spoke very little Vietnamese, but he insisted he would be fine. So I left my husband at the hotel by himself and felt a little guilty about it.

Ma wanted to come with us for emotional support, which I was grateful for. Thao's boyfriend also wanted to come, so the four of us got in a taxi and headed to visit Thao's grandparents. I was very nervous on the way there, asking myself many "what if" questions. The taxi dropped us in front of an alley, based on the information Thao had gotten from her dad. I asked the taxi driver to wait for us on the street, just in case. As soon as we got out of the taxi, I saw three of my ex's siblings walking toward us with big smiles. They recognized me.

"Oh my God! Lien. Wow! You look the same," Thu said.

"Hi Thu, hi Thai, Hien. This is your niece, Thao." I introduced everyone and turned to Ma. "You remember my ma, right?"

They said hello to Ma in a very respectful way, then they called to everyone in the house to come out.

"Where is Ba and Ma? Go get them now," Thu told one of the siblings, then turned to me. "Let's go inside, Lien, Thao, and...?"

"This is my boyfriend, Martin," Thao said.

"Hi, nice to meet you," Martin said.

"American?" Thu asked.

"No, he's German. We met in college," Thao said.

"Hello. Please come in." Thu held Thao's hand and led us to a big house in the back of the alley.

"The biggest house is your grandparents'." Thu pointed it out to Thao. "And all the houses around it belong to your aunts and uncles. We own this whole alley, and everybody lives around here."

My ex's parents came out crying. They hugged my daughter for a long time. They turned to us and invited everyone inside. By that time the whole commotion had really gotten started. More of my ex's siblings came to welcome us. They asked so many questions about my son. Why hadn't he come too? How was he doing? I told them Toan was busy with work and couldn't come, but he sent his regards.

My ex's family was very nice to us. There wasn't even one mention of the divorce.

"You all have to stay for lunch," Thao's grandfather said.

"Thank you, but we don't want to cause any trouble," I said.

"It's no trouble. It's a celebration." He turned to Thao. "Your uncle's restaurant is right here. It's no trouble at all."

"Please stay and eat with us," Thu said.

We couldn't refuse the warm invitation, so we said yes. Thu went out to tell the taxi guy to leave, since it was going to be a while. Thai set up the VIP room in his restaurant for us, and he cooked up a storm. The food was delicious, and we all had a good time.

Thao's uncles brought out some beers for all the men

at the table. Thai raised his glass and asked me to teach Martin the Vietnamese way to say "cheers."

"Lien, tell him to say yô before he drinks it."

"Martin, say yô before you drink your beer. It means 'cheers,'" I told him.

Martin did, and they gave him a round of applause for trying.

"Amy, can you tell them I want to share my culture too?" Martin waited for me to translate, then continued. "In Germany, when we say 'cheers,' we have to look each other in the eyes, otherwise it's seven years bad luck."

"Oh, we don't want bad luck. Let's do it." Thai and Martin both clinked their glasses and stared at each other's eyes. They both said "yô!" and gulped the beer down.

There were many rounds of yô, stares, and laughs. Thao's grandparents, uncles, and aunts were bonding with her and Martin, exchanging their stories and cultures. My daughter was so happy, I could tell. She smiled a lot and was asking so many questions. I translated for them back and forth. She was delighted, and I was glad I was there for her.

Before we left, Thu invited us to go for breakfast the next day. "Of course!" my daughter said, and she gave her aunt the address of the hotel.

The next morning Thu showed up at the hotel with a big van. The whole group stepped out of the van to say hello to me. Thao's other aunt, Hong, had come with her Canadian husband and her two eight-year-old identical twin daughters. Hong had met her husband when he'd gone to Vietnam for a vacation. They fell in love and got married, and the twins came along shortly thereafter. They all had Canadian citizenship but chose to live in Vietnam instead.

Thao's youngest uncle, Hien, was also there. Hien had married his high school sweetheart, a Chinese girl. They were both nineteen years old when they got married and had a son and a daughter.

"It's just going to be my boyfriend and me. Ma can't come," my daughter said.

"Lien, you're not coming? Why not?" Thu asked in

surprise.

"You guys go and have fun. I can't leave my husband. I left him at the hotel by himself yesterday. He doesn't speak the language, and he doesn't know much about Saigon. I can't do that to him again," I explained.

Thao's aunts and uncles were disappointed that I wasn't going to breakfast.

"Come on, Lien. It wouldn't be the same without you," Thao's aunt Hong said.

"Why can't he come with us? Tell him we invite him to breakfast, so he can find out what a Vietnamese breakfast is like," Thu said.

"No, that would be weird," I said.

"No, it's not weird at all. You're like a sister to us," Thu said.

"Tell him we want to meet him, and we need to practice our English," Thao's uncle Hien added.

"Please!" they all said in unison.

"It would be nice if you came with us, since my Vietnamese is so rusty." Thao looked at me and smiled.

"All right, let me go and ask him. I'm not sure if he'll agree to come, but I'll try," I said and ran back to the hotel room.

My husband was surprised that my ex's siblings had invited him to breakfast, but after some convincing from me, he got ready, and we went. I introduced my husband to the group, then we all got into the van. The driver took us through the morning rush hour of Saigon, then he got on the highway. I didn't think anything of it at first; maybe he was avoiding the traffic and taking a shortcut to the restaurant. We were joking and laughing in the van; nobody seemed to pay attention. Then all of a sudden, we saw rice fields and cows.

"Where are we going?" Don asked me.

I translated that to Thu.

"Breakfast," Thu said with a smile.

"I thought we're going to have breakfast in Saigon. We're not in Saigon anymore, are we?" I said.

"No, we're going to have an authentic Vietnamese

breakfast. You'll see." Thu kept on smiling.

Luckily my husband and I had eaten breakfast already, so we were fine, but my daughter hadn't. She was hungry and confused. She looked at me, wondering what was going on. I shook my head, saying, "I don't know."

After an hour and a half of driving by green fields and fruit farms, the driver pulled into some sort of rest stop right next to the Mekong River. We all got out and followed Thu on a footpath to the restaurant. It was a countryside restaurant with a huge thatched roof and lots of trees and flowers around. Waitresses were wearing traditional ao dai. It was nice. The food was good; everyone seemed to enjoy their noodle soup and rice dishes. Yeah, that was breakfast.

"What do you think of Vietnamese food?" Hong asked my husband.

"I love it. I even know how to cook Vietnamese food," Don said.

"Really? What kind of food have you cooked before?" Hong asked.

"I can cook phở and fried rice, and I know how to make bún—you know, the noodle salad."

"Wow, is it true, Lien, that he knows how to cook phở?" Thu turned to ask me. "I don't even know how. Phở is complicated."

"Yes, he's very good at it," I told her.

"I'm impressed. You can teach Vietnamese men a thing or two," Thu said.

"And a Canadian man!" Hong said, and everybody laughed.

I was so glad they all liked Don. They treated him with respect and really wanted to know more about him. I had never thought my husband and my ex's family would sit at the same table. It blew my mind that they were having a good time.

After we were done with breakfast, Thu took us to a boat dock a short walk from the restaurant, and there she bought a countryside tour for the group. I realized then Thu had planned this trip all along. She hadn't just invited us to breakfast; she wanted us to see the countryside as well. We got on a big wooden boat with a tour guide and a captain. The tour guide told us a little bit about the countryside and what to expect while we were sailing deeper into the Mekong Delta, toward Mỹ Tho. My daughter was very surprised and happy that her aunt was giving her such a unique experience.

We saw lots of fruit farms and learned how to cross a monkey bridge—a single bamboo tree bridge. It spanned across a pond or a stream. Monkeys were the masters of crossing, but the local people also passed over it with ease.

We visited a coconut candy factory to see how they made candies, all by hand. Mỹ Tho was famous for coconut goods. We drank some young coconut juice for refreshment. Everything was really interesting. Then we paired up, got in some wooden canoes, and went deep up a small river, where we saw how the locals lived.

After another meal we headed back to the boat landing and went back to the city. I couldn't believe we had spent an entire day in Mỹ Tho. It was nice to know that my ex's family had no hard feelings about me. Thu and Hong invited us out again the next day, but we were flying to Da Nang. Thu made Thao and me promise to call her after we got back from Da Nang. She wanted to take Thao to the tailor for an ao dai fitting. Thu wanted her niece to have a traditional dress to wear for Vietnamese New Year's—and something to remember her aunt by.

***

Da Nang was a small city right next to the ocean. It was clean and quite beautiful, with mountains on one side and beaches on the other. My aunt Gai lived there with her son and a stepdaughter that Aunt Gai adopted when she was a baby.

Aunt Gai was a realtor and lived in a big house. She offered to have us to stay with her, and Ma said yes. Thao decided she and her boyfriend would stay there so they could learn more about Vietnamese culture. My husband and I liked to have our privacy, so we stayed at a small, quaint boutique hotel instead, located one block from the beach. It was nicely decorated, with modern amenities like Wi-Fi and cable television. We got a nice spacious room with an ocean-view balcony for forty-two dollars a night. Breakfasts were included, and they were surprisingly good. We walked on the beach every morning, then headed to Aunt Gai's to spend time there during the day.

My two cousins, Ly and Loc, drove from Hue to Da Nang to spend some time with us. This was the first time I met them, although I had met their younger sister, Loi, in Saigon and had dinner with her. Their father, Uncle Tu, was an honorable man and was shown a lot of respect by family members. My uncle Thien talked about him all the time.

I could tell Ly and Loc were well to do. They drove a nice car and wore fancy clothes. While Aunt Gai and Ma cooked an amazing meal for us, they told us the fascinating story of how they had become rich.

The Communists came to their house in Hue after the fall of the South in 1975. They took Uncle Tu to a reeducation camp, because he was a soldier for South Vietnam. They then took his family into the jungle, where they were told to build a new community. It was a horrible time in their life. Ly was the oldest of three girls, and she was only twelve. Loc was eight, and their mom had just had a new baby, Loi. How could a weak woman and three very young daughters survive in the jungle? They cried a lot but did what the government told them to do.

The government assigned them a piece of land to farm. Their new neighbors helped them to build a small hut out of wood, with a thatched roof. Everyday their mother tied baby Loi on her back and went to work in the fields with her two girls. They worked hard, but the result was minimal, since they didn't really have the strength or experience. They planted all kinds of vegetables, and it was Ly's job to bring them to the market to sell.

"I had to walk three kilometers each way, with two baskets of vegetables in my arms. I don't know how I survived all of that walking from the field to the market. It was very hard," Ly said, choking up.

"Then all of a sudden, they released our father. Thank goodness," Loc said. "Our father picked up the farming so we could go to school."

"We learned to work and to live a hard life like everyone else," Ly continued. "After ten years the government changed their policies. They allowed citizens to open private businesses or do whatever they liked with their pieces of land. Some people chose to plant coffee; others planted tea. We chose to plant rubber trees. It was small at first, then we did so well we bought more land. Now we have a whole plantation, with hundreds of employees working for us."

"Wow. Congratulations! I'm so glad you're doing well," I said to her after translating the story for my American family.

"Thank God," they both said.

"Amy, please tell them I appreciate them so much for sharing their story," said Martin. "I came from West Germany and heard a lot of stories about East Germany during Communist times. I have so much respect for your family and Uncle Tu. Despite their hard life, your family stayed together and turned the hardships into good fortune. I'm glad you're all doing well now."

"Thank you, Martin. It's very nice of you to acknowledge that," Uncle Tu said.

"Let's drink to the future," my husband said and raised his beer glass.

"Yô!" Clink. "Yô!"

The dinner went on till late, with lots of talking and exchanging of cultures. By the time we got back to our hotel, it was past midnight.

The next day Ly and Loc took us to Ba Na Hill, a mountain resort recommended by Aunt Gai. We took a long cable car ride above the rich green jungle. We saw beautiful waterfalls, going through clouds and it kept on going up and up. That was the longest and the most beautiful cable ride I had ever been on. They called this a hill? Obviously it was a huge mountain.

There was an even better surprise when we got to the top of the mountain. Apparently the French had built a village up there for themselves. It had been abandoned for decades, but recently the government fixed it up and opened it up to the public. We were all awestruck by how beautiful the village was. I felt like I was walking in Europe for a moment. The square was so beautiful, with an elegant old stone church. The restaurants and shops were uniquely beautiful; the air was so crisp, with clouds below us.

We walked to the other side of the mountain, where there was a Buddhist temple gleaming in the sun. Thao climbed up to the highest point of the temple. She was taking a lot of pictures of this gorgeous mountain. We had lunch back at the square and walked around some more before heading down for a drive to the ancient town of Hoi An. My cousins had planned it all out for us, where to go and what to eat. I told my husband it was going to be another long day, and he said, laughing, "What's new!"

Hoi An was a charming four-hundred-year-old town that was so picturesque, like an old painting. It was even better at night, when all the decorative lanterns lit up. There were a lot of tourists in this area. I saw Australians, Europeans, Japanese—it was cute and quaint, but it was overrun by tourists. For dinner my cousins took us to a seafood restaurant near Hoi An. The food was good, but the place was noisy, with people singing karaoke in the background. Overall it was a good, fun day, and I slept like a baby when we got back to the hotel.

The next day I was still tired, so we decided we would spend a day on the beach to relax. It was still winter, so there were very few people on the beach. The air temperature was perfect; it was about seventy-five degrees, but to the Vietnamese it was cold. We went for a swim, then had some delicious seafood for lunch. We all met up for dinner at Aunt Gai's house, and Thao told me about her adventurous day. Her two cousins had taken her and Martin on scooters to see all of Da Nang's nature and beaches. Thao liked Vietnam a lot.

"It's really a beautiful country. I'm so glad I have a chance to see it. Thank you, cousins," Thao said in Vietnamese, and I was surprised to see how good her pronunciation was, considering she had been there only a short time.

Ma would stay in Da Nang with Aunt Gai for another month. I was happy for her to be able to spend real quality time with her sister. I thanked Aunt Gai's family for their hospitality and ended the night with good-bye hugs. Who knew when we would see each other again?

Don and I flew back to Saigon with Thao and her boyfriend. They wanted to see more of Vietnam and asked me for help to book a jungle tour. I was surprised she felt confident enough in her Vietnamese to travel without me. I told Thao to be careful, and off she went with her boyfriend the next day to the jungle of Cat Tien.

***

One more thing I wanted to do before heading home was to visit my other aunts in Can Tho. I knew they still lived there, according to letters I received from them. It had been thirty-eight years since I'd seen my childhood home. Even though they were my stepfather's siblings, I still loved them very much.

We had only a few days left in the country. Thao and Martin were still on their jungle tour. Don and I couldn't wait for them to return, so we decided we would go to Can Tho without them. We took a speedboat there to save time. It was quite pleasant, because there wasn't any traffic on the river, and we got to Can Tho in less than three hours.

A taxi dropped us off in front of my childhood home. I still recognized the house, although it looked a lot smaller than I remembered. There wasn't much of a garden anymore, and the house had lost some of its old glory. I thought of those days, those birthdays and Christmas parties, when we'd had so much love and fun in this house. I was glad my aunts got it back after the government basically borrowed it for ten years.

I rang the doorbell, but it was broken, so I called out their names. "Aunt Sau, Aunt Bay! Hello!"

They didn't know I was coming to see them; in fact they didn't even know I was in Vietnam. This was totally a surprise visit. I called out their names again and saw Aunt Sau appear at the door.

"Aunt Sau, it's me, Lien." I waved.

"Lien! Is that you?" Aunt Sau's jaw dropped. She ran to open the gate without realizing she still had a bunch of curlers in her hair. We embraced each other.

"Oh my God! I was taking a nap, and I heard your voice. I thought I was dreaming. What a nice surprise," she cried.

"How are you, Aunt Sau? How is everyone?"

"Everybody is doing well. Come on in."

"Aunt Sau, this is my husband, Don." I introduced them to each other.

"Nice to meet you, Aunt Sau," Don said in Vietnamese. He had been practicing the whole morning. Sau is a difficult name to pronounce; the tone of your voice has to go up. There is a Vietnamese word, sạo, that means "liar," and Don didn't want to call Aunt Sau a liar!

We went inside, and Aunt Sau knocked on Aunt Bay's bedroom door. "Bay, wake up, Lien is here."

Aunt Bay opened the door with sleepy eyes. She had been napping as well. This was our old tradition when I used to live there. After my cousins and I came home from school, we took naps. Aunt Bay cried out of excitement. She couldn't believe I was right there in front of her.

My aunts brought out fruit and drinks for us. We talked about everything and everyone. Aunt Sau and Aunt Bay had stayed single, living together in the same house. Aunt Bay retired after thirty years of working for the government. Aunt Sau wasn't able to find a job as a lawyer for all those years.

The government had returned the house to Grandma when she was still alive. She had owned two houses next to each other and decided to sell one. She kept the one I grew up in, and Aunt Sau rented some of the rooms out to college students. Thank goodness Can Tho University was nearby. Aunt Sau also cooked for the students for a small fee, and that was how they earned their living.

Touring the house, Aunt Sau took us upstairs to the ancestors' altar. She lit a candle and three incense sticks for me to pay respect to my grandparents. Their pictures were side by side, next to photos of their young children, Uncle Tu and Aunt Nam. After I paid my respects, Aunt Sau showed us around the rest of the house. I saw my old room that I used to share with my cousins. Aunt Sau told me stories about when I was young; some of them I remembered, others I had forgotten. Then a woman walked into the house and smiled at me.

"Guess who?" Aunt Sau tested my memory.

I blanked out, trying hard to think, but I just couldn't remember her.

"Here is a clue," Aunt Bay said. "She used to work at the hospital in Saigon."

"Aunt Tam!" I jumped to hug her.

Aunt Tam had aged so much, I didn't recognize her and felt so guilty about it. Her two older sisters looked much younger than she did. I cried and told her I was sorry for not recognizing her right away. Aunt Tam cried too. She said life hadn't been kind to her, and it showed.

Aunt Tam had married her Northerner boyfriend even though Grandma was against it. Right after they got married, the government fired them both, and their life had been difficult ever since. They couldn't find any decent jobs, so they had to move back home and had lived in this house ever since. I could only imagine the tension between Grandma and the newlyweds. Aunt Tam had two grown children now. Her daughter got married and moved out. Her son still lived with his parents at my grandparents' home.

Aunt Chin and her husband came as soon as they heard we were in Can Tho. They owned a farm and lived an hour and a half away. Aunt Sau and Aunt Bay cooked a delicious dinner, and the house was bubbling with laughter and jokes. Aunt Tam's children were also there, and I was glad I had a chance to meet them.

We stayed there two nights, catching up and talking about the old days. Aunt Sau took out some of my old report cards from grade school and gave them to me. I couldn't believe she had kept them after so many years.

Aunt Sau and Aunt Bay took us on their scooters to my old Catholic French school. It was a now a public school and had a new name. Unlike my other school in Saigon, this one still looked somewhat the same. I stared at it for a little while, and memories rushed back. I saw my cousins and me running around in that schoolyard. My French was so rusty now, but the memories were still there. Beautiful childhood memories, where I was loved and protected by my aunts. I was half-American; to society I was an eyesore; but to them I was their niece, even though I wasn't blood related.

I thanked all my aunts for the love and support they gave me. I would have loved to stay longer, but unfortunately we didn't have much time. Aunt Sau insisted we should go to see the floating market on the Mekong River before we left. I had heard of it but never had the chance to go there. My husband couldn't wait to see it either, so we booked a tour for the next day before we headed back to Saigon.

We got up at the crack of dawn to go to the boat dock. Our appointment with the boat owner was at five, because the floating market started at four and lasted until eight in the morning. By the time we got there, the sun was just about to rise, giving us enough light to see the action. The boat owner took us to the heart of it, our boat squeezed into the middle of the hustle and bustle of the floating market at Cai Rang.

It was a crazy traffic jam on the Mekong River at that time of the day. Everything from fruit, vegetables, and rice to cooked food was available for sale on the boats. They were all farmers, and this unique market was the place for them to sell their produce. Each boat hung some of their produce from a tall bamboo stick. From faraway you could tell which boat was from the pineapple plantation, which boat was from the mango farms, which boat sold rice, which sold vegetables, and so on.

All different size boats were weaving past each other to sell, to buy, and to eat breakfast. We saw some houseboats there too, with families and dogs. A lot of people were paddling their small canoes around to buy their food for the day.

We saw a boat selling iced coffee in little plastic bags with straws sticking out—that's how the locals drank their morning coffee. Some boats were selling bánh mì sandwiches; others sold coconut sweet rice, even noodle soups. How did they do that on the water? How did they balance the boiling broth on the wooden boat? It was fascinating to see how the locals lived.

My husband and I were glad we had the chance to see something so unique. Who knew if the floating market would still exist later on? It might disappear, with the way the country was changing; people might go to a supermarket instead. So much had changed in Saigon. I hoped Can Tho would stay the same.

We got back to the dock around seven thirty, after the market thinned out and disappeared. My aunts took us out for a good-bye breakfast, then we headed back to Saigon.

My daughter and Martin were also back from their jungle hiking tour and said they loved it. We spent our last day in Saigon together. I took them to see Notre Dame Cathedral and the city's beautiful post office that had been built by the French architect Eiffel when he was young—the same architect who built the Eiffel Tower in Paris. Thao was in there for hours, writing postcards to her professors and friends.

My sister Anh and her kids joined us for a last dinner before we left. It was an emotional dinner for me and for Anh as well. We had come from the same womb; I was lucky to live in America and she wasn't. My children got to go to college, and her children did not. I tried not to cry, because if I started, I wouldn't be able to stop. Anh and I both put on brave faces for the kids. She looked really sad when we left the restaurant. I told her I love her and that hopefully we would see each other again soon, maybe in America.

The next day Thao and her boyfriend flew to Hong Kong for her conference. Don and I headed home. For Thao it had been a trip to see her roots that she'd heard so much about. For my husband it had been an adventure, learning and understanding more about his Asian wife. For me it had been a healing trip, to visit the past and the people I loved.

As we took off, I looked down at my old country one last time. "Bye, Saigon," I whispered.

"Are you OK, Em?" my husband asked and squeezed my hand gently.

"Yes, honey, I'm all right."

I held Don's hand and leaned on his shoulder, thinking how lucky I was to find him. What were the odds of a little half-American girl from Saigon ending up being married to a Swedish boy from Minnesota? It had been a long journey to find my happiness. Along the way I had learned so much, and it shaped me into the person I am content with today. I still don't know who my real father is, and I still don't know my real birthday, but it's all right. I have my family who loves me, and I found peace knowing that.

Acknowledgments

I hope this book helps to represent all the half-American and half-Vietnamese children out there who suffered so much during and after the war. Some might have gotten lucky to find their fathers and were able to leave the country. Others were orphans and got treated badly by society until some got a chance to go and live in America.

I would like to thank my husband, Donald, for his encouragement and support; without him this book would not exist. Thanks to my children for giving me unconditional love and strength. I'm very proud of them. Thank you, Ma, for being strong and not giving me up for adoption. Thank you, my guardian angel Aunt Hai, and many thanks to my entire big family for loving and supporting me.

I am indebted to Susan Harper Berliner for her valuable opinion and suggestions in helping me to improve this book. Sincere thanks to Rebecca Taub for believing in my story and encouraging me to keep writing. Many thanks to William Booker for always being there when I needed help. Thank you Professor Nancy Noguera for telling me I have a voice and my English teacher Mr. Loi, wherever you are, for giving me the foundation and the confidence to write.

Made in the USA
Las Vegas, NV
20 September 2021